Padua

Plays from the Padua Hills Playwrights Festival

Padua
Plays from the Padua Hills Playwrights Festival

Produced by Sideshow Media LLC, New York, NY

Editorial director and project manager: Dan Tucker
Cover and interior design: CoDe. New York Inc., Jenny 8 del Corte Hirschfeld and
Mischa Leiner
Padua editor: Guy Zimmerman

Printed in the United States of America

Distributed in the United States and Canada by Theatre Communications Group,
520 Eighth Avenue, 24th Floor, New York, NY 10018-4156.
ISBN: 0-9630126-4-9

Cover photograph: Jenny 8 del Corte Hirschfeld

Contents

When There Is Nothing to Sell

by John Steppling

Theater is, if nothing else, a social art form and a way to introduce us to ourselves. How and why we engage with the medium of theater usually says a lot about the state of the society we live in. The theater in America is suffering the various viruses of political correctness (with buzzwords like *diversity*), consumerism, entertainment, and the ubiquitous sentimentality that seems to infect everything. An addiction to celebrity and the marketing of social redemption are everywhere. For over a decade, the Padua Hills Playwrights Workshop and Festival was doing something very different.

The Padua Hills Playwrights Workshop and Festival created a community in the best sense of the word, and from within that community evolved a genuine aesthetic style in both playwriting and performing. I rarely have attended any theater or performance in Los Angeles (before I left in 1998) or even in New York where I didn't instantly recognize the influence of Padua. At this point, one might reasonably ask why the Padua Festival has never garnered the press that so many other similar yet trivial enterprises have. I suspect the answer lies somewhere amid the principles founder Murray Mednick set in place at the inaugural festival.

The first was that the festival developed writers and not plays. In an age driven by marketing and advertising and where the "product" must be foremost in our minds lest the sales of that product suffer, it's easy to see how Padua never acquired a "franchise." Padua had nothing to "sell." Second, Mednick never encouraged the vapid sociology that so appeals to the modern liberal critic. He had the audacity to take theater seriously and to insist that the writers, whatever they wanted to do at Padua, at least maintain the sense of importance he himself felt about the medium. Mednick believed that the theater should ask questions. If answers were available, that was fine, but not necessary. One didn't come to Padua, as either audience or participant, expecting reassurance.

The workshops and the physical demands (that the company both work and live together) served to underscore the community I think we all felt. The teaching and involvement of the students created a conscience for the festival. The attention given to the (much abused) word *process* was critical in the evolving of this sense of conscience. The manner in which all involved approached the crafts of both writing and acting (and directing) came to be understood in an almost Buddhist-like way, which is not to say everyone was even aware of these things let alone doing them. Still, the doing of things took on a resonance few had experienced before, and much of the work seen at Padua shared this sense of dignity. The plays may have been sometimes or even often failures, but they were never (or nearly never) silly or flippant. Even the "comedies" took on a shadow they carried with them.

The search was regional to some degree; this was a festival of the West, and as such it seemed to embrace the empty deserts and to exist in the darkness cast by the Rocky Mountains. The mythic expansiveness of American art from Melville to Pollock was always there, and the occasional swooping hawk or howl of a coyote only seemed to be the latest directorial choice from this "sight-specific" group. The festival had a masculine quality as well (and I trust nobody will take this remark as meaning in some way that the women artists weren't fully themselves or didn't help form the essence of the festival as much as the men. It seems absurd to include this disclaimer, but there you are) and a lack of attitude; it wasn't kitsch, and its irony was real and not just cleverness. To be different is to be a threat: So it has always been and so it is today.

Somehow the plays and performances, at their best, seemed to reflect the sense of having reached the end of something. You can migrate no farther than California, and artists have, for years, shared in their work a quality of rootless alienation. From Hammett and James Cain, to Chandler and West, to *noir* directors (mostly German Jews) who fled to Hollywood from their homeland, the strategies of fatalism have always seemed to be primary out here in El Lay (unless you were groveling for the crumbs from the table of some CEO at Fox or Paramount). The dynamics of the westward migration from the 1800s through to the Dust Bowl generation, and now from Latin America, have given the area a haunted sensibility that its artists have consistently responded to. Orson Welles said the south of anywhere was a different kind of place from the north (or something like that) and far more seductive.

The seductions of El Lay and SoCal are well documented (and constantly televised), but the dusty, barren inner life, like the inner valleys of the state itself, the brutalized psyches of the forgotten and overworked, the callused and lonely, are invisible and rarely chronicled. The Padua Festival looked for a way to engage with a medium that had been sold out and made irrelevant, in equal parts, by the cultural arbiters of the entertainment industry and the middlebrow safety of academic and institutional theater. In entertainment, "art" is your friend, but of course it isn't, it's only a salesman. Padua listened to the ghosts lost to the media, and the images it created were not of wealth or youth, but of the margins and of a hidden American mythology. Peter Brook has talked of "theater not pretending to be other than theater," and I think Padua came close to achieving this. Not much from the festival had series potential, and I remember few agents or producers bothering to drive out (and the ones who did had a terrible time).

Theater asks for collective attention from the audience, and modern audiences are more used to an isolated individual unreflective consensus with the cultural ideology. There is little true appreciation in such agreement; it is the ego shrieking "yes," and at Padua it was difficult to find this comforting response. The community of the festival seemed to insist the audience take part in this communal experience, and for some (or many), this was very uncomfortable, but, I would argue, valuable. In its inherent social dynamic the theatre will ask for a civic self-awareness and reflection on the individual's role in his world. This era tends toward a knee-jerk approval of all that is commercially successful while distrusting to the point of official derision the transformative potential of art; the trope of irony is a catchall apologia for a faux-populism, and a way to hide from the deeper levels of human consciousness.

The Padua Festival wasn't auditioning, and it didn't pander. Its doom was written in its ethic and integrity, and I hope the revival Murray is undertaking will plug back into those increasingly rare forces of creativity.

Padua: Wild in the Hills

by Wesley Walker

I first attended the Padua Hills Playwrights Festival in 1991, but Padua occupied a place in my imagination long before that. In 1984 I acted in a play Michael Farkash had written when he was a student at Padua, and what he described hooked me: each summer, a renegade troupe of writer-directors would gather at Cal-Arts to teach weird classes and stage subversive, avant-garde plays in various clearings and loading docks around the campus. The workshop leaders were brash, vigorously anti-commercial and dedicated to formal exploration. I wanted to write plays myself and had attended a class or two, but nowhere had I encountered exercises such as the one Michael recalled, where Padua students were asked to render on paper a drawing of their heart, then instructed, without discussion, to write. The workshop sounded both threatening—where is there room for the writer's ego in such an exercise?—and invigorating. Though I did not attend for years, Michael's depiction of Padua began to fuel my writing.

By the time I saw the festival in 1991, it had moved to Cal State, Northridge, but Padua's mysterious heart was beating strong. The plays were performed deep into the night and one got the notion, sitting in the cold, that there was something primal and right about keeping the festival out-of-doors, some link to theater's ancient Greek roots. There was mystery in these plays and humor and sex, but beyond this, driving them forward, there was *thought*. This may be why, though the plays were often set in Southern California, something about them felt alien. They were hyper-verbal, ironic, urbane. I learned later the Padua heart was a transplant: it had originally resided in New York City.

In the early sixties Ralph Cook, a character actor from California, founded Theatre Genesis at St. Marks Church in the Lower East Side of Manhattan. Similar in his venturesome spirit to the other Off-Off-Broadway theatre impresarios—Joe Cino of Caffe Cino, Al Carmines of Judson Poet's Theatre and Ellen Stewart of La MaMa—Cook was singular in his aim to create a *writers'* theater. He encouraged young playwrights, such as Sam Shepard and Murray Mednick, to search for new theatrical forms. He mentored them and directed their plays. These new writers, in turn, spoke to a young, radicalized audience, hungry for new modes of expression. In a forum where experimentation and seriousness of intent were prized above all, these young writers thrived, generating increasingly daring, complex work. Cook called it "subjective realism." Maria Irene Fornes and others similarly flourished in the other Off-Off venues. It was a galvanizing time and place.

When Mednick left New York for the West Coast, he carried the ethos of Cook and Genesis with him. At the invitation of Robert Woodruff of Laverne University, he formed the Padua Hills Playwrights Festival and Workshop in Claremont in 1978, asking five other writers, including Shepard and Fornes, to join him. As Padua's artistic director for the next eighteen years, Mednick remained just as dedicated to protecting the voices of young writers as his mentor had been.

By the time I attended the workshop as a student in 1995, I had studied with Padua-alum John Steppling and with Mednick, among others. I had written plays that had been produced and was, compared to other students, a veteran. Still the workshop was a challenge. On Saturdays the teachers, actors and hangers-on would gather to hear what we students had written during the week. It is difficult to imagine a more sophisticated audience. The student-author would sit in a chair before the audience and, after the actors had read his piece, without explaining or defending his work, he or she would *listen*. The critique was high-level, and utterly varied. Often, arguments over form and content grew heated—I remember O'Keefe and Mednick going at it over the notion of a Nazi play—but this contentiousness only served to illustrate the seriousness of intent being cultivated in the students with regard to their own work. There was little room for received notions of political correctness. No one would soften their views to soothe the feelings of their students or peers. It is in the spirit of those Padua critiques, with their multifarious opinions and voices, that I would like to offer this former student's thoughts as to what is most powerful about the plays that make up this collection.

Writing in free-form verse, Neena Beber infuses her play, *Failure to Thrive*, with a sense of loss that seems emblematic of Padua plays. Her characters are unable to articulate the psychic and material pressures that shape their lives, and this is part of what pulls us into Beber's funny, poignant conflation of memory, domestic squabble and misapprehension. The text is full of acute observations about its middle-class Floridian milieu. As the characters vie for what they think they want, the nature and depth of their actual needs elude them. The play serves to delineate, and mourn, the gulfs that separate us from each other, and from our actual lives.

The brilliant *Terra Incognita*, by Maria Irene Fornes, illuminates how a quintessentially Paduan approach to writing for the stage can resonate powerfully with politically subversive energies. Though free of diatribe or overt dogmatism, her text is animated by a profound disgust at the violence of Europe's conquest of the New World. With disorienting humor built on simple interactions—three American friends tour to Spain, they drink tea, they read newspapers—Fornes brings us up close to mysterious and unsettling questions that underlie the bloody founding of the Americas. A steady presence at the Padua festivals, and an old compatriot of Mednick's from Off-Off Broadway, no anthology of Padua plays would be complete without her work.

Politically potent also is Joseph Goodrich's *Steak Knife Bacchae.* This one-man play brings out hidden familial likeness between DIY punk, Joy Division and the tragedies of Euripides. As performed by the author, this boiled-down production proved one of the high points of the 1995 festival. Crouching behind a plastic shower curtain, the author worked himself into a controlled fever, hurling lines of absurdity, death and woe at the spellbound crowd. The choral refrain that closes the play, "You'll sleep soon enough," brought home the Greek tragic vision with blunt intensity.

Freeze, by Padua founder and artistic director Murray Mednick, provides another example of a Padua playwright echoing the techniques and concerns of the Greek tragedians. Those who have studied with Mednick will recall the dictum with which he sums up Greek tragedy: "you can't take it back." In *Freeze*, a young woman, Tracy, runs a cruel scam on a childless Jewish couple who hope to adopt her unwanted child. On one level, her act goes unpunished. But, as the play unfolds, we gradually come to view her as indelibly marked...by *our* awareness of her crime.

In this way, we in the audience begin to play a role in the unfolding drama. The unsettling aspect of *Freeze*, as in other Mednick plays, is how the text works on our awareness, slowly transforming us into an impassive, but powerful witnessing presence: a divine auditor drawing out the truth. The effect of the playwright's tightly woven dialogue is to open in the mind of the listener a vertiginous multileveled space, full of moral peril. (see the director's "Note on *Freeze*," in the endnotes.)

Marlane Meyer's *The Chemistry of Change*, in turn, exemplifies the theatrical potential, often realized by Padua writers, of sheer *attitude*. The play is very funny, the characters skewering each other with such merciless abandon that we end up bleeding ourselves. At the same time, of course, the text challenges our fixed ideas of family and the role women play in it. Attenuated by pressures fiscal and man-related, the protagonist, Lee, supports her fractured family by performing abortions. While mustering a wise courage, she refuses to capitulate or grow bitter.

Susan Mosakowski's *The Tight Fit*, in turn, demonstrates how an artistic sensibility of the Padua variety can deliver decidedly postmodern effects. Through an overlay of thematic juxtapositions, the playwright achieves an effect similar to that of the "cut-up" fictions of William Burroughs or Kathy Acker. Mosakowski's stage pictures support, and also undercut, the vivid imagery of her language, resulting in a disturbing hilarity. The night I saw the play, I felt as if the entire history of the human mind, gorgeous and flawed, was waiting near at hand, dancing in the wings.

The anarchic political ethos of the Padua festival is vividly embodied by John O'Keefe's *Disgrace*, which transformed a large, steeply sloping hill at Woodbury College into a stark wilderness from the pre-Victorian era. Like escapees from a novel by Emily Brontë, three sisters experience the exhilaration of transgressive sex and murder. Like Goodrich's piece, the startling sight of O'Keefe's three women—dressed in white, running and laughing through the night—points back to the wild bacchants: women gone crazy in the hills. The women here are in flight from a crime against the ruling patriarchy, from capture and confinement, and, in running, they reach for a vivid but terrible freedom: the freedom a suicide might come to know between window ledge and ground.

John Steppling's unnerving *Understanding the Dead* carries us to a new land as well: an India of quiet nightmare, mocking Western aspirations. Skip, who works for a multinational hotel and development group, speaks in the optimistic tones of American capitalism, but against the hissing silence of this third-world village, his exhortations seem thin and false. Steppling's India is an underworld where the dead commingle with the living and convey unwanted knowledge. It is the mirror image of sun-filled Los Angeles, a necessary counterpart that will not be forgotten. Similarly unnerving is the corporate hell of Kelly Stuart's *Demonology* where questions of morality also loom large. Stuart's play, though sharp and farcical, is oddly mythic as well. The play's harried single-mother heroine is an ironic version of the archetypal mother, a goddess in disguise who makes war against the death-realm of the repressed and repressing corporation for which she works. This sadistic hierarchy cannot contain or survive her: with her plain, matter-of-fact pragmatism, she is too potent, too true.

The Padua Hills Playwrights Festival was *theater*, theater in its oldest sense. It shared more with the Greeks and the Elizabethans than it did with any of the current television-inspired situation comedies or musicals based on Disney cartoons or "edgy" well-made satires, or 1940's-style social statement dramas or glittering campfests. These are jagged, wildly human plays. They reach deep for what is noble and terrible in human life and bring to the surface an evanescent, ever-mysterious bounty.

Failure to Thrive

by Neena Beber

Failure to Thrive *was first presented at the 14th Annual Padua Hills Playwrights Festival, Woodbury College, Los Angeles, California, in 1994. The play was directed by the playwright with the following cast:*

Lola: Jessica Hecht
Jack: Mike Shamus Wiles
Miriam: Kara Westerman

Dedicated to Charles and Joyce and Jennifer.

Characters

Jack *a father figure*
Lola *a would-be mother*
Miriam *a captive daughter*

The Scene

Near the Everglades (Florida). Inside, outside. Dusk.

JACK wearing binoculars around his neck.
Holds them up, stares out, drops them.

Jack   I want it understood
that I did not at any time touch or harm or inflict bodily
that the girl was not at that time, was not in the
inhabitation of her body, of her then body
and nothing of my own doing as I am in full
recollection and authenticity of my own knowledge at
this time and then also. May the mistake of my, of my
injustice present and otherwise, serve as a reminder of
the fallacy of human and the human the human
intercourse.
Then when she comes on that day forward of her own will
and retribution may I then and only then be exonerated
as it shall be transparent before all who can see
bodily.
May I also say now as I would like duly recorded on
behalf of those among me
I had a loving home and tried to duplicate in as much
as my financial
stability
in that also the world no longer and has changed
undoubtedly you will see
what I have been, or better,
meant to be
truth
in what I have recorded
unto you: impossible to nourish
impossible to sustain

impossible in the soil dead soil to take root...

Blackout. Lights up on JACK *in doorway of house, staring out through binoculars.* MIRIAM *sitting looking at a book.* LOLA *waiting for an answer.*

Lola   *(After a while)* Well?

Are you listening to me?
Jack? Huh?
I don't want to be someone who has never been there,
who will go through life, their whole life, without—

Jack   Roseate spoonbill on the premises.
You don't see them often, not alone like this.

Lola   She should go, she should see.
The door, Jack, would you mind? The door?

Jack   It's like I'm seeing this bird
for the first time, because you can't imagine this,
a perfect thing, you can never remember
or imagine in your head
this kind of perfection.

Lola   Air conditioning has been invented
and we don't have it.

Jack   It's important to experience
the changes in temperature
the variation.

Lola   I don't take pleasure in being uncomfortable. Close
the door.

He doesn't close it.

Jack	The roseate spoonbill is a beautiful bird, the most beautiful fucking awesome bird.

JACK turns his binoculars from outside onto MIRIAM. He does this periodically throughout.

Lola	Stop it. Stop watching her. Stop it, stop, stop it, the way you watch her.
Jack	I'm not watching her. *(He turns binocs back to outside)* If I had to choose a favorite bird: roseate spoonbill, hands down.
Lola	You don't have to.
Jack	That or the great blue heron. Because of the stillness. Not since I was a boy have I observed the heron known as great blue. Remarkably still. Remarkable balance. I'd have to say that between the two species, roseate and great blue, it's a toss-up. Miriam!
Lola	She's reading.
Jack	She might learn something here. *(To MIRIAM)* The roseate spoonbill has a bill shaped like a spoon, hence its name, spoon-bill.
Lola	It's good for her to read. I've tried to encourage her in that area.
Jack	She doesn't need to read.
Lola	Nobody ever encouraged me.
Jack	What I think about reading books is that fundamentally

it's a machine, a machine that feeds the Great Machine,
and what you have here in this book is paper,
inks, toxins, dyes, a pollution
of words
while right here
in our yard, in our own yard
right here is the real
thing
the thing about which
it is written
and therefore read
in books.
All she needs is on the earth and in my
head and I am here
to teach.
(To MIRIAM)
The roseate spoonbill is a bird
of the color pink
it is a migratory bird that comes
from Manitoba, the North, all the way here
each winter, and the individual
is not often seen
away from the flock unless sick so we perhaps have here
a sick or outcast bird of the species roseate
spoonbill.

Lola We should go there, Jack,
we should take her
there
a child's vacation should be
there.

	Miriam, which would you rather do, would you rather
	see this, see this bird
	or go to Disney World
	and they have birds there, too
	that talk I think
	and countries
	whole foreign countries
	Mickey Snow White all that
	huh? Which would you rather?
Miriam	*(Softly)* New Zealand...New Zealand...it's better in New Zealand.

Jack lets go binocs.

Jack	What's that? What's that? What?
	You have something to say
	you say it
	you say it loud and clear go ahead
	What?
Lola	Leave her alone.
Jack	There's a toxicity in her brain, a kind of toxicity
	a poison
	and that poison comes from where
	that seeping, it seeps from
	where—tell me, the reason we are here
	why are we here we are escaping what
	What?

MIRIAM stands.

Miriam	There is a poison in my brain, a kind of poison,

Miriam   There is a poison in my brain, a kind of poison,
          a seeping...into my brain.

Jack   Very good, very good, you see? You see that?

MIRIAM sits.

Jack   And you want to take her where? To Disney World?
          To the Magic Kingdom, to what? To the place, the
          center, the source of the toxic seep?

Lola   I thought she would enjoy it.

Jack   *You* would, you would enjoy it.

Lola   Yes. I would.

Jack   In place of nature you have
          an imitation of nature through the machine
          the machine that is not imagination but
          the failure of imagination
          the decay, erosion, and grotesquerie of what we call
          imagination.

LOLA goes out. JACK stares at MIRIAM through binocs.
LOLA comes back, carrying portable typewriter. JACK stares
out again. LOLA starts typing—she's slow.

Jack   I'll tell you
          the roseate spoonbill is not an ordinary bird. It's
          unique. That color pink
          on a creature
          is unique. Birds, flowers, fish are the most colorful
          creatures and we desire an imitation of such can you
          explain this?

Doesn't anybody want to see?
In our own backyards, dammit.
Not in a magazine. Not on television.
Here.

MIRIAM stands.

Jack   It's gone now. Doesn't matter. Gone.
The roseate spoonbill has gone.

MIRIAM sits.

Lola   *(Typing)*
All good men must come to the aid of their country.
All good men must come to the aid of their country.
All good—shit.
All good—shit, shit, double shit.
The "d" is too close to the "s."
It doesn't make sense, for the "d" and the "s"
to be so close.

Jack   Have you ever seen a mother feeding her young?
You've probably never seen that.
How it is in nature.
How it is supposed to be.

Lola   You don't catch any fish and you don't kill the birds
and you don't grow any vegetables and here's what else:
There's half a bottle of shampoo. Forget about
conditioner.
Do you know what my hair gets like without conditioner?
I slashed the bottom of the tube of toothpaste

to get more out. But:

You are not growing anything.

You are not catching anything.

Even if you were

that's not enough.

Your plan—what is your plan, do you have a plan?

I didn't think so.

My plan—I have a plan—I'm going to type.

And then I'm going to find people,

people who will pay me

to do their typing.

Jack   Who, Lole? Who? Have you thought about that?

About who, where, who? The reality is not aligned

with where we are living, with the needs

of the community.

Lola   The reservation, the trailer park

the old people in that trailer park.

Everybody has letters, government letters,

papers that should be typed.

Jack   I don't.

Lola   They'll find you. When they find you

you'll have letters

that should be written, papers

that should be typed.

Jack   Crap, all of it.

Lola   Yes, Jack.

Jack   Where did you get this, Lole?

From where did you purchase

this thing?

Lola   My father said if you know how to type you will always

be able to make a living
in this world.
My father said that, not my mother, *he* did.
No matter where you are, there will always be people
who don't know how to type or who lack access and who
need things typed. Letters, papers, official things,
so forth.

I traded it for old magazines.

Jack My magazines? My *Geos*? My *National Geos*?
There were maps, there were things in there—
maps, and things that I would need
that I would potentially need.

Lola *Where* were you planning to go?
We're out of shampoo.

Jack I have tried and
an honest effort has been made but
they don't let you, you can't
you can't just live anymore
off the land out here
being down here they don't let you just live.
If I were alone, yes, if I were on my own that's
another story because my needs
are smaller
because I am not susceptible to the wants they create
the artificial needs—

Lola We need food, Jack.

Jack My hunger is something I can feed
my own hunger
but I am maintaining a family, maintaining you

with your desires, all kinds of desires

for crap

conditioner

the right conditioner

the brand-name conditioner

and that desire, where does it come from?

It comes from the Jews, who make advertising,

who make us want want want,

and even the Indians,

the damn fucking Indians over there with their

used Trans Ams, and nobody lives like an Indian anymore

not even the Indians.

Lola You're full

of hostility

Jack, and you don't know whom

to blame.

Jack You can walk out this door and I'll tell you

you're on your own then, go drown in the poison

of the city, go wade through the pesticides.

Take your choice, Miriam. You can stay

with me

on this land

and build, renew, live, thrive

or you can go back out and finish the rot stink piss

taking over your brain out there,

finish off the job.

Miriam *(Hushed)* New Zealand...New Zealand...where it is better

is New Zealand—

Jack Speak up, girl!

Make your position known!

You have something to say?

Is there something you are trying to say?

Say it!

Lola   She should be in school.

Jack   That's where they get you, is in school.

That's where they get your brain the worst.

Give us your report, Miriam.

Speak up. In your own words.

MIRIAM stands and recites.

Miriam   New Zealand.

New Zealand is the last place.

Jack   In your own words!

Miriam   It is the last place on earth, we should go there, to

New Zealand.

Many birds in New Zealand, rare and beautiful birds and

exotic.

When the world blows itself up *it* will *be*, the last

place, the only place,

left of the world

and the birds only

will fly.

The birds of New Zealand will fly, they only, to lift

from the fire and cancer and poison and find

to start again to start over. (*Keeps standing, then sits.*

Pause)

Jack   C-plus.

Lola   I thought it was a B, at least; A-minus even.

Jack   I'm the teacher. Feedback:

syntax, sloppy; specificity, lacking; ornithology, lacking; vocabulary, improved.

Lola
It was better than that. Miriam,
it was better.

Jack
Once the mind has been poisoned it takes work
to come clean. Freeing the brain at this stage
of toxic seep, my God, look at her.
It's bad, Lole. It's toxic, Lole. We gotta detox,
Lole.

LOLA *stands, doubles over, stands.*

Lola
Phantom pain.

Jack
You gonna have children, Lole? You think? Ever?
You think you're ever gonna have children
of your own?

LOLA *sits.*

Jack
You can't get far enough away
anymore. From the contamination, you can't escape it,
there's no place left to go. New Zealand maybe.
That's it.
And I say maybe.

Lola
We're all going to die of cancer.
We're all going to die, isn't that what you say,
eventually, of cancer?

Jack
Something else, another kind of death, may occur first.
And if not, well then,
eventually there is always cancer.

Lola	I can agree with you on a few things
	and that's one of them.
Jack	When we have money we'll go
	to New Zealand.

LOLA begins typing again, slowly.

Lola	These machines, these are solid machines.
	Smith-Corona is a brand name, a reliable name.
	I had a Smith-Corona in high school.
	Mine was red.
Jack	If you think about a machine and what happens to a
	machine ultimately
	where it goes, ultimately,
	doesn't go anywhere, does it? Unlike the living,
	everything of living substance: trees and bark and dead
	animals and human tissue.
	That which goes back, into the earth, into the live
	source. Transforms from root to tree to man to bird to
	food to shit are you with me on this?
	The smell, rancid smell, of the dead living,
	will a machine ever go bad
	with that smell?
	Not this, this poison, this synthetic thing, machine,
	it has no death and therefore no life,
	a terminal existence and I am not a militant,
	not one of your anti-synthetic militants,
	take polyester now that's useful
	up to a point, and I can live
	with that, that's a good fabric, polyester, a soft

thing not this hardness
of a machine, this
is a poison
creating more poison
an endless seeping
to our brains.

JACK picks up the typewriter, drops it to ground. LOLA picks it up, begins typing again.

Lola   These machines, they're built to last. I had one in
high school and I'm sure it has lasted
somewhere as a fully functional piece
of equipment.

You've jammed the keys.
The "r" and the "t" are stuck now,
stuck together.

Jack   And you expect a financial gain
a monetary compensation for your typing
expertise?

Lola   A hand was found by the reservation, this for example,
hand of a girl,
third part of body in a row,
and that will require an investigation requiring
extensive official papers to be typed.

Jack   Don't you think that official people requiring official
papers to be typed already have official means of doing
their typing, i.e. official typists and you
at twenty-five words a minute are not one of them,

	don't you think, Lole?
Lola	I think something is bound to come up.
	Body parts are being found
	around here
	and I might as well try to get a piece of that.
Jack	The world is a sick place.
	I would tell Johnny that.
	I would tell Johnny that the world is a kind of a place
	to make you want to weep for it.
Lola	Johnny wouldn't be listening.
Jack	I have anecdotes, I could tell him anecdotes
	about birds, the lighter side
	of bird-watching, do a few birdcalls
	for Johnny. One look at Johnny Carson you can see
	the man has compassion.
	Compassion is a thing you can tell right off if a man's
	got or not and Johnny, he's got it.
Lola	You don't like television.
Jack	That's not it, not the point, you don't—
	Johnny is a man I could buy a drink, say,
	he's like somebody I've known
	all my life.
Miriam	(Loudly) It's lovely in New Zealand. Clean and pure and
	waters crystal clear. There's all variety of flora and fauna
	in New Zealand.
Jack	Johnny is probably there right now,
	a man like Johnny could retire
	to fucking New Zealand.
Lola	Palm Springs.
Jack	And me and Johnny would unwind

	in New Zealand, start over in New Zealand.
	Miriam! Assignment! In your own words!
	Something you know, tell me, what you know.
Miriam	*(After a moment)* A man like Johnny could retire to fucking New Zealand.
Jack	What *you* know, Miriam, something *you* know.

She is silent.

I'll tell you what you know:
I am the real parent. I am the real father and the
real flesh and the answer. I found you and you are
mine.
That's family. That's a child. That's security:
ownership.
Love is ownership.
Freedom is ownership.
That's America, the American Way, got it?
You know this, you get this straight.
Okay?

Lola	Leave her alone.
Jack	She's learning something here.
	How to be loved.
	She wants to be loved.

MIRIAM stands. Sits. Goes back to book, folding over corners of pages as she turns them.

Lola	*(Typing throughout)*
	When I was a girl my father encouraged me to learn

how to type. He gave me a red Smith-Corona portable
typewriter and this was a gift
from him.
He gave me advice and I think now it was because
I was not pretty enough and he saw that this might be
an obstacle
in the future, might prevent me
later in life
from certain privileges,
this fact that I was perhaps
plain.
In my typing classes at the Y we typed
in rows on black
machines
that had
no letters
only blank
tabs to make us memorize
the keys
with our hands. And I looked down, at my hands,
when I typed
which was a way
to cheat
and type faster
at first
and I never did learn
correctly so now,
looking down
at my hands
the way

	I do,
	I am at a disadvantage,
	a distinct disadvantage
	in my typing.
	I have to slow down to get it
	right, and thus improve; to learn
	the correct way, the system
	of touch typing,
	a marketable skill,
	see.
Jack	*(Pause)* Do we have any money left at all?
Lola	Not at the moment. No.
Jack	I came back here for the birds.
	You see species here that you don't find anywhere else.
	What you see—what you can see here—it's
	remarkable.
Lola	The reason we're here
	is because of your failure
	among people
	your inability to handle
	life and I think we should recognize that,
	your anger
	number one first
	and foremost.
Jack	To be sent into the world as a man is something you
	cannot, I repeat cannot, understand.
	You are protected as you have always been by the men
	of the world.
Lola	So why are we here again?
	Tell me again why we're here?

Jack   To be able to walk outside onto grass,
have your feet touch the ground,
have it be there not ten twenty a hundred stories below
is critical absolutely critical.
And that is the secret, the key
to our lives here,
our detoxification.

Lola   And your job is to maintain
tell me if I'm getting this right but as the self
proclaimed head of the family unit it falls
upon your shoulders to maintain
the family burden by that I mean money
food, sustenance, shampoo, so on
when I speak of failure it would be
in that area to which I am referring.

*MIRIAM, unnoticed, balances book on her head, paces
room in long, exaggerated strides.*

Jack   Dammit. Dammit dammit dammit, shit.

I worked for Avis, I was an Avis man,
red jacket, name tag, could have been promoted and
what.
Marina del Rey, ten years ago, beach community.
And the renters were these barefoot girls,
literally barefoot coming in, sandy toes.
This was ten years ago and the girls
they wanted cute cars, they all wanted
cute little cars,

Rabbits and Camaros in bright colors
and these girls wore bathing suits
right into the Avis office
located in the Marina del Rey Holiday Inn
I had a name tag and my jacket
was red.
What we had rarely suited these girls,
the kinds of cars:
Family cars, American cars, in blue
or white
colors least likely to offend.
I never saw the beach. Never saw the fucking beach
which was six blocks down I was never interested
in that kind of beach
lifestyle.

Miriam, what are you doing? What are you,
what are you doing? *(He lifts book from her head)*

How to be a Model? This? You read this?
You would like, someday, to be a model?
Do you want to try to achieve what you cannot, what is
not in your cards, in your nature, in your stature? *(He
drops book, exits to outside)*

Lola   I'll do your makeup real pretty. Just like a model's.
Okay? I used to work at a fancy drug store in New York
that sold makeup to movie stars and model stars,
to the big important makeup artists who do the
magazines and the movies

and the television shows.

I learned a lot from them 'cause I was curious and I asked
questions and I learned:

Shading. Highlighting. Blending.

Blending is key.

You can change a whole face if you know how to blend
properly. That's the secret and you find you can
change everything with a simple and skillful
application
of makeup properly blended.

I used to want to be a model.

I had bad skin.

*MIRIAM studies herself in mirror. JACK is outside, looking
through binocs.*

Jack   You will note that in almost all of the species it is
the male who is endowed with coloration, markings, and
plumage such that would attract the attention of
possible future mates. This is the way of nature with
one exception, the human species. This use of makeup
by the female human is a clear departure from nature
and bespeaks the disintegration of the natural through
civilization. Are you with me, Johnny? Because I have
a few theories about what has come to pass in terms of
sexual demarcation in the species. I have theories.

JACK enters. LOLA doubles over, straightens again.

Lola	The pain is here, right
	here, right
	where there is nothing
	to be in pain.
Jack	They cheated you. They lied to you. They fucked with
	your body and your head.
Lola	I was seventeen so I found
	the doctor's name in the yellow pages
	Dr. Z it said
	I wanted the pill but he told me about
	a new thing miracle thing a wonder.
Jack	Machine, Lole. Metal. Toxic. Seeping.
Lola	I found his manner to be efficient
	and the place was clean
	enough and he gave me a robe,
	white, of paper, and said to leave on just
	my bra "brassiere" he said, and left
	the room and when he came back he took that off
	unhooked the bra and removed it, all very clinical
	hardly touching my skin at all
	not looking at me at all
	and talking the whole time about
	this wonderful invention
	this mechanism that would be
	inside me
Jack	Before you speak, Lole, maybe you should think
	"Is this really an appropriate story to tell
	in front of a child, in front of my child, would I
	perhaps be better off refraining from telling it?"
Lola	When I went back because of these cramps

he said to leave on just
my skirt, a green wrap skirt I left on
under the robe, according to instruction, and
later he undid the skirt let it slide
down which was odd but he seemed to follow
procedure in some precise way how his fingers
barely touched me except to look for the miracle
contraption—

Jack   The machine within.

Lola   —which he never found and therefore
my uterus was removed and the machine, yes,
was never retrieved, had disappeared
into my body
somehow

Jack   A poison seeping
into the brain
into the brain of the child that is not
yours

Lola   And the pain was gone
for awhile but now
it comes back

Jack   The poison seeps from you to her and that
is your tie, the tie to the child, the mother-daughter
tie that leaves the wombless to haunt the brain
of the unwanted child, the orphan

Lola   It's worse than ever for the brief
visitation, I can hardly stand
and then
it's gone
that pain that filled the place where something

should be.

Jack They lied to you, Lole.
They lied, cheated, and stole
your children. The Jews of Madison Avenue
were behind it in order to make
a fast buck, just another scheme to market
poison, make you feel you need it.
The pain is good, Lole.
You're detoxing, Lole.
It's leaving her brain and back to your body
then you'll flush it out.

LOLA doubles over, straightens, suddenly no longer in pain.

Lola Where is she?
Where is she, Jack?
Where did she go?
Miriam!

JACK picks up binocs. Room falls away into outside, marshland, sound of birds, night soon.

MIRIAM is very still, her pose birdlike.

Lola *(Not seeing her)* Miriam! Miriam! Miriam!
Jack Shhhhh.

I used to come out here with my father. I didn't know
the names of any of the birds
back then. My father

is the one who taught me the names.

He had books on the subject and after he died

I put the books into boxes.

You didn't know me then.

Lola   Yes, I did.

Jack   You didn't know me, knew nothing about me, it was then

I drove across the country

the boxes of my father's books

in the back seat of the car.

I got tired of having those boxes

there, behind me, filling the back seat

Lola   Like a coffin.

Because you might have wanted to pick up a hitchhiker

and she might have wanted to stretch out

in the back seat

with the girl who was with her

the girl she said was her daughter

but that didn't seem possible because the ages

were close and the looks

vastly different

and though the girl said "Mom" you suspected right away

there was another story that they

weren't telling.

Jack   I got off the interstate and there was a sign,

Storage for Rent, the sign was right there

off the interstate.

The first locker I opened had people living in it.

They'd been traveling with a circus but the circus had

run out of money and they were waiting,

a circus family,

waiting together. No one was interested in their

little family circus and they promised to keep an eye

on my books.

I don't recall what exit that was so I can't

get back.

The lockers were pale green tin in rows of six.

I put the boxes in locker 103 next to the large circus

family.

It was somewhere in the Midwest I believe.

I don't know where, exactly.

Lola   Delaware.

Jack   It may have been Delaware.

But I doubt it.

Lola   You picked me up in Delaware.

You'd gotten rid of the books right before you picked

me up.

Jack   I'd like to have those books now.

For purposes of identification. For clarification.

I could use them now, my father's books

on birds.

Lola   I've never seen the point to bird-watching.

Never seen a point to it at all.

Jack   My father kept a list of the birds he had seen.

He was able to identify hundreds of birds,

all in this area. Literally hundreds

of species observed

over the course

of a lifetime.

Lola   Your father was a cruel man who made you puke on

rattlesnake soup at Tiger Tom's Family Restaurant
when you were a child and it is this cruelty
in him that allows me to forgive it
in you, although I wonder sometimes
why I should.

Jack   You never knew my father and you don't know.

Lola   How old were you, ten? When you went to the
reservation to see an Indian
wrestle an alligator
to the ground, man against reptile, no tricks,
were you nine or ten?

Jack   You didn't know me then and you certainly
didn't know me then.

Lola   Afterwards you went to Tiger Tom's,
you and Mom and Dad, and there it was on the menu—
rattlesnake soup.
And you wanted to order it, begged and whined and when
it came you lost your nerve. The soup, however, was
already
on the bill and your father
being the kind of father that he was
made you drink the whole big bowl of soup in one long
gulp.
Afterwards you threw up.
Your mother watched it all and said
not a word
just wiped the dribble from your chin and then you all
climbed back into the car after the day's outing.

Jack   My father, if your story were true which it isn't,
did the right thing (although I couldn't see it then)

	and the thing that I myself would do.

and the thing that I myself would do.
As a matter of discipline
and of love.

Lola   I know. I know it. That's what I know and that's
what bothers me, that I
like your mother would say nothing but wipe
with a clean hanky and tenderness of a sort
the dribble from the chin.
They try to help me
in my twelve-step
in my twelve-step program
they try to help me with this issue
of passivity, compliance, co-dependency,
and I'm working on it,
see,
and I think once my business,
once my typing business starts to take off
and I have a sense of self derived from financial
independence, solvency, and by my own hands—
Where is she? See now, where did she go, what,
where is she?

Miriam   *(Unnoticed)*
They had horses.
It was hot and we weren't allowed to ride still
they had them, the horses
I saw them in the barn
for some reason we were not allowed to ride.
It was hot and the people
whose place it was were paid I think
to take us in, a few of us

who got to see a farmer's life
for the first time, but then they worked us too.
It was Okala, Florida, that's north of here, I think,
but hotter even, and the pills we took
were salt, to put back quick the salt that we were
sweating.
It was a sleep-away camp which sounded good but all
night long the sleep was such you could not sleep,
and horses there we could not ride though once
I saw a loose mare walking round like she was
freely hers to be
who she wanted, whatever she wanted,
unowned.
The beautiful horse with a black mane
I saw from my window, I ran outside
I thought to take a ride, or just stand next to,
and it was night, you know,
and when I got to her
she was gone.

Lola   She's run away again. It's your fault
that she's run away again.

Jack   You've got to be quiet while trying to observe.
There's a great blue,
a great blue somewhere near,
that's my sense.

Miriam   The top model of the year of my two weeks
at sleep-away camp on a farm in Okala, Florida,
was Christie Brinkley, the blonde, the blonde blonde
blonde.
I had a picture of her above my bunk from an ad

	for *Cover Girl*. She looked in the ad like the kind
	of girl who got to ride horses all her life I think
	and later she married
	somebody famous.
Jack	The stillness here would indicate the presence
	of a great blue.
Miriam	At the sleep-away camp in Okala they killed
	pigs and they grew
	oranges, limes, avocados,
	it was a working farm we got to see working, and do.
Lola	She'll get hurt on her own,
	she may have been hurt
	already.
Miriam	And we worked on the farm, those of us sent
	to the farm, we had chores
	and woke early from a sleepless night
	to do them. We did chores early before the heat
	worsened.

JACK staring through binocs at MIRIAM.

Jack	Man can profit off of nature. I'm not against that,
	you understand, the use of nature for profit
	by man.
Lola	Miriam?
	It's getting dark and I worry in the dark
	about my daughter.
Miriam	When I was little my mother—the one
	before now—she kept a suitcase for me and whenever
	I did something bad she'd put something

of mine in it, "when this gets full

I'll send you away,"

she said. And she filled it

to send me to the camp, the sleep-away camp

though that was supposed to be a treat maybe

'cause we were poor and it was free

and anyway she had been the longest mother I'd had till

them, 'cause I'd had

several and I think they were paid, all of them,

to feed me.

And Lola was there, at the camp, she said one day

to call her Mom and we would go away

and ride horses

but first she had to find a job

or a man

preferably a man with a job

she was a counselor at that camp I guess

or just another of the girls who was older

and she chose me.

Jack	You see the great blue, how still it is,
	how it comes into view
	into your consciousness
	all of a sudden, because it is more still
	than anything else around it,
	more still than water, trees, or stone,
	and what you observe most
	is that unnatural stillness.
Lola	I don't see it.
Jack	The great blue heron is the most remarkable of all
	birds. Remarkable for its stillness poise and balance

	its absolute grace.
Lola	And what I see is nothing, nothing
	at all, it's like I'm blind when the night comes,
	it's like my eyes turn inside-out and see
	the space inside, the hollow…
Jack	The great blue was once hunted down for its plumage.
	You could profit off of birds when ladies' hats
	were in fashion. That would be a business you could do
	nicely. It's best to profit off of nature
	when there is a balance
	to the hunt, an understanding of equal forces
	in a match, a wrestling match, that is not without
	cooperation, an understanding
	of order, need, and ownership
	which is also love.
	The plumage of the great blue heron stuck on top of a
	lady's hat was considered the height of elegance
	at one time.
Miriam	What I keep wondering is, did the roseate spoonbill
	die? Did it die?
	I never got to see it. I came out here
	and it was gone and if it came here to die
	did it want to be left alone like that,
	to be left alone
	by us, to die in private
	without a bunch of people watching
	like it was theirs to name?
	But maybe that's all wrong. Maybe it came looking for
	us, and we let it down.
Lola	Sometimes I am so close

to the pain, I can almost touch and that's
okay, that's better then.
Other times it settles far away, I cannot hold it
here, I cannot close in
on the one place
and then it's like a poison gas everywhere
in the air.
I met him and I felt it
again, pain a solid thing
between us, something to hold
like a stone
or a piece of fruit; heavy and bruised; like that
I can live with it
better.

LOLA doubles over.

Miriam   I didn't see her, the pink
bird but I know
she was beautiful.
Beautiful things hurt your eyes, and my eyes
stung. Beautiful things have a way
of making you hold you breath out of not believing
that they are possible.

He's staring at me, he's staring and I can't
think I can't feel I can't fly
he's staring and his eyes burn and burn and burn.

MIRIAM disappears.

Jack	It's not easy to kill a thing of great beauty.

It's a struggle—am I right, Johnny?—a constant
struggle—to stay on top.
On top of nature. It is therefore necessary to kill
with compassion, cooperation, with an understanding and
total knowledge of your prey.
Some people don't like killing birds,
don't think it's an even match, a man against a bird
like that, a man with a gun.
Nonsense, of course it is.
Of course it is.
Those people who say that, they don't understand
the prey, don't understand
the bird. Have no respect
for birds.
Because if you look at it, it's clear that the human
species doesn't come close.
Not in my book.
Not at all.

Long pause. Back inside the house LOLA *typing.* JACK *with binocs, holding them at his side now, as in opening.* MIRIAM *gone.*

Lola I named her Miriam because
it was a name that did not suit her,
a name I would remember
for being wrong. Renamed her I should say
and about the hand I should say
the girl's hand, when found, could not have been hers,

not ours, not Miriam's.
Because of the polish,
on the nails, coral polish, and that would not be
her hand, that would have to be the hand
of somebody else's girl.
Maybe she was with us still by then.
I don't remember.
I don't know what's made up and dreamt and what
has come to pass.
I think I know
where she went, where she was trying to get to
at least.
I think that's obvious, that she would try,
try to go there.

LOLA stops trying. Closes eyes.

Lola	New Zealand...New Zealand...it's better in New Zealand...

JACK with binocs, looking out. LOLA opens her eyes. Alone and apart.

Jack	I love you, Lola.
Lola	I guess I like to hear that.
Jack	I know.
Lola	I guess I like to hear that a lot.

The End

Terra Incognita

by Maria Irene Fornes

A Libretto For An Opera
For Roberto Sierra

Terra Incognita *was originally produced by INTAR Hispanic American Arts Center and Women's Project and Productions in New York in 1997. Commissioned by INTAR Hispanic American Arts Center and Theatre for the First Amendment.*

An earlier version of the play was presented at the 14th Annual Padua Hills Playwrights Festival, Woodbury College, Los Angeles, California, in 1994. The play was directed by the author with the following cast:

Georgia: Kimberly Flynn
Amalia: Jennifer Griffin
Rob: Leo Garcia
Columbus: Leon Martell
Steve: Joel Goodman

Characters

Amalia *A delicate and intelligent American of Spanish descent. Twenty-eight years old.*

Georgia *A curious and thoughtful American. Twenty-eight years old.*

Rob *Amalia's brother. Sensitive and intelligent. Going through a difficult time emotionally. Twenty-nine years old.*

Burt *A derelict. Cheerfully demented. Sometimes he recollects Christopher Columbus experiences.*

Steve *A man who sits in thoughtful repose. Except for the sailing speech he speaks words from Fray Bartolome de las Casas's "History of the Indies," 1512.*

Index

The Scene

Summer—1996. An outdoor terrace of a café in the port of Palos, Spain. The building of the café is behind the audience. Upstage of the terrace is an elevation, a plateau, ten to fifteen feet high, which extends beyond the width of the stage on both sides. Along the edge of the plateau is a dirt road. On the down side of the road and on the slope there are some trees, plants and bushes. On the left there is a partial view of a kiosk. Next to the kiosk there is a milk crate. On the terrace, or lower level, there is a table and three chairs. On the table are two road maps, a travel brochure and magazine, a dictionary, a phrase book, a notebook, a pencil, a pen. Three American travelers in their mid-twenties are around the table. GEORGIA sits center, AMALIA sits left, ROB stands to GEORGIA's right looking over her shoulder at a travel brochure. The sound of "saetas" (religious Flamenco chanting) is heard in the distance. ROB, AMALIA and GEORGIA go up the promontory. They look to the right as a ship with black sails approaches. The ship is pulled by a hooded monk. ROB, AMALIA and GEORGIA watch the ship as it crosses and disappears to the left. AMALIA and GEORGIA return to the lower level. ROB disappears to the left. AMALIA sits to the left. She writes in her diary. GEORGIA sits center. She looks at a travel brochure. After a few moments ROB sits on the milk crate.

1. Prince Henry

Amalia	*(Reading what she just wrote)*
	Rob is getting coffee
	For himself and for me.
	Is Georgia getting coffee?
	(She turns to GEORGIA)
	Georgia…
Georgia	Yes?
Amalia	Are you getting coffee?
Georgia	Tea.
Amalia	*(Writing)*
	Georgia is getting tea.
	Rob and I
	have not had
	an argument yet.

GEORGIA laughs. AMALIA laughs.

Have you?

GEORGIA shakes her head. AMALIA writes.

The day started well.
It's 9:20
and there's been
no argument yet.

*AMALIA and GEORGIA look up toward ROB. ROB looks at
them questioningly. He puts his hand to his ear. They put*

their thumbs to their own ears and wave their fingers. He
points to them. Then, with finger pointed, he indicates circles
around his ear and points to them again. He, then, waves
and exits left. They wave back. AMALIA *closes the diary.*
She is elated.

I think we should drive
to Sagres tonight.
Let's go to the place
on the cliffs
where Prince
Henry built
his ships.

Let's go to the cliffs
where he thought
of ships
to sail
the ocean sea.

He did.
Is Prince Henry's castle still perched on those cliffs?

Let's go to Portugal,
Georgia.
Let's go tonight.

Does Prince Henry still sleep in a hairshirt?

Georgia   Did he?

Amalia   Yes.

(Pause)

Do you know he died a virgin?

Georgia No.

Amalia So they say.

(Pause)

He gathered men of knowledge—
navigators from the East,
from Greece, Syria, Egypt
round him. Engineers,
shipbuilders, instrument makers.
Inventors came to him, worked for him,
from Greece, from Syria,
from Egypt.
Oh, Prince!
The Navigator.

She does a Flamenco singer's intonation. ROB in mockery makes the sounds of a dog.

Let's leave him behind. Let's take the car and leave him behind. Oh, let's!

AMALIA giggles. GEORGIA giggles.

Both Yes!

*

2. A Picture

GEORGIA points to a picture in the brochure.

Georgia   Look at this.

(She looks at the building behind the audience.

Then, she looks at the picture and points to it again)

See this café?

(Pointing to it again)

This café

(Pointing to the café downstage)

is this café

(Pointing to the café)

is this café.

(Pointing to the picture)

This here is our table.

You're sitting here.

I'm sitting here.

At this table.

(She points to another picture)

See this?

It's a picture

of the inside

of the café.

(Pointing to the café)

Of this café.

(Pointing to the café)

See the picture on the wall?

It's a picture of the inside

of the café.

(Pointing to the café)

Of this café.

On the wall of the café
in the picture, is a picture
of the inside of the café.

And in the picture of the inside of the café. On the wall of
the café—

Is a picture of the inside of the café.
And on the wall of the café,
in the picture
of the inside
of the café
is another picture
of the inside of the café
and on the wall
of that picture,
of the picture
of the inside
of the café
is again another picture
of the inside
of the café
with
another picture
of the inside of the café
inside that picture
of the inside of the café
is again

another picture
of the picture of the picture
of the picture
of the picture
of the picture
of the picture.

It's a picture of the picture
of the inside of the café.

A picture of the inside of the café;
of the picture in the
picture on the wall of the café.

Now, look here,

the picture's just a dot
on the wall of the café.

Now the picture

is not even a dot.
There is nothing on the wall
of the café.
Now there's just a dot.
Then the dot is the café.

Now the dot is gone.

Puff.

No picture.

No wall.

And no café.

GEORGIA and AMALIA put their hands to their mouths and gasp in amazement.

...Ahh...

ahh

ahh

ahh

They faint.

ROB is on the top level. He holds a tray with drinks and a pile of old newspapers under his arm.

Rob   Coffee!

AMALIA and GEORGIA walk a few steps up the slope. They take the cups from the tray and walk to the table. AMALIA and GEORGIA sit.

*

3. A Virgin

Rob   Why do you think Prince Henry died a virgin?

Amalia   Because he was dedicated.

ROB sits.

Rob	To what?
Amalia	To his work.
Rob	And what does virginity have to do with work?
Amalia	...It helps.
Rob	It does not.
Amalia	It does.
Rob	It does not.
Amalia	Does.
Rob	Does not.
Amalia	Does.
Rob	Does not.
Amalia	Does.

Rob	Not. Not. Not. Not.	**Amalia**	Does. Does. Does. Does.
	Not. Not. Not. Not.		Does. Does. Does. Does.
	Not. Not. Not. Not.		Does. Does. Does. Does.
	Not. Not. Not. Not.		Does. Does. Does. Does.
	Not. Not. Not. Not.		Does. Does. Does. Does.
	Not. Not. Not. Not.		Does. Does. Does. Does.

AMALIA opens her book. She mouths the words "first argument" as she writes. She looks at her watch. She mouths the words 9:13 as she writes.

Rob	*(To himself)*
	Not.
Amalia	*(To herself)*
	Does.
Georgia	Heavens!

She looks at the brochure. ROB places a newspaper on the floor to the right of the table. He looks at the front page of the paper and places a stone on it. Through the following he repeats this until he has placed seven papers on the floor.

*

4. Isabel

Georgia	*(Looking at a brochure)*
	Why do Spaniards say Isabel?
Amalia	Why not?
Georgia	For Elizabeth. Why don't they say Isabella?
Amalia	Because Isabella is not Spanish for Elizabeth.
Georgia	I thought that's how you say Elizabeth in Spanish.
Amalia	No.
Georgia	Queen Isabella.
Amalia	No.
Georgia	That's what I thought.
Amalia	Well, it isn't.
Georgia	Oh.
Amalia	You think the "La"
	In "La Católica"
	Is part of Isabel.
	It's the "La"
	Of "La" Católica
	That makes you
	Think that.

	It's Isabel "La"
	Católica.
	Not Isabella.
	That's all.
Georgia	...Not Isabella?
Amalia	No! It's Isabel!
	Not.
	La, lalala-lalala lala
	La, lalala-lalala lala
	La, lalala-lalala lala

But
La, lalala-lalala lala
La, lalala-lalala lala
La, lalala-lalala lala

It's
La, lalala-lalala lala
La, lalala-lalala lala
La, lalala-lalala lala

Ca to li ca.

Georgia and Amalia

Not
La, lalala-lalala lala
La, lalala-lalala lala
La, lalala-lalala lala

But

La, lalala-lalala lala

La, lalala-lalala lala

La, lalala-lalala lala

It's

La, lalala-lalala lala

La, lalala-lalala lala

La, lalala-lalala lala

Ca to li ca.

Amalia	That's what it is.
Georgia	I see.
Amalia	They even call the Infanta of Castille an elephant.
Georgia	An elephant?! Who does?
Amalia	The English do. They call the poor Infanta an elephant.
Georgia	Is she fat?
Amalia	She's not fat.
Georgia	Who is the Infanta of Castille?
Amalia	The Princess Heiress of Spain.
Georgia	Do you mean Elephant and Castle?
Amalia	Yes.
Georgia	Is that what Elephant and Castle means?
Amalia	Yes.
Georgia	Oh, dear.
Amalia	That's right.

*

5. Amerigo

Amalia	Like Amerigo
	Which is
	What
	American comes from
	And sounds American
	But it's not.
Georgia	Not American?
Amalia	It's Italian.
Georgia	Italian?
Amalia	Amerigo Vespucci.
Georgia	United States of Amerigo Vespucci?
Amalia	Si.
Georgia	The word America is not a Greek word or something?
Amalia	Greek...?
Georgia	Something that means...Nirvana or...New World...or Land of Possibility?
Amalia	No.

(Reading in the magazine)

Vespucci, Amerigo, 1454–1512, Italian navigator. Discovered and explored the mouths of the Amazon river in 1499 and sailed along the north shore of South America.

Georgia	Not North America?
Amalia	...No.

(She reads)

The name America was used to honor him.

Georgia	Used to name South America?
Amalia	North America, too.

Georgia	I see.
	(She looks at the travel magazine)
	Listen to this. This is a puzzle.
	(Reading)
	Two women have just met.
	Woman 1: Were you ever in the States before?
	Woman 2: No never.
	Woman 1: Did you just come from Spain?
	Woman 2: No, I've been traveling in America for the last two years.
	Woman 1: You said you never were in the States before.
	Woman 2: Yes.
	Woman 1: Yet you just said you have been here for two years.
	Woman 2: No. Two days. I arrived here two days ago.
	(She turns to AMALIA)
	What's the answer?
Rob	I know the answer.

AMALIA and GEORGIA turn to him.

The woman is using "America" correctly as the name of
the continent from the North to the South Pole is America.
The name given to the union of the colonies in the northern
hemisphere is the United States of America. It's a descrip-
tive name. It was suggested by John Adams and it stayed.
The woman was living or traveling in Canada, or any
of the Central or South American countries for the last
two years.

Georgia	It's a descriptive name? You mean they could have called

it...South of Canada?

Rob   Well, the Spaniards did that in the Southwest.

A place with mountains was "Montana."

That means mountain.

A yellow place was "Amarillo."

That means yellow.

A place with snow was "Nevada."

That means snow.

A red place was "Colorado."

That means red.

States that are united

Is United States

And if they are

In America,

They are of America.

Georgia   We called America after an Italian who discovered South America!

Amalia   The whole continent is America. We are the U.S. of it.

Georgia   And the rest?

Amalia   The rest of the countries have names.

(Reading)

A German mapmaker—

Engraved a map of the New World—

Where Amerigo's discoveries

Were outlined.

On it was engraved Amerigo's name

From that

Amerigo's Map.

From that

America.

Georgia	When I hear "America."
	I see the star-spangled banner
	And the stripes.
	I see red, white and blue.

AMALIA gradually becomes distressed by what she reads.
GEORGIA looks at one of the maps.

*

6. Maps

Georgia	Look at this.
	(Looking more closely)
	Look here.
	(Pause)
	There's no Palos.
	(Looks at the other map)
	Now look at this.
Amalia	What?
Georgia	Look here.
	(Moves her finger around till she finds what she is looking for)
	Here's Palos.
Amalia	Ah.
Georgia	We're not lost.
Amalia	What do you mean?

GEORGIA points to the first map. She slides her finger in
the area where Palos should be.

Georgia	Well, in this map there's no Palos.
	(Indicating the other)
	But in this one there is a town called Palos. Here it is.
	(Pointing)
	Look at these two maps. They are of the same area.
	Southern Spain. Look at this. They look different, don't
	they? Does this look the same as this?
Amalia	No.
Georgia	Do these two look like maps of the same place?
Amalia	No.
Georgia	Look at this map.

They look at it.

And look at this one.

They look at the other. Then GEORGIA points to the first.

Look here. See this road here?
(Pointing to the other)
It's not here.
(Pointing at the same)
Look at this. This,
(Pointing at the other)
it's not here. Why is that?

AMALIA is closely looking at both maps.

Things are built—then abandoned—
then rebuilt. A bridge is built—

it's repaired—then it collapses.
A dam is built—the land is razed—
there's a landfill—a town is built.
It starts to crumble. This town is abandoned—
this town prospers—it's beautiful.
Then, it falls apart. Then it's abandoned—
then it's rebuilt—the ashes pile—
and pile again. Layers—upon layers
of ashes pile and pile. There are ashes
in the air—the air is contaminated—
animals cough—the race is contaminated—
the senses atrophy. Fumes disintegrate
brain cells—common sense atrophies.
We don't recognize ourselves—we can't
see the physical world. Common sense
is replaced by non-ideas expressed by
non-words, and non-gestures—

AMALIA notices that ROB is distressed. He starts walking to the table.

Amalia   …What's the matter?

ROB sits. He stares.

… Rob…?

*

7. Newspapers

Rob   *Note: He will read a couple of items about war,*
injustice, violence. (Indicating the newspaper) Well...this.

Amalia   What...

Rob   This.

Children have to fight wars,

have their little bodies blown apart.

Women are raped and gorged.

Why do we do such terrible things?

The gods look at us

and we're in a state of shame.

As we need.

And need.

And need!

Need and need more.

Need more

and more

and more.

Have more

and more.

Not yet enough!

Not enough!

Not yet enough!

Till we bury ourselves

in garbage

pestilence

bitterness

and abuse.

*

8. A Drop of Water

Amalia   *(Nervously)*

Where are we in relation to all this?

Georgia   Us?

Amalia   Yes, us here in Spain.

How do these people here see us?

As part of what? As part of that?

Are we a part of that?

How do they see us in relation to all this?

Will they think

we're responsible?

Will they think we're a part of it?

(She stands)

Are we in danger?

Will someone tear the clothes

off our backs?

Beat us? Spit at us?

Hate us? Tear our limbs off?

Walk on our mutilated bodies?

Will they think we're guilty

of these things?

Georgia   Don't worry, Amalia.

Amalia   ...because we're Americans?

Does the world hate us?

Do they blame us for those things?

Does the world hate us?

Are we guilty

of those terrible things?

I don't want to

think we're a part of it.
(She starts to cry and sits)
People are so unkind
to those who're not
exactly like them.

They beat someone
because he is
of a different race,
because he speaks
a different tongue,
because he's poor,
because he loves someone
of his own sex,
because she is
of a different sex.
They hate children.
They torture them
and mutilate them.

What is happening to us?
People kill
for a gadget.
They kill
for a pack
of cigarettes.
They kill
just to kill.
(She sits, still breathless)
I'm not talking about being nice.

Just to know that others exist.

To be curious about others.

To want to know someone other than yourself.

Not just to be nice,

but to be curious.

"Oh, look at this—look at that.

Oh, look at that man. What's he doing?"

"Oh, he's picking up something. I wonder
what it is?" "Oh, that woman is leaning over.
She's telling him something." "I wonder what
she's saying?" Just that.

You don't have to weep.

Just be curious.

That's how you know other people exist.

If you are not curious, you are alone.

What do you think bliss is?

To go outside yourself. That's all.

If you experience nothing but yourself
you'll feel no relief.

To get lost outside yourself is bliss.

Not always thinking "I, I, I, I." "I enter."

"I exit." "I'm up." "I'm down."

"I wear this." "I wear that." "Do I like this."

"I don't like that." "I drink."

(She pants as if hyperventilating)

"How do I look?" "How am I doing?"

"How does this look?"

You go around in circles.

Around and around.

And you lose your balance.

You get crazy and wild
and mean and cruel.
But if
you look outside yourself,
you feel
a natural person.

You see,
and you wonder,
and you feel
another, and you learn.

And you love and
that's how you feel
a natural person.

If you think only of yourself
you get crazy and frustrated
and wild and mean and cruel.
That happens to the ones who
are in power
as well as to the ones
who're not.

They also loot and kill and rape.
The same as the ones who are not in power.
They steal and kill
for petty things.
They never think beyond themselves.
What do you think is the reason for cruelty

and oppression
and bigotry
and racism
and a desire
to be drugged
and numbed
and anesthetized.
If God could,
he would
(As she puts her finger in a glass of water)
come back
(As she lets a drop of water fall on the table and points to it)
and say,
"Look at this drop of water.
Therein lies
everything."

*

9. Christian Mystics

BURT enters. He stands between GEORGIA and ROB. He indicates a large circle with his arm. Musical arpeggios accompany his movements, gestures, and words.

Rob, Georgia and Amalia

(Covering their noses and gagging in reaction to his bad smell)
Ugh.

Burt   *(Speaking in an intense and eccentric manner and illustrating his words with gestures)*

Christian mystics saw the earth as a circle. And they saw the moon as her mother.

(He raises his arms. The others gag and cover their noses)

A great white bird who spends the night

(He opens his legs and pantomimes a large egg coming out of his groin)

brooding over her egg.

Others saw the earth

(Indicating a large circle with his arms. The others gag and cover their noses)

as the yolk of an egg.

(He puts his finger in the imaginary egg and licks it. The others gag)

Yum yum—

(Lifting his arm. The others gag and cover their noses)

How does that strike you?

(Lifting his arm. The others gag and cover their noses)

The air around the earth was the white of the egg.

(Lifting his arm. The others gag and cover their noses)

The blue above the clouds was the skin inside the shell.

(Indicating a large circle with his arms. The others gag and cover their noses)

And the fire around it was the shell that binds it?

(He lifts his arm to point to the others)

How does that strike you?

(Silence)

No one has any comments? No comments?

ROB raises his hand. BURT points to him.

You.

Rob   Is the egg hard-boiled or soft-boiled?

They laugh. BURT growls.

Burt   *(Indignant)*
Some—
(Pointing to each)
one-two-three—
*(He gestures as if throwing something on the floor and
presses his foot on it as if crushing a cockroach)*
can't conceive things beyond their noses. Some,
(Pointing to each)
one-two-three—
(He repeats the above)
can't even conceive their noses.
(They laugh derisively)
It's hard-boiled. Close to the surface it is. It's hard-boiled.
Deep inside it isn't. It's soft. Volcanoes. Hot egg yolk.
(He licks his fingers)
Yum-yum.
(He laughs. Then, he speaks to STEVE)
Don't look at me like that. I can't stand that look.
You think I've done something wrong or something?
Are you a faggot or something? I bet you he's a faggot.
Don't look at me like that. I don't feel right about
that. I get a feeling in my stomach, like it's going to
turn. It makes me feel like puking. *(He makes sounds*

as if vomiting all over the floor. The others huddle togeth-
er, cover their noses and make sounds of protest. He then
speaks to STEVE)
What's the matter with you?
(He mumbles to himself. Then, he speaks to the others)
I have this plan. It's a thought.
(As he does a karate chop)
It's like walking through walls.
(As he does a karate chop)
It's like walking through walls.
(As he does a karate chop)
It's like walking through walls.

It's like thinking
you're walking through walls
because you know you can.
It's reality that comes
(He sits on the floor)
from the depth of the earth.
And from the outside.
(Moving the tips of his fingers against each other as if
weaving minuscule threads)
Like mathematics:
insignificant signs
that attest to forces
not yet known to man,
but are clear as sound.
You can go
through the center of the earth
(He does a backwards shoulder roll)

and come out the other side.

(Intensely)

You think I'm crazy?

(Coyly)

I'm not.

(As he skips to the right)

I speak symbolically.

(He sits on the floor on the right)

Others know what I know.

They too are obsessed.

They too feel compelled.

Compelled, like only those

who imagine things,

can be compelled.

We have experienced it

in the mind.

And we must experience it

in reality.

Because we know we can.

That's why we're compelled.

(He turns to STEVE)

Have you ever experienced that?—Hm?

(Pointing to each coyly)

You? You? You? You?—

(He laughs)

It looks like this.

(He turns his back to the audience and lifts his buttocks with his hand while he lets a Bronx cheer out of his mouth)

Some don't understand this.

(Standing and turning his back)
Others understand it and sit on
(He wiggles his buttocks)
their asses. I won't stop till I put it to work.
I'm a modern man!
No one knows that.
Don't you know that?
(He does a spin down kick)
I'm a modern man!
(He does a spear hand crescent)
I'm a modern man!
(He does a spear hand crescent)
I am a modern man!

He does a spear hand crescent. Then he exits talking to himself, laughing, singing, whistling and doing a Charlie Chaplin walk.

*

10. The Indies

Steve   *(With his eyes fixed front)*
As beehives are filled with bees,
the Caribbean islands
were filled with natives
whom the Spaniards called Indians.
Of any soul that ever existed,
God chose the purest and the noblest

and in one fell swoop,

he placed them there.

Let it be known that because of the Spaniards' insatiable
greed and ambition and their desire for riches and for
gold and their desire to improve their position in dispro-
portion to their worth, and because the Indians were so
humble, patient, and easily subdued; because the Spaniards
did not deign to treat them even as they would treat
beasts (would that they had treated them as beasts instead
of as dung in the public square) because of this, hundreds
of thousands died without pity and without faith or
holy sacrament.

(Gospel)

What I'm about to say

is a truth

that everyone even the tyrants

and killers,

know and confess to.

Never,

in all the Indies,

did an Indian

cause any harm

to a Christian.

Instead they thought

they came from heaven

even though they received

nothing but harm, theft, death,

violence and humiliation

from them.

Amalia	*(In a whisper. Referring to* STEVE*)*
	Who's that?
	GEORGIA *and* ROB *look at* STEVE.

*

11. The Church with the Steps

AMALIA looks at her book and reads.

Amalia	"May 9th. Train to Burgos.
	Slept there near the station.
	At 7 am went to Vigo.
	From there went to Lisbon,
	Portugal.
	Very beautiful Lisbon.
	Left Lisbon on Friday
	went on to Cordoba
	got good rooms with three beds each
	and hot water in the bathrooms.
	From there we went through Seville
	on the way to Cadiz
	with the beautiful
	cathedral
	and waterfront promenade
	like Havana."
	(To the others)
	Is this right? Are the dates right?
Rob	Yes, they're right.
Amalia	*(Reading)*

	Then back up to Seville. We went to the church with the steps and saw the tall tower and the courtyards with the potted plants hanging on the walls.
Rob	Amalia, you are my sister and I know you're very smart. But is that all you can say about the cathedral in Seville? "The church with the steps?"
Amalia	Yes.
Rob	Oh, Amalia, Amalia, Amalia.
Amalia	Where the people dance Flamenco and sing like they have their souls in their throats.

AMALIA does a Flamenco intonation. GEORGIA is tickled by this and giggles. In unison, all three make sounds as if giggling and talking while they put on sunglasses, pick up their drinks, cross their legs and drink while they continue making sounds of laughter and fake animated conversation, as children imitating sophisticated adults.

*

12. The Red Hat
GEORGIA puts down her drink.

Georgia	This morning I went out looking for the store where I saw the red hat and I got lost.
	I went this way

and that way
but I couldn't remember

where I was.

So I walked to a man and I said,

"Puede ayudarme?
I am lost.
Estoy partida.

Puede ayudarme
Estoy partida. Partida."

And he smiled and said,

"Mmm mmm mmm mmm
Mm Mm
Mm mm Mm mm mm."

So I went to a woman and said,
"Puede ayudarme?
I am lost.
Estoy partida.
Puede ayudarme
Estoy partida. Partida."

And she looked worried and said,

"Mmm mmm mmm mmm

Mm Mm
Mm mm Mm mm mm."

Then, I came upon a man in a café and I said,

"Puede ayudarme
Estoy partida. Partida."

And he offered me his glass and said, "Drink red wine. It
will help you." And I said, "I don't need red wine. I'm
already partida. Tell me where's that store. Estoy Partida."
Partida.

And he said, "Red wine will ease the pain." I am partida
but I have no pain. Why won't they show me the way?
Rob   You said, "I'm broken." Lost is "perdida."

They laugh.

Georgia   Oh, well. Then. I just walked and walked. Hopeless—
discouraged.
Walked and walked
When suddenly.
I was standing
in front
of the store
with-the-red-hat!
In front of the store
with-the-red-hat!

	And how was your day?
Amalia	I lost my passport, but then I found it. And—I got a date—for tonight.
Georgia and Rob	
	What!
	(Clapping)
	With whom?—With whom?
Amalia	With-the-clerk-in-our-hotel!
Georgia	*(Clapping)*
	He's cute! He's cute!
Amalia	And he found my passport! I left it on the counter! And I gave him a kiss!
	(To ROB)
	And what did you do today?
Rob	I did fine.
Georgia	What did you do?
Rob	I was looking
	for shoe polish.
Georgia	Shoe polish?
Rob	To shine my shoes.
Amalia	And?
Rob	I said "shoe polish" and no one understood. I said "Shoe polish." And no one understood. Then I went
	(Moving his arms as if holding the end of a rag on each hand to polish a shoe)
	like this,
	and someone said,
	"maracas!"
Georgia and Amalia	
	(Disappointed)

Oooh...

Rob   Then someone said,

"Betun."

And that was right!

(He lifts a foot and points to the polished shoe)

Betun!

Amalia and Georgia

(This is a kind of "bebop")

Betun, betun,

Betun-betun-betun.

Rob   Be-bebe Be-be

Be-bebe Be

Be-be-be Bebe

Be-be-be Tun.

Georgia   So that's how you say shoe polish...

Rob   *(Pointing to his shoe)*

Sure. Betun.

(To GEORGIA)

So. Did you buy the hat?

Georgia   I bought it.

Amalia   Where is it?

Georgia   *(As she goes to where she has hidden it)*

I bought it. I bought it. I bought it.

(As she puts on the hat)

The red hat!

Rob   The red hat.

Amalia   The red red hat.

Georgia   Hat, hat, hat.

Rob   *(As GEORGIA returns to the table)*

The red hat.

The red red hat.

Georgia   *(As she sits)*

Hat, hat, hat.

All Three   The red, red hat.

Hat, hat, hat.

Hat hat.

In unison, all three put on sunglasses, cross their legs, and pick up their drinks while they make sounds imitating animated and sophisticated conversation as children do and miming, laughing, and drinking.

＊

13. A Malady

Rob   This coffee's terrible. Whose idea was it to come to this place?

Amalia   I don't know whose idea it was.

Rob   From now on I'm taking charge of the travel plans.

Amalia   You're not taking charge of the travel plans. You're terrible at making plans.

Rob   Of all places you had to choose this?

Amalia   *(To Rob)*

You always have to blame someone else when things go wrong.

You always do.

In your life,

you always blame
someone not you.

When something
goes wrong.
You blame anyone
but yourself.

You manage to find
someone to lead you.
So you can blame
someone not yourself
if something
goes wrong.

So you can feel
superior and oppressed
at the same time.
And pout and
lose spirit.
And feel obedient
and rebellious
at the same time.
And righteous and
ineffectual
at the same time.
How can you manage all that?
How can you manage to be righteous
and ineffectual at the same time?

Rob   It's a defect of my generation.

Amalia	Well, quit it.
Rob	Can't help it. It's there and it's going to stay. So forget it.
Amalia	You're stupid!
Rob	That's right and I can't help that either. And you're more stupid. And you don't even know it.
Georgia	You're both stupid. So quit it.
Amalia	You quit it! He just must blame someone else for everything that goes wrong.
Rob	Whom have I blamed?
Georgia	A malady in his mind and in the minds of so many, many, many, many, many.
Amalia	It's a malady.
Georgia	Blaming other people.
Rob	I haven't blamed anyone.
Georgia	Something is not right. So we think someone else is responsible.
Amalia	Never us.
Georgia	No one is responsible.
Amalia	It's always them.
Georgia	Whoever appears to be responsible.
Amalia	Whoever is in charge.
Georgia	When you make someone else responsible for your own life…
Amalia	That's how the world ends.
Georgia	It just dies.
Amalia	Simply.
Georgia	Simply.

*

14. Socializing

Burt   *(Entering)*

That's nice. Very nice. It sounds nice.

(He sits on GEORGIA's lap and puts a piece of candy in front of her)

Candy for you.

(He puts another piece of candy in front of AMALIA)

And this is for you. You don't have to thank me.

(To GEORGIA)

My father had a tavern.

(Pointing his finger to GEORGIA's head like a gun)

And yours? What does your father do?

Georgia He's an accountant. Why?

Burt   *(Crossing his arms and pointing the fingers of his other hand at AMALIA)*

And yours? What does your father do?

Amalia   Why do you want to know?

Burt   To hold him up. Ha ha ha ha ha ha. I want to hold up your father.

(To GEORGIA)

And your father, too. Bang bang.

(He laughs and snorts. Then, to AMALIA)

Bang bang.

(He laughs and snorts. Then blows on both fingers like guns)

I'm being sociable.

(He laughs)

Amalia   That's not a way to be sociable.

Burt   I'm not talking to you. I'm talking to her. When I talk to you I'll be sociable to you.

(He makes sounds of pleasure as he moves his eyebrows)

Now I'm being sociable to her.

(He makes sounds suggesting friendly conversation)

You ask me how is one sociable? You ask the person what their father does. You tell the person what your father does. And you get to know each other. Socialize. You want to know what my father does?

Georgia *(Pushing him off her lap)*

I don't care what your father does. You want to socialize? Socialize with someone else. Don't socialize with me.

Burt Why not madam? I'm a gentleman and I think you're cute.

(To AMALIA)

You're cute, too. Yum, yum.

(He licks his lips. Then, to both)

I was married once to a nice woman. Nice family. Nice house. Solid middle class. But it didn't mean anything.

Georgia It didn't?

Burt *(Standing)*

Not a thing. Except I had a son. One can have a son very easily.

(Thrusting his pelvis forward)

Hump. Hump.

(Pulling his pelvis back)

If you pull out two seconds before, you don't have a son.

(Thrusting his pelvis forward)

If you don't pull out you have a son. Having a son takes two seconds.

(Thrusting his pelvis forward twice)

Hump-hump. You can have a son in two seconds.

(Pulling his pelvis back)
If you pull out two seconds before, you don't have a son.
There are people who believe the Earth is square.

They all laugh loudly.

Ancient Peruvians did. The Aztecs thought the universe
was in the shape of five squares.
(Pantomiming five squares around Georgia's head)
One in the center and one extending from each side.

They all laugh loudly.

Some have seen the earth as a wheel.

They all laugh.

And so on and so on. What do we think now? Or do we
think? Think-think. They said I went crazy because I started
seeing mermaids. What's wrong with that?
(He becomes agitated and speaks rapidly)
It's better than seeing people who want to destroy you and
want to take advantage of you. Better than seeing people
take everything from you. Everything that you worked for
day and night every day of your life. It's better to see...
(Starting to pull at his leg)
your leg rot while it's still attached than to see it cut off.
Better to see it gangrene and give you pain worse than you
ever imagined than to let it be taken off—because it's
yours—

(He starts to walk down off the table)

just like those islands were mine. They said I saw mermaids. I didn't see mermaids. I said I saw mermaids. Because I saw something that resembled mermaids.

(He sits on his haunches and emulates the sensuality of the manatee)

Round faces, big eyes, long eyelashes. Sensual bodies with breasts like women. When a man sees a manatee he can get a hard-on. They're something like seals, only a lot more attractive. A lot more human. It still turns me on to think of them. Round shoulders like girls. Round breasts. Soft skin. Like mermaids.

(He starts going upstage and up the slope)

They said I lied. I didn't lie. It was partly lies and partly ignorance. What does that make me? Good? Bad?

(To STEVE)

You have something against me?

Steve   I have nothing against you.

Burt   *(Continues going up)*

You have nothing against me because I cut the hands off Indians?—I didn't. Didn't you know that? They were laughing at me.

(He falls to the floor and convulses as if with an epileptic attack)

I didn't! I didn't! I didn't!

Amalia   What's wrong with him?

*

15. The Holy Fathers in the Desert

Steve

The Spaniards came into the lands of the Indians and they saw the Indians as ravenous wolves and tigers and lions. Since their arrival all they did was mangle them and butcher them and impale them, and dismember them, and torture them and drive them to despair and inflict upon them every imaginable form of cruelty that man has ever suffered from man. Because of their cruelty, those islands were despoiled and left desolate. Christians started by taking the Indian women and children to serve themselves and to misuse them. They ate the Indian's food which was the fruit of their sweat and toil. Because they wanted more than what the Indians gave them of their own free will (what was enough meat for three Indian families of ten for a month, a Christian ate in one day). Because of these and other ills perpetrated, Indians started to understand that those men could not have come from heaven. Indians were clean and had clear and quick minds. They were capable and docile and were open to any good teaching that was taught to them. Of all people the Indians possessed the least amount of material goods and had little desire to possess more. They were not ambitious, not greedy. They were not presumptuous. Their food was so plain, the Holy Fathers in the desert could not have eaten more plainly. Except for a loincloth, they walked in the nude. They slept on a simple mat on the floor, or sometimes on a net that hung from trees. The Christians overpowered them. The Indian's weapons were too weak to defend them against

the Spaniards' horses, spades and lances and such cruelty
as they had never known.

*

16. The Bottom of the Well

Burt In the town of Syene
in the Greek colony of Egypt,
on the first day of summer
(Pointing upward with the pointer)
at exactly noon,
the sun shines
exactly overhead.
Now, on that day at noon,
(He places the bottle on the floor)
if you look down the deepest well,
(He puts his eye to the mouth of the bottle)
you will see the sun
shining on the bottom
of the well.
In the third century A.D.,
Eratosthenes knew this.
And listen
to what he did.
He looked
for the tallest tower
*(He places the stool at a distance from the bottle. He taps
the bottle with the tip of the pointer and draws a line to
the tower)*

following the straightest line due north from the well, 517 miles north of Syene, was Alexandria. On the first day of summer, at exactly noon, when the sun was hitting the bottom of the well in Syene, in Alexandria the tower threw a shadow of 7.5 degrees, which is 1/48th of the 360 degrees in a circle. Eratosthenes multiplied the distance between Alexandria and Syene by forty-eight to complete the circle and arrived at 24,816 for the miles of the Earth's circumference which is only fifty miles off the actual measurement of the earth's circumference through the poles. In the third century A.D. they not only knew the Earth was round but they knew the measure of its circumference.

(Expecting a reaction)

What do you think of that?

(Wielding his pointer)

You're not impressed? You think you could've figured it out? Never!

(He growls)

You think you could've?

(He throws the pointer on the floor and walks away)

*

17. The Shrouded Ship

The shrouded sailboat crosses the stage. The black cloth is now tattered. The ship is filled with garbage bags.

*

18. Sailing

Steve *(Setting himself as the mast of the boat, he illustrates what he describes)*

The front part of the boat
is the bow,
and the back is the stern.
"Abeam" means
to either side of the boat.
If I am the boat
and things are
in relation to me.
The right side of the boat
is called
the starboard side.
The left side is called
the port side.
On a sailing boat,
let's say a sloop,
there is one mast.
My neck and my head
are the mast.
And this arm,
is attached to the mast,
and it's called the boom.
Now the main sail is a triangle
formed from the top of the mast
coming down to the end of the boom
and running along my arm.

Maria Irene Fornes Terra Incognita

107

Sloops have another sail
attached to the top of the mast
called a jib or a foresail.
Now it can run free on either
side of the mainsail.
So, here we have two sails;
a mainsail and a foresail.
I'm sailing and
I want to get to
(Indicating the direction of the house)
that house over there.
The wind is coming
(Indicating to the same direction as the house)
from that direction.
I can't sail directly to the house
because that would be sailing
into the wind.
What would happen is my sails
wouldn't fill.
They'd "luff."
Which is like a rustle and shake
and the boat doesn't move.
So, what I have to do
is zigzag, or tack
towards that house—
(Pointing)
there's the house.
To do that,
I steer a little
off from the direction

of the wind.
My sails will fill
and I'll begin to move
and I would be
on a starboard tack
because the wind is
coming over
the starboard beam
of the boat.
Then, after a while
I have to zag or
"come about"
which is changing
to the other tack.
Now I steer the boat
to starboard
and the sails
come across
and fill this way.
The wind is coming over
the port beam
of the boat,
and we're now on a port tack.
After a while
I have to zag or
"come about" again
and now we're on
our way
tacking towards the house.
There's also something

called "a reach"
where the wind comes from off of
either beam.
The wind is a beam.
Now the sails can be let out
a little further,
but not too much.
If you let the sails out
too far. They'd luff again.
The sails still have to be
pulled in order to catch the wind.
Now, the big maneuver is
"running free" where the wind
is behind you—Either directly
aft or only slightly off the aft.
Here the sails can really be
run out
because the wind's pushing directly
and going just where we want to go.
You could have one sail on each
side which is called "wing in wing"
where the mainsail and
foresail are over either beam.
But that's rarely done.
If the wind's fluky
or very strong
you can't do that.
Now, if you're "running free"
and you need to change direction,
you have to "jibe"

and that's a lot trickier
than "coming about."
Because what that means is,
you have to bring the stern
through the wind.
And you have to really know what
you're doing
because if you don't
and the wind is very strong.
You can either capsize the boat,
or the boom can come across
with such force
that it can rip the boat apart.

Burt   *(To GEORGIA and AMALIA)*
See? You thought it was easy? It's not that easy.

*

19. In Perpetuity

Burt   The land where you're standing is mine, in perpetuity. How
could I not be fit to govern what is mine in perpetuity. They
owe me ten percent of all the profits from all the lands I
own and still own and will own in perpetuity, by contract
which I hold.
*(He takes an old stained piece of paper from his pocket.
He shows it to GEORGIA)*
Here it is. In perpetuity.
(To AMALIA)

See? In perpetuity. See it was a business. A business enter-prise. I was supposed to get ten percent in perpetuity. Like a patent. It was supposed to be a business...like any other, but it was too big. So I was left out.

(To ROB)

See? In perpetuity.

(He puts the paper in his pocket)

*

20. Conga Line

Burt	*(Taking GEORGIA by the hand)*
	Ok. Come, let me show you around. Have fun.
Georgia	*(As she goes with him)*
	Why?
Burt	I've been around. Get it? Round?
	(As he starts doing a conga step)
	Tata tatata ta. Ta ta tatata ta.
Georgia	*(To AMALIA as she joins BURT in the conga step)*
	You wanna come?
Amalia	*(To GEORGIA)*
	You're going?
Georgia	Yeah.
Amalia	Why?
Georgia	It may be fun.
Burt	I've been around. Get it?
Amalia	*(Joining the conga line)*
	Okay.

>   *(To Rob)*
>   You're coming, Robbie?
>   *(Rob shakes his head)*
>   Ciao.
>   *(They exit singing)*

Amalia, Burt, Georgia

>   Ta-ta Ta-ta Ta Ta
>   Ta-ta Ta-ta Ta Ta.

Georgia   Ciao.

Burt   Ciao.

*

21. Crystal Ball

Rob goes towards the café. He stops and turns to Steve.

Rob   Would you like some coffee?

Steve   No, thanks.

Rob takes a few more steps and turns to Steve again.

Rob   Would you like anything else?

Steve looks at Rob

>   Soda?

Steve   Yes, please.

Rob   I'll get it.

ROB exits. STEVE goes to the table, sits down. ROB enters with a bottle of soda and gives it to STEVE. STEVE lifts the bottle to offer a toast and drinks. ROB sits across from STEVE and watches him drink. Then, he stands and walks a few steps to the left.

When I was seven I lived in fear of a tall skinny boy who was crazy. I was afraid of him and he knew it. When he saw me in the street he came to terrorize me. I'd continue walking but he'd catch up with me and tap me on the shoulder. I would become paralyzed and break into a cold sweat. He would reach for my pencil box and take whatever he wanted as he said strange things in a strange voice. When he finished he threw the box at me and walked away whistling. I've tried to protect myself against being wounded or humiliated by anyone.

He is despondent and puts his head down. A car enters on the stage left area. GEORGIA is at the wheel. AMALIA noticing that ROB is upset comes out of the car and takes a few steps towards him.

Amalia   ...Rob...let's go...

ROB moves to the table.

Rob
...It's time to go...*(Pause)* What's the matter?
(Speaking in a very intense manner, with his eyes blank, as if in a trance)
If you look into a crystal ball and ask, "Crystal ball, will there be such a thing as the end of the world?"

(Short pause)

The crystal ball doesn't answer. Why don't you answer, crystal ball? Will there be such a thing as the end of the world? *(To AMALIA)* It doesn't answer—do you know? *(There is a moment's silence)*
Why don't you answer?
(To STEVE)
Is this the end of the world?
(Pause)
Why don't you answer?

AMALIA *tries to help* ROB *up.*

*

22. Christians

Steve   Christians slapped them, punched them and beat them with sticks and even raised their hands to the chiefs.

AMALIA *and* ROB *take a couple of steps left.* ROB *turns to* STEVE *violently as* AMALIA *tries to restrain him and pull him away.*

Rob   *(Swinging his arm towards* STEVE*)*
Shut up! Shut up! Shut up!

AMALIA *pulls him towards the car.* ROB *speaks over* STEVE'S *lines.*

Shut up! Shut up! Shut up!

AMALIA forces ROB into the car and gets in herself. The car starts moving slowly.

Steve
They entered the town and without sparing either children or elders or pregnant women or new mothers, they tore them to pieces as if they were sheep in their flock. They made bets that with one slash of their knife, the could dis-embowel and rip a man in half, cut off his head, or cut open his belly. They took infants from their mother's breast and by their feet flung them against boulders. They threw them in the river and pushed them under shouting, "Float whoever you are." They put a sword through both the infant and the mother and anyone else whom they found in their path. They hung thirteen men close together in a bunch with their feet just touching the ground. And, in the name of our redeemer and the twelve apostles, they lit a fire under their feet and burned them alive. Others were wrapped in dry straw and were set on fire. Others had their hands slashed and with their hands still dangling from their wrists they were sent walking into the hills where rebel Indians were hiding. They trained fierce dogs to tear the Indians to pieces and eat them as if they were pigs. They tied Indians and put them on a grill to roast under slow burning embers.

The car appears in the promontory. AMALIA and GEORGIA get off the car and walk to the edge to listen to STEVE. ROB follows. He stands next to GEORGIA. Soon he starts to sob.

While they screamed in pain, their souls left them. Once the Indians screamed so loudly that the captain, either because he felt sorry for them or because the screaming kept him from sleeping, he ordered that they not be burned but drowned. The guard did not drown them, instead he put sticks in their mouths to make them silent. He kindled the fire and let them roast even more slowly while he waited.

GEORGIA has put her arms around ROB. She starts to lead him back to the car. AMALIA follows. Saetas are heard in the distance.

I saw all the things I have said and even more. I know the name of the guard and even his relatives in Seville.

The car starts. The lights begin to fade slowly all around STEVE.

Because once in a great while, though ever so rarely, an Indian did kill a Christian; they passed a law that for every Christian killed, Christians could kill one hundred of them.

The last light begins to fade as the volume of the music increases and is heard through the actors' bows.

The End

Steak Knife Bacchae

by Joseph Goodrich

Steak Knife Bacchae *was first presented at the 15th Annual Padua Hills Playwrights Festival, U.S.C., Los Angeles, California, in 1995. The play was directed by Michael Hacker and performed by the author.*

It was subsequently presented by Asylum at the Zeitgeist Multi-Disciplinary Arts Center, New Orleans, LA, in 2000, with the same director and cast.

One actor plays all the parts in **Steak Knife Bacchae**. *The "characters" are figures made from the cheapest material available (cardboard, house paint, etc.) and mounted on large steak knives—hence the title.*

The CHORUS enters.

Chorus   WAR ALL THE TIME
NO MORE
NO LESS
WAR ECONOMY
TROUBLE WITH THE SLAVES
OUTPOSTS CRUMBLING
WE'RE NOBODY'S FRIEND
BIG FAMILIES TUMBLING
TO THE BLOOD BANQUET BLUES
WE CAN'T GET CLEAN
THINGS ARE TURNING MEAN
EVERYONE'S BEAT TO SHIT
FLAYED TO RIBBONS
PULVERIZED
BY LIES
BY A LOT OF LIES
LAWS SHUCKED
JUSTICE JUST AS FUCKED
NO MERCY
LESS BEAUTY
NO FUTURE
IF WE'RE LUCKY
HISTORY'S BLEEDING FROM THE NOSE
IT'S DOWN FOR THE COUNT
IT'S OUT
FROM NOW ON
ONLY LESS
NO MORE MORE

NO MORE MORE AND MORE
ONLY LESS AND LESS
SENSE*LESS
MIND*LESS
HOPE*LESS
MORE AND MORE OF LESS AND LESS
MORE AND MORE LOSS
LOST IN LOSS
LOST IN DEATH AND NOSTALGIA
STUCK IN THE CHUTE
WAITING FOR THE HAMMER
HOPING FOR THE HAMMER
CRYING FOR THE HAMMER
PRAYING FOR THE HAMMER
NO MORE
NO LESS
ANCIENT TIMES FOR ANCIENT CRIMES

(I'M SO GLAD
I DON'T LIVE
IN THEBES...)

A STRANGER HAS ARRIVED AT THE GATES!

DIONYSUS
BORSTAL BOY
BAD LUCK KID
BOUNDER, ROUNDER, FOUNDER
OF THE FESTIVAL
A STAMPING BULL

A YELLOW*EYED LION
A SERPENT*HEADED SEDITIONIST

(I MYSELF MET HIM
IN THE FORM OF AN INDIAN
GREYHOUND DEPOT
MINNEAPOLIS
1982

DENNIS BLACK FEATHER
HE WROTE IN MY BOOK
A.K.A. DIONYSUS, GIVER OF THE GRAPE
ON HIS WAY TO DIE IN DENVER
SEEN AGAIN IN TUCSON
BORN AGAIN IN MEMPHIS.)

DIONYSUS
FATHERED BY A GOD
MOTHERED BY A WOMAN

BENT, INTENT
ON MENDING WHAT'S RENT—
THE RAVELED SLEEVE OF CARE, ETC.—
THROUGH THAT WHICH BRINGS
THE POOR MAN SLEEP:
MUSIC, WINE AND DANCE

MUSIC, WINE AND DANCE:
STILL ENOUGH TO
RAISE THE HACKLES AND SHACKLES

OF THE ONES WHO SHOOT
THE PIANO PLAYER
SMASH THE URN
AND BREAK THE LEGS OF DANCERS

A STRANGER WAITS AT THE GATES
FILL THE CITY WITH NOISE
DIONYSUS... HAS ARRIVED

Dionysus DON'T STAND AT THE PARTY WITH THE GIFT IN
YOUR HANDS.
OPEN IT UP. IT'S YOURS. UNWRAP IT. GO ON...
GOOD. YOU'VE UNWRAPPED IT.
NOW LIFT THE LID...GOOD.
REMOVE THE TISSUE PAPER. THAT'S RIGHT...
TELL ME: WHAT'S IN THE BOX?
WHAT COULD IT BE?
THERE'S A HEAD IN THE BOX.
WHOSE HEAD COULD THAT BE?
IT'S YOUR HEAD.
THOSE ARE YOUR EYES
STARING INTO YOUR EYES.
IT'S YOU IN THE BOX.
TELL ME: WHO PUT YOU IN THERE?
TELL ME: HOW LONG HAS IT BEEN?
SO LONG YOU FORGOT
THERE WAS ANYTHING ELSE?
TELL ME: IS THE BOX YOU'RE IN TOO SMALL?
WOULD YOU LIKE A BIGGER ONE?
THEY'LL GIVE YOU ONE.

BIGGER BOXES ARE COFFINS.

WHO PUT YOU IN THERE?
DON'T YOU WANT TO KNOW?
IF I WERE YOU
I'D FIND OUT WHO
AND I'D SMASH THEM.

THAT'S A GOD'S ADVICE:
IF IT DOESN'T SERVE YOU—
SMASH IT.

IF IT LOCKS YOU UP—
SMASH IT.

IF YOU DON'T LIKE
YOUR PRISON—
SMASH IT

FIRST THINGS FIRST.

Chorus GODS THEMSELVES MANY MANY ENDS MAKE/
AND IS HAS HERE GODS MANY/THEY LEAST/GOD
HAPPEN TODAY/IS HAPPEN/DOES HAPPEN/FOR THE
EXPECTED MANY/SURPRISING WOULD HAPPEN/ TO
THINGS HAPPEN UNEXPECTED/ AND HAS WAYS/
MOST HAPPENS AND EXPECTED/MAKES WHAT IS
HERE THEMSELVES/MANY ENDS/ EXPECT NOT
LEAST TODAY/FORMS MANIFEST FORMS/ SUR-
PRISING WOULD HAPPEN/THINGS THOUGHT

HAPPEN NOT/THEMSELVES UNEXPECTED/ UNPRE-
DICTABLE/ EXPECT NOT FOR TODAY/TAKE FORMS
MANIFEST IN WAYS/MOST FIND WAYS/MANIFEST
IN FORMS UNEXPECTED/AND IS HAS HERE/GODS
MANY GODS/THEY EXPECT FOR GOD HAPPENS/
TAKE MANIFEST WHAT MANIFEST/FORMS SUR-
PRISING WOULD HAPPEN/THOUGHT NOT MAKES IS
HERE/MANY THEMSELVES IN WHAT DOES/HERE
HAPPEN/HAPPENS/MAKES/IS HERE.

PENTHEUS—
GRANDSON OF CADMUS
SON OF AGAVE
PENTHEUS POSSESSES ALL THE STATELY VIRTUES
ALL THE KINGLY GRACES
BUT HIS MIND'S A BADLY KNITTED BONE
A TWISTED FISTFUL OF CRIPPLED KNUCKLES
HE'S A WALKING IRON LUNG...
PENTHEUS STANDS ON THE PALACE STEPS.

Pentheus   ORDER. ORDER. SANITY. TRUE. CHAOS. UPROAR.
ORDER. PROMISCUOUS. SECRET. LEWD. HOLY.
ECSTASY. WINE. PIETY. IRON. DRUNKEN FILTH.
ROT POISON. ORDER. ROASTED. WOMB. PROFANITY.
ORDER. ORDER. SANITY. TRUE. WINE PIETY. IRON
DRUNKEN. DISGUSTING. CAMPAIGNING. PROMIS-
CUOUS HYPOCRISY. CHAINED. CAGED. WOMB.
CUNNING SUBVERSION. CUNNING ORDER. ORDER.
SANITY. ORDER. ORDER. CHAOS. UPROAR. ORDER.
FILTH. ROT. POISON. HOME. WOMB. BASTARD.

SUBVERSION. ORDER. CHILDREN. DEEP PROFANITY.
OBSCENITY. ORDER. SANITY. LEWD. HOLY. ECSTASY.
ROASTED. DETAIL REALITY. CHILDREN. DEEP
SERVICE. WOMB PROFANITY. OBSCENITY. DETAIL.
REALITY. PROMISCUOUS. DISEASE. DRUNKEN.
HYPOCRISY. CHAINED. CAGED. CUNNING SUBVER-
SION. CUNNING SANITY. ORDER!

*Two old men—*CADMUS *and the blind* TIRESIAS*—enter.*
Both have canes. Both move slowly.

Tiresias	STANDING POSTURE?
Cadmus	PLANTIGRADE FEET. REASONABLY SO.
Tiresias	HIPS?
Cadmus	EXTENSION IN EXTERNAL ROTATION EXCEEDS EXTENSION IN INTERNAL ROTATION.
Tiresias	KNEES?
Cadmus	NO MEASURABLE ATROPHY IN THE QUADRICEPS.
Tiresias	JOINTS?
Cadmus	NO EFFUSION. SYMMETRICAL EXTENSION.
Tiresias	LIGAMENTS?
Cadmus	INTACT.
Tiresias	MENISCI?
Cadmus	NEGATIVE MCMURRAY MANEUVER.
Tiresias	PATELLA?
Cadmus	POSITIVE PATELLO/PELVIC COMPRESSION. MINOR SCARRING OF LATERAL COMPARTMENT. A TENDENCY TO LATERAL LUXATION.
Tiresias	PROGNOSIS?
Cadmus	PATELLAR REHABILITATION. GENTLE STRETCHING

	AND ICE SHOULD HELP. TAKE STAIRS SLOWLY.
Tiresias	YOU'RE OLD.
Cadmus	I MAY BE OLD, BUT I'M NOT BLIND.
Tiresias	I MAY BE BLIND, BUT I'M NOT STUPID. WHEN IT'S TIME TO DANCE, WE DANCE.
Cadmus	IS IT TIME?
Tiresias	ARE YOU STUPID?

CADMUS dances.

| **Tiresias** | ...WHERE ARE YOU? WHAT ARE YOU DOING? |
| **Cadmus** | I'M DANCING...DANCE! |

Both old men dance.

Cadmus	ARE YOU DANCING?
Tiresias	ARE YOU ASKING?
Cadmus	I'M DANCING...I FEEL YOUNG AGAIN!
Tiresias	YOU LOOK YOUNGER. ALL PRAISE AND POWER TO DIONYSUS!
Cadmus	ALL PRAISE AND POWER TO DIONYSUS!

PENTHEUS enters.

Pentheus	I AM THE POWER HERE!
	WHAT'S WORSE THAN AN OLD MAN WITH NO SHAME?
	TWO OLD MEN WITH NO SHAME.
	OLD MEN SHOULD:
	GET UP WITH CHICKENS

GO DOWN WITH THE SUN
PLAY CARDS IN THE MORNING
NAP AFTERNOONS
STAY INSIDE IN THE EVENING
CRACK WALNUTS AND WAIT TO DIE
WITH DIGNITY
EXERCISE HUMILITY
LET OTHERS HELP YOU
WAKE UP FIVE TIMES A NIGHT
WORRY ABOUT FALLING
ENVY THE YOUNG
CRY UNEXPECTEDLY
FEEL ABILITY COLLAPSE
DESIRE SHRINK
BONES GET BRITTLE
SERVE ON COMMITTEES
SIT ON THE PORCH AND REMINISCE
AS YOUR MIND FRAYS AT THE EDGES
KNOW YOUR PLACE
KEEP YOUR PLACE
BE THANKFUL WE'VE KEPT A PLACE FOR YOU
CULTIVATE HARMLESS PASTIMES
STAY OUT OF TROUBLE
NO DANCING
NO ECSTASY
DECORUM
DIGNITY
ORDER!

PENTHEUS exits.

Tiresias	PUNK!
Cadmus	MY OWN FLESH AND BLOOD.
Tiresias	I THOUGHT YOU RAISED HIM RIGHT.
Cadmus	HE'S LOST HIS MIND...I BET HE'S ON DRUGS... I FOUGHT IN THE WAR, YOU KNOW!
Tiresias	YOU FOUGHT—I PREDICTED IT.
Cadmus	YOU KNOW WHAT I PREDICT? TWO OLD MEN GO TO THE MOUNTAINS. THEY GET DRUNK. THEY DANCE. THEY FALL ASLEEP IN A PILE OF LEAVES.
Tiresias	YOUR GRANDSON WON'T LIKE IT.
Cadmus	"HE WHO FUCKS NUNS WILL LATER JOIN THE CHURCH"...LET'S GO. COME ON. YOU DON'T WANT TO GET CAUGHT AND LOCKED IN YOUR HOUSE, DO YOU?
Tiresias	HE WOULDN'T DO THAT...YES, HE WOULD—COME ON!
Chorus	A MESSENGER ENTERS!
Messenger	TELL. TELL. MUST TELL. CAN'T. CAN'T TELL. TELL WHAT? WHAT? WHAT TELL WHAT? CAN'T. WON'T TELL? CAN'T. WOULD TELL. CAN'T. WHAT TELL? HOW TELL? WHAT TELL HOW TELL WHAT I SAW? TELL? TELL YOU? CAN'T. CAN'T TELL. WHY CAN'T? HOW TELL WHAT TELL TELL HOW WELL TELL YOU? WHERE HOW START? START. STOP. STOP? CAN'T STOP. CAN'T? TRY? START...
	TRIPLE TIGHT DRUM BEAT. TRIPLE TIGHT DRUM BEAT. TRIPLE TIGHT DRUM BEAT. BREATHING.

TRIPLE TIGHT DRUM BEAT.

WOMEN.

BREATHING. GLASSY GLADE. CAVERN. COVE
FIELD. FLOWER LUSH. FLOWER LUSH BRIGHT OAK
SOUL FLESH. FLOWER. FLOWER LUSH. FLESH
FLOWER. FLESH OAK. FLESH LUSH.

DIONYSUS.

TRIPLE TIGHT TIMBREL FEAST. SKIN STREAM.
SNAKE IVY. SNAKE HAIR. GOLD. GOLDEN. HORN.
HORNS. PINS. GOLD FIRE FLESH SWEET WEARY
LABOR WEARY SILENCE SONG SILENCE.

TIMBREL FEAST. FEAST WEARY. HUNT. BLOOD RAW
FLESH RIBS HOOVES BLOOD AIR UHHHH...UHHH-
HHHHH...UHHHHHHHH.

EEEEEAAAAARRRRTTTTTTTHHHHHHHHHHHH!

Chorus THE MESSENGER IS REVIVED, AND HIS STORY TOLD.
SEVERAL SHEPHERDS AND HERDSMEN ATTEMPTED
TO CAPTURE THE BACCHAE AND BRING THE
WOMEN—LED IN THEIR FRENZIES BY AGAVE—
BACK TO TOWN, THEREBY WINNING THE LOVE
AND ADMIRATION OF PENTHEUS, AND (NOT TO
PUT TOO FINE A LINE ON IT) A BOUNTY. BUT THE
WOMEN, IN THEIR DIONYSIAN RAPTURES, THIS

MULTITUDE IN TRANSPORTS OF JOY—TO QUOTE
THE OLD IRISHMAN—TORE THE FLOCK AND HERDS
APART. THE SHEPHERDS AND HERDSMEN BARELY
ESCAPED ALIVE. THE BACCHAE CONTINUED
ONWARD, RIPPING THROUGH A SMALL HILLSIDE
COMMUNITY. FLAMES PLAYED ABOUT THEIR
HEADS, BUT NOT A HAIR WAS SINGED.

PENTHEUS JUMPS SALTY. HIS FIRST IMPULSE IS TO
SEND IN THE TROOPS. DIONYSUS ASSURES HIM
THAT SOLDIERS ARE NO MATCH FOR THE BACCHAE.
THIS IS BORNE OUT BY THE SHEPHERDS' STORY.
ANOTHER APPROACH IS NEEDED. DIONYSUS
SUGGESTS THAT PENTHEUS VISIT THE BACCHAE
HIMSELF. PENTHEUS RELUCTANTLY AGREES.
HIS DESIRE TO SEE WHAT'S HAPPENING IN THE
HILLS KILLS CAUTION.

SETS HIM ROILING AND BOILING WITH ATTRACTION
AND REPULSION.

GETS HIM ITCHING LIKE A HANDFUL OF ANTS.

SOMETHING'S RIPPING LOOSE INSIDE HIM
SO THAT HIS REASON, HIS REASON
HIS REASON MUST ALLOW
WHATEVER WILL HAPPEN
TO HAPPEN.

Pentheus   WHEN DO WE START?

Dionysus   AS SOON AS WE'VE DISGUISED YOU.

Pentheus	WHAT?!
Dionysus	THE ONLY WAY TO SEE THE BACCHAE IS TO BE ONE OF THE BACCHAE. NO DECEIVERS, UN-BELIEVERS OR STRANGERS ALLOWED. YOU UNDERSTAND THAT, DON'T YOU?

DIONYSUS disguises PENTHEUS as a woman.

Pentheus	DISSEMBLERS QUELLED INCUMBENTLY. FACT FINDING MISSION. OBSERVER STATUS. ADVISORY CAPACITY. STATED GOAL TO DETERMINE AREAS OF CONTAMINATION AND CONTAIN INCIPIENT THREAT. CATCH THEM IN THE ACT AND ERADICATE THEM. SHOCK. CONCERN. SCANDAL. LICENTIOUS SUCKLING OF WOLF CUBS. SAME SEX. ANY SEX. SEX. REPORTED REVELATIONS REVEAL REVELS CONDUCTED IN CONDUCIVE DARKNESS. MY OUT-FIT WILL BE SENSUAL BUT RESTRAINED. FEMININE YET MASCULINE. OVERALL EFFECT TO SIMULATE BACCHIC GARB. FLOWING GOWN. LONG SILKEN TRESSES. BIT OF FACE PAINT. BUT THAT'S IT. NO SILKEN UNDERTHINGS, PUSH*UP BRAS OR TIGHT SKIRTS. ABSO*FUCKING*LUTELY...ABSOLUTELY NOT. I ASSURE YOU IT'S A DISGUISE ASSUMED FOR THE PURPOSES OF INFILTRATION AND DISSUASION. I WILL BE ESCORTED...LED...ACCOMPANIED BY THE AMBASSADOR FROM THE EAST, DIONYSUS, AND BY A SHEPHERD WELL VERSED IN THE LOCAL TERRAIN. I HAVE NO DOUBTS AND HIGH HOPES FOR A QUICK CESSATION OF CONFLICT AND CIVIL

UNREST STEMMING THE SUDDEN OUTCROP OF
SEEMING MADNESS APROPOS THE DISTAFF POPU-
LATION. I AM DOING THIS FOR YOU. I KNOW WE
ALL SHARE THE SAME FEELINGS VIS*A*VIS THE
PUTATIVE EVENTS HERETOFORE BROUGHT TO OUR
SHOCKED ATTENTION. I AM NOT A DEGENERATE.
ALL POWER TO THE GODS.

Tiresias   PENTHEUS, DIONYSUS AND THE MESSENGER MAKE
THEIR WAY INTO THE MOUNTAINS. PENTHEUS ISN'T
USED TO CLIMBING—HIS BREATHING IS RAGGED,
HIS LEGS BUCKLE, HIS HEART SLAMS AGAINST HIS
CHEST. YET SOMETHING DRIVES HIM THROUGH
THE WOODS, UP THE PATH TO THE EDGE OF THE
CLEARING.

BUT THE WOMEN ARE GONE.

THE MESSENGER WANTS TO LEAVE, BUT CAN'T.
HE FEARS THE CONSEQUENCES OF LEAVING
MORE THAN HE FEARS THE CONSEQUENCES OF
STAYING. HE IS HAPPY WITH NEITHER. I PITY THE
POOR MESSENGER, WHO WISHES HE WOULD'VE
STAYED HOME.

DIONYSUS BENDS A TREE TO THE GROUND.
PENTHEUS SETTLES HIMSELF IN ITS BRANCHES.
DIONYSUS SLOWLY LETS THE TREE ASSUME ITS
HEIGHT. FROM THE CROWN OF THE TREE,
PENTHEUS CAN NOW SEE THE WOMEN. HE

WATCHES THE SACRED RITES OF DIONYSUS. HIS
MOUTH FALLS OPEN. THE BRANCHES GROW
SWEATY IN HIS PALMS. HE WATCHES. HE IS VERY
THIRSTY. HE SWALLOWS REPEATEDLY. HE CANNOT
CATCH HIS BREATH.

WHEN DOES HE REALIZE THAT THE WOMEN CAN
SEE HIM, TOO?

HOW DID THEY KNOW?...DIONYSUS.

WHAT WAS THAT MOMENT LIKE?...AND WHAT
WAS HE THINKING WHEN HE HEARD THE DEEP
ANIMAL CRIES AS THEY CIRCLED THE TRUNK—
AND RIPPED THE ROOTS FROM THE GROUND?

FALLING THROUGH SPACE, WHAT WAS HE
THINKING?

WAS HE THINKING AT ALL?

HAD HE FINALLY GIVEN UP THOUGHT?

HE NEVER TOUCHES GROUND. THE WOMEN
GRAB HIM OUT OF THE AIR AND TEAR HIM APART.
HIS ARMS ARE TORN FROM THEIR SOCKETS. THE
LIVING SKIN IS CLAWED OFF HIS BONES. THEY DIG
OUT HIS VISCERA WITH THEIR FINGERS—STEAMING
GUTS IN THE HIGH MOUNTAIN AIR. THEY POP
THE EYES OUT OF HIS HEAD. THEY EMASCULATE

HIM. BLOOD DRIPS OFF THE BRANCHES.

IN THEIR FRENZY, THEY THINK THEY'VE CAUGHT
A LION. THEY PRIDE THEMSELVES ON THEIR SKILLS
IN THE HUNT. AGAVE WILL LEAD THE PROCESSION
BACK INTO TOWN. SHE WILL ASK THAT HER SON
NAIL THE LION'S HEAD TO THE CITY GATES IN
HONOR OF HIS MOTHER'S KILL. SHE WILL OFFER
THE FLESH TO ALL.

CADMUS WILL ASK HER SIMPLE QUESTIONS.

Cadmus WHAT IS YOUR NAME?...WHAT IS THE COLOR
OF THE SKY?...WHAT IS THAT YOU HAVE IN YOUR
HANDS?

Agave AGAVE...BLUE...THE HEAD OF A LION.

Cadmus WHAT IS YOUR NAME?

Agave AGAVE.

Cadmus WHAT COLOR IS THE SKY?

Agave BLUE...BUT NOT SO BLUE AS BEFORE.

Cadmus WHAT IS THAT YOU HAVE IN YOUR HANDS?

Tiresias AGAVE LOOKS INTO THE DEAD EYES. SHE SEES
HERSELF. SHE OPENS HER MOUTH. NOT A SOUND
EMERGES. THE CHORUS WATCHES, BUT NO ONE
MOVES TO HELP HER. THIS IS A MOMENT OF
GRIEF SO INTENSE, SO EXQUISITE IN ITS WAY,
THAT NO FURTHER COMMENT IS NEEDED. A
MOTHER HAS KILLED HER CHILD. SHE MUST LIVE
WITH THIS KNOWLEDGE FOR THE REST OF HER

LIFE. A SUPREMELY PRIVATE AGONY.

Agave
I DIDN'T KNOW
IT WASN'T ME
I DIDN'T KNOW
THIS ISN'T ME
I DIDN'T KNOW
I DIDN'T DO THIS
I DIDN'T KNOW
I WAS SOMEWHERE ELSE
I DIDN'T KNOW
IF I COULD DO IT AGAIN
I DIDN'T KNOW
THIS WOULDN'T HAVE HAPPENED
I DIDN'T KNOW.

I DIDN'T KNOW
SOMETHING CAME OVER ME
I DIDN'T KNOW
I DID WHAT I HAD TO DO
I DIDN'T KNOW
IF I'D KNOWN
I DIDN'T KNOW
IF I'D KNOWN
I DIDN'T KNOW
IF I'D KNOWN
IF...I'D...KNOWN...

Chorus
THE BEST WE CAN HOPE FOR
WHEN THE SPELL WEARS AWAY

WHEN THE BOTTLE'S EMPTY
WHEN THE MOMENT HAS PASSED—
IS THAT THE HEAD ON THE STICK
THIS TIME
THANK GOD
ISN'T MINE
NOT THIS TIME, NOT THIS TIME.

ALL WE CAN HOPE FOR
ALL WE CAN ASK FOR
IS THE STRENGTH TO LIVE WITH WHAT
WE'VE DONE
ALL WE CAN HOPE FOR
ALL WE CAN ASK FOR
IS THE STRENGTH TO KEEP ON LIVING
UNTIL OUR STRENGTH GIVES OUT.

TOO MUCH TRAGEDY
HOW MUCH CAN YOU TAKE?
TOO MUCH TRAGEDY
HOW MUCH MORE CAN YOU TAKE?
WE THINK WE'RE IMMUNE BUT WE'RE NOT
NO ONE'S IMMUNE ANYMORE
SOMEWHERE SOMEONE'S WORSE OFF THAN YOU
SO ENJOY WHAT YOU'VE GOT WHILE YOU'VE
GOT IT.

Dionysus   HA HA HA HA HA HA HA
HA HA HA HA HA…

Chorus   SO MANY BLOODY HEADS AND BULLET HOLES

EXPLODING PLANES AND CRASHING CARS
SINKING SHIPS AND WOMEN RAPED IN PARKS
SO MANY SKULL*FUCKED BABIES SMASHED
AGAINST THE WALL
SO MANY BURNED*OUT VOCAL CORDS
SO MANY EARS FRYING ON RADIATORS
SO MANY FINGERS SEVERED
SO MANY TESTICLES RIPPED OUT AND EATEN
SO MANY TONGUES REMOVED WITH PLIERS
SO MANY LIPS CUT OFF WITH SCISSORS
SO MANY NOSES BUSTED WITH CROWBARS
SO MANY JAWS DISLOCATED
SO MANY CURLING IRONS SHOVED UP RECTUMS
SO MANY EYES
SO MANY DRILL BITS GOUGING OUT EYES
SO MANY BLOWS TO THE BACK THAT THE KIDNEYS
SHATTER
AND WE PISS BLOOD
WE SHIT BLOOD
WE SPIT BLOOD
VISION JELLY RUNNING DOWN OUR CHINS
SO MANY TRAGEDIES
DAY AFTER DAY
AMNESIA SETS IN...

WHERE WAS I?...WHERE WAS I?...I WAS...WHERE
WAS I?...WHERE WAS I?...OH, RIGHT...YEAH,
RIGHT...RIGHT. UH-HUH. YEAH, THAT'S RIGHT...

SO MANY WORDS

SO MANY PICTURES
AMNESIA SETS IN

THE SPECTACLE NEEDS IT
THE SPECTACLE FEEDS IT

SOMETHING HAPPENS
IT CAN'T BE EXPLAINED
IT CAN ONLY BE ENDURED
COMFORT YOURSELF
WITH THE HUNDRED EXCUSES
THE THOUSAND EVASIONS
THE MILLION EXPLANATIONS
ALL OF US
EVEN THE GREEKS
NEED JUST TO WADE THROUGH
THE TRAGEDY.

...WHERE WAS I?

*DIONYSUS appears above the palace walls. The CHORUS
trembles.*

Dionysus   YOU DENIED ME.
CALLED ME A LIAR.
SPAT, SHAT AND RATTED ON ME.
SO I DROVE YOUR WOMEN MAD
WITH A SHOT OF REDEMPTION.
YOU PUT ME IN CHAINS.
THREATENED ME WITH DEATH.

BUT THE CHAINS TURNED TO RAIN.
THE STABLE SHOOK TO PIECES.
AND DEATH STARTED RUNNING
LIKE AN IDIOT BOY IN A THUNDERSTORM.
YOU'D RATHER BUST YOUR SKULLS
THAN BOW YOUR HEADS
I JUST WATCHED WHILE YOU KICKED OUT THE
TRACES.
AND NOW YOU HAVE NO CITY
YOU HAVE NO PEOPLE
YOU HAVE NO HOME
ALL YOU HAVE IS YOURSELF
AND THE MEMORY OF A BETTER PAST.
LEAVE ME.
GET—OUTTA—HERE!
YOU ARE FREE TO WANDER FOREVER IN THE
PALACE OF NOWHERE.

Chorus   WE FORGET. WE IGNORE. WE KILL.
WE REMEMBER. WE ACKNOWLEDGE. WE KILL.
FOR ALL THE BEST REASONS.
A PIECE AT A TIME OR A MOUTHFUL OF BLOOD
WE KILL
UNTIL WE
DIE

ALWAYS ENDLESS ALWAYS
NEVER ENDING NEVER
HEAR US

IN THE EMPTINESS OF CROWDS,
COMFORT US

WHEN PAIN IS STRIPPED OF PAIN
WHEN PLEASURE'S STRIPPED OF PLEASURE
WHEN MEANING'S STRIPPED OF MEANING
WHEN WORDS ARE STRIPPED OF WORDS
HAVE MERCY ON US
CHOICE OF NO CHOICE
OUTDATED FATE
BROKEN ENGINE OF THE SUN
FORGIVE US…

Agave   MY FATHER CADMUS AND MY SISTERS PREPARE
FOR EXILE. WE PACK WHATEVER MEAGER, NECES-
SARY POSSESSIONS WE HAVE LEFT, AND PART AT
THE CROSSROADS. DISTANCE ACCUMULATES.
SOON WE ARE WELL INTO THE DAY, WITH ALL
THE TIME IN THE WORLD TO THINK.

CADMUS, CADMUS OF THE DRAGON'S TEETH,
REMEMBERS AN OLD MAN AND A BOY WALKING
UP A STEEP HILL AT SUNRISE. THEY ARE ON THEIR
WAY TO THE FAIR. THE OLD MAN HOLDS THE
BOY'S HAND AS THEY CLIMB. SOON THEY REACH
THE PLATEAU WHERE THE TENTS ARE PITCHED.
MEN ON HORSEBACK CUT THROUGH THE GROW-
ING CROWD. THE OLD MAN TIGHTENS HIS GRIP
ON THE BOY'S HAND. HE LOOKS FORWARD TO
WATCHING THE BOY GROW UP. NOTHING MUST

HAPPEN TO HIM. THE BOY THINKS OF NOTHING
BUT THE FAIR. THE OLD MAN STOPS AND PRESSES
THE BOY TO HIS CHEST. THE BOY STRUGGLES,
IMPATIENT. THE OLD MAN SMELLS OF CANDY
AND TOBACCO. THIS IS HOW, IN YEARS TO COME,
THE BOY WILL REMEMBER THE OLD MAN.

AT MIDDAY, CADMUS STOPS TO RINSE THE SWEAT
FROM HIS BEARD. HE KNEELS AT THE EDGE OF A
POND AND LOWERS HIS FACE TOWARD THE
WATER. HE NOTICES SCALES FORMING OVER HIS
EYELIDS. "I'M TURNING INTO A SERPENT," HE
THINKS.

HIS MOUTH MEETS HIS MOUTH IN THE COLD
SHOCK OF THE POND. HE DRINKS UNTIL HIS
BELLY SWELLS. WATER IS HARD TO FIND IN THIS
COUNTRY.

"THIS ISN'T RIGHT," HE THINKS. THE OLD
SHOULD DIE FIRST.
THE OLD SHOULD DIE FIRST.

TWENTY MINUTES HAVE PASSED. PERHAPS TWENTY.
CADMUS RISES, LEANS INTO HIS STICK, AND
MOVES ON DOWN THE ROAD.

Chorus LIFE IS HARD. LIFE ISN'T HARD.
GOD RULES OVER ALL. NO GOD RULES OVER ALL.
YOU CAN DO SOMETHING. YOU CAN DO NOTHING.
YOU ARE HELPLESS. YOU ARE NOT HELPLESS.

HAVE A CIGARETTE. DON'T HAVE A CIGARETTE.
GO TO WORK. DON'T GO TO WORK. GET DRUNK.
STAY SOBER.
GO TO CHURCH. DON'T GO TO CHURCH. LIVE
ALONE. LIVE WITH FRIENDS.
SLEEP WITH MEN. SLEEP WITH WOMEN. DON'T
SLEEP AT ALL. YOU'LL SLEEP SOON ENOUGH.

MAKE YOUR CHOICES. LET SOMEONE ELSE MAKE
YOUR CHOICES. AGREE. DON'T AGREE. DISAGREE.
BE CONCERNED. BE UNCONCERNED. YOU'LL
SLEEP SOON ENOUGH.

LISTEN TO MUSIC. DON'T LISTEN TO MUSIC.
DRIVE A CAR. DON'T DRIVE A CAR. TAKE THE BUS.
IT'S CLEANER. SAFER. CHEAPER. WALK. DON'T
WALK. STAND STILL.

YOU'LL SLEEP SOON ENOUGH.

THINK. THINK HARD. THINK OF THE DEAD.
THINK OF YOUR DEAD. THINK OF YOU DEAD.
DON'T. DON'T THINK. DON'T THINK OF THE
DEAD. DON'T THINK OF YOUR DEAD. DON'T
THINK OF YOU DEAD. DON'T THINK. THINK.
DON'T THINK.
WORRY. DON'T WORRY. SOMETHING'S WRONG.
NOTHING'S WRONG. DON'T WORRY. WORRY.
WORRY. DON'T WORRY. DON'T WORRY. WORRY.
YOU'LL SLEEP SOON ENOUGH.

DON'T WORRY. DON'T THINK. DON'T DIE. DIE. DON'T DIE. DIE. DON'T DIE. DIE. DON'T DIE. DON'T THINK ABOUT DYING. DON'T WORRY ABOUT DYING. THINK ABOUT DYING. WORRY ABOUT DYING. DON'T THINK ABOUT DYING. DON'T WORRY ABOUT DYING. DIE. DON'T DIE. DIE. DON'T DIE. DON'T DIE. DIE. DON'T. DON'T DIE. DO DIE. DIE. DON'T DIE.

LIFE IS HARD. DEATH IS HARDER. IS IT? IT IS? NO IT ISN'T. IT IS AND IT ISN'T. DON'T LIVE. DON'T DIE. DON'T WORRY. DON'T THINK. DON'T DOUBT. DON'T DOUBT DYING. DOUBT DYING. DON'T. DON'T. DON'T. DON'T. YOU'LL SLEEP SOON ENOUGH.

DON'T WORRY. DON'T DOUBT. DON'T THINK. DON'T DIE.

WORRY. DOUBT. THINK. DIE.

IT MAKES A DIFFERENCE. IT MAKES NO DIFFERENCE. IT DOESN'T MAKE A DIFFERENCE. IT MAKES A DIFFERENCE. IT DOES. IT DOESN'T. IT DOES AND IT DOESN'T MAKE A DIFFERENCE.
BE HAPPY. DON'T BE HAPPY. TRY TO BE HAPPY. DON'T TRY TO BE HAPPY. LET HAPPINESS SURPRISE YOU. EXPECT HAPPINESS. DON'T EXPECT HAPPINESS. DON'T LET IT SURPRISE YOU. IT'S POSSIBLE. IT'S COMPLETELY IMPOSSIBLE. IT'S POSSIBLY

COMPLETELY IMPOSSIBLY POSSIBLE.

BUT DON'T BE SAD. DON'T BE. BE HAPPY. DON'T
BE HAPPY. BE SAD. BE HAPPY AND SAD. BE SAD
AND HAPPY.

DON'T LOVE. DON'T LOSE.

LOSE. LOVE. LOVE AND LOSE. DON'T.

RELAX. DON'T RELAX. BREATHE DEEPLY. DON'T
BREATHE DEEPLY.
SUCCUMB. DON'T SUCCUMB. GIVE IN. DON'T GIVE
IN. DON'T GIVE IN, GIVE UP. DON'T GIVE UP, GIVE IN.

CHANGE THE WORLD. DON'T TRY TO CHANGE
THE WORLD. TRY TO CHANGE THE WORLD AND
FAIL. TRY TO CHANGE THE WORLD AND SUCCEED.
DON'T TRY TO CHANGE THE WORLD AND FAIL.
DON'T TRY TO CHANGE THE WORLD AND SUCCEED.
SUCCEED AND FAIL. DON'T SUCCEED AND FAIL.
SUCCEED OR FAIL. DON'T SUCCEED OR FAIL.
DON'T.

BE A GOOD WINNER. BE A GOOD LOSER. BE A BAD
LOSER AND A BAD WINNER. BE A GOOD WINNER
AND A BAD LOSER. YOU'LL SLEEP SOON ENOUGH.

YOU'LL SLEEP SOON ENOUGH.

TORN TO PIECES. HAPPY IN BED. HIT BY LIGHTNING.
RAISING A SPOON. WAVING A FLAG. SCREAMING IN
PAIN. SNAPPING A TENDON. KISSING A SHOULDER.
OPENING A LETTER. READING A LETTER. BURNING
A LETTER. SCATTERING ASHES.

THERE ARE MANY THINGS IN HEAVEN AND ON
EARTH. IF THERE'S A HEAVEN AND IF THERE'S AN
EARTH, THERE ARE MANY THINGS. THERE ARE
NOT TOO MANY THINGS IN HEAVEN AND ON
EARTH. IF THERE'S NO HEAVEN AND NO EARTH,
THERE ARE NOT TOO MANY THINGS. IF THERE'S
NO HEAVEN AND NO EARTH, THERE ARE TOO
MANY THINGS. THERE ARE TOO MANY. THERE
ARE NOT ENOUGH. THAT'S ALL RIGHT.

YOU'LL SLEEP SOON ENOUGH.

CODA

A MAN PUTS HIS SHOES ON
IN THE MORNING
AND TAKES THEM OFF AGAIN
AT NIGHT
AND WALKS ANOTHER HUNDRED MILES IN HIS
SLEEP

THERE IS NO REST
NO RESPITE
ONLY FASTER AND SLOWER

WE ALL SHARE THE SAME RUIN
ALL THAT REMAINS IS PAIN

WE ALL SHARE THE SAME RUIN
UNDERSTAND THIS, AND MOVE ON

WE ALL SHARE THE SAME RUIN
UNTIL THEN
KEEP SHUF*SHUF*SHUFFLING TO THAT GHOST
DANCE BEAT

I'LL SEE YOU THERE.

The End

Freeze

by Murray Mednick

Freeze was first presented at the 15th Annual Padua Hills Playwrights Festival, U.S.C., Los Angeles, California, in 1995. The play was directed by Guy Zimmerman with the following cast:

Tracy: Amy Raasch
Joan: Denise Poirier
Rick: David Weininger
Kurt: Michael Matthys
Jamie: Angelique Valente

Characters

Tracy *Twenty, light-complected student at a trades or community college in the San Fernando Valley. When we first meet her she is four-months pregnant.*

Jamie *Twenty-three, another student; Tracy's best friend.*

Kurt *Twenty-one, Tracy's ex-boyfriend and father of her child; an apprentice investment banker.*

Joan *Forty-five, Tracy's mother.*

Rick *Forty-seven, Tracy's father; he is a journalist and talk-show host for a local radio station.*

Voice of Sara

1. (Tracy, Joan & Rick)

Rick	You are in error, and you must pay the consequences. Without killing the innocent result.
Tracy	I don't want to.
Rick	Of your stupidity.
Tracy	I wouldn't. I don't want to kill it.
Joan	Someone of your age and background. And discipline.
Tracy	What can I do?
Joan	You can stew in your juices. Someone of your training.
Tracy	I don't know what to do.
Rick	Smart girl like you.
Joan	Not smart.
Tracy	Okay. Great.
Joan	You won't get a penny from us, if that's what you're thinking.
Tracy	Well, great. But I have to live somewhere.
Joan	You can stay here sometimes. I suppose. Until you start to show.
Tracy	No. Not here.
Joan	You'll soon start to show.
Tracy	Not here.
Joan	We do have the church to think of.
Rick	And KCIV. My program. My listeners.
Tracy	I don't want to stay here, and I'd like to continue with my classes.
Rick	We'll give you a little money.
Joan	If you can go on with your classes. We'll pay for the classes. How far along are you? Do you know?
Tracy	I told you, three or four months.

Joan	She'll show in a month.
Rick	Who's the father? Is it Kurt?
Tracy	It's Kurt.
Rick	Let him pay some. Let him put you up and pay a few bills. Let him do what he can.
Tracy	He can't do anything.
Joan	If he's the father, then he has to do it. Let him pay.
Tracy	He has no money.
Rick	Let him go to his father.
Tracy	He has no father.
Rick	Let him go to his stepfather.
Tracy	His stepfather is dead.
Rick	He left him nothing?
Tracy	He left him money to go to school.
Rick	Doesn't he have a job?
Tracy	He's an apprentice. I don't think he'll pay, but I'll ask.
Rick	Why not?
Tracy	We broke up months ago.
Joan	So what?
Tracy	I can't ask.
Joan	Don't be a fool, Tracy.
Rick	This is shattering for us.
Tracy	Me too, Dad.
Rick	We preach the Time of Advent, when we don't make these kinds of errors.
Joan	Kurt does have a job.
Rick	Publicly. We preach against both sins—that of fornication and the taking of innocent life.
Tracy	I'll think of something.
Rick	For the sake of the Coming, and life everlasting.

Tracy	It's the end of my life. My life is over.
Joan	Don't start feeling sorry for yourself. You got yourself into this, now you can get yourself out of it.

Blackout.

*

2. (Tracy & Kurt)

Tracy	They won't help.
Kurt	I knew that.
Tracy	It's the principle.
Kurt	It's his stupid radio program.
Tracy	It's their religion. Mine, too. Don't forget that.
Kurt	You have anything saved?
Tracy	Are you crazy? Do you care?
Kurt	I knew they wouldn't help.
Tracy	Kurt?
Kurt	My stepfather had them figured out, before he died. Germans, Seventh Day Adventists. They're so cheap.
Tracy	So are you, Kurt. You're so cheap.
Kurt	You want to have the kid?
Tracy	What else can I do?
Kurt	I don't know how you told them.
Tracy	I had to tell them.
Kurt	You freaked them out.
Tracy	I'll start to show.
Kurt	That must have been a scene.

Tracy	What do I do now?
Kurt	There must be something.
Tracy	It's expensive. We can't afford it.
Kurt	There must be something.
Tracy	I'll talk to Jamie.
Kurt	I'm with Yvonne.
Tracy	I'm too young for this.
Kurt	So am I!
Tracy	I'm too young to be a mother.
Kurt	I won't leave her.
Tracy	You're immature.
Kurt	We broke up. I'm with Yvonne, now.
Tracy	She's married to someone else.
Kurt	I'm with Yvonne.
Tracy	I won't commit murder.
Kurt	We broke up, then you got pregnant.
Tracy	You're the father, Kurt.
Kurt	I know.
Tracy	You're the father.
Kurt	I know.
Tracy	So don't think stupid thoughts.
Kurt	I'm not stupid.
Tracy	What we need is cash, that's all. A little cash, get us over. Then we'll see. You know?

Blackout.

*

3. (Tracy & Jamie)

Jamie	You could give it up for adoption.
Tracy	Oh, no.
Jamie	Why not?
Tracy	I couldn't give it up for adoption.
Jamie	You want to be a mother?
Tracy	I don't want to be a mother. I'm too young.
Jamie	That's why I'm saying.
Tracy	Give it up for adoption?
Jamie	What about Kurt?
Tracy	He's a nothing, he's a jerk.
Jamie	Women are infinitely superior.
Tracy	What would I do? Stay home?
Jamie	You would be a mother. You would have a baby. People do it all the time.
Tracy	I'm not sure about that.
Jamie	Well, you're twenty years old. You're old enough.
Tracy	Would you?
Jamie	What?
Tracy	Have a baby?
Jamie	Oh, yeah, I would. Of course, the money.
Tracy	I know!
Jamie	The money would be an issue.
Tracy	The money is a big issue.
Jamie	Knowing your parents.
Tracy	Would you?
Jamie	I wouldn't give a baby up for adoption.
Tracy	You wouldn't?
Jamie	No. But that doesn't mean.

Tracy	I could.
Jamie	You could?
Tracy	Sure. Kurt. Fuck Kurt.
Jamie	Give it away.
Tracy	Right.
Jamie	Men are much too stupid.
Tracy	I could do that.
Jamie	He wouldn't know the difference.
Tracy	Ha! That's funny, Jamie!
Jamie	You could show him a paper doll.
Tracy	Oh, my goodness!
Jamie	They're in a dumb fog anyway.
Tracy	I could never give it up. To strangers?
Jamie	That's what happpens. Or you put it in an orphanage. Or in a box!
Tracy	Yeah!
Jamie	Or in a basket! And you leave it in a supermarket!
Tracy	Ha! Okay! At the Mall!
Jamie	It happens.
Tracy	I'm sorry I let him, Jamie. I'm really sorry now.
Jamie	This happens to girls, Trace. This happens.
Tracy	I know. Why? Why me? Shit!
Jamie	We can do without sex.
Tracy	I'll think of something.
Jamie	We don't need it.
Tracy	It's like Russian roulette.
Jamie	Penises.
Tracy	Ha!
Jamie	Welfare?
Tracy	No!

Jamie	Well, something.
Tracy	I can't. My parents. Especially my father. We're white. We're the religious white!
Jamie	That's funny, Trace!
Tracy	Strictly white. Seventh Day.
Jamie	I know a person. Down the street. Mary. "Virgin Mary." She got it paid for, the whole thing.
Tracy	Mary?
Jamie	Down the street. In Agoura.
Tracy	How?
Jamie	She gave it up.
Tracy	The baby?
Jamie	For adoption.
Tracy	I don't know.
Jamie	You don't have to, actually. She got support, medical, payments. The whole thing. Plus.
Tracy	From who?
Jamie	The adoptive parents.
Tracy	She sold it?
Jamie	No. Like, you can change your mind. Smart. You make arrangements. You get support. You have the baby and you can change your mind. Mary. She got this couple. They maintained her. And now she has a toddler.

Blackout.

*

4. (Tracy & Kurt)

Tracy   I call this group, it's an adoption group.

Kurt   A group?

Tracy   For an adoption.

Kurt   They'll take the baby?

Tracy   No, they don't do that. They find people. They bring people together.

Kurt   An agency.

Tracy   No, it's not an agency. They're like...consultants. You call them, "I'm pregnant, I can't have a child, the father doesn't want it, I'm looking for a couple." Then there's a meeting. They check you out, you check them out.

Kurt   Me?

Tracy   No, not you personally. I do it. Then there's an agency, then there's a lawyer.

Kurt   Who pays?

Tracy   They do, the parents. The prospective parents. The adoptive. They pay. Then they pay you. They pay expenses.

Kurt   Are you serious?

Tracy   I have to do it.

Kurt   It's not true.

Tracy   Maybe it's the best idea.

Kurt   That I don't want the child? Not true.

Tracy   Otherwise, it's our life. Not yours so much.

Kurt   No?

Tracy   Mine. Responsibility. You want it?

Kurt   I don't have a career yet.

Tracy   That's what I'm saying.

Kurt   So how can I?

Tracy	You can't.
Kurt	But don't speak for me.
Tracy	I'm thinking of the best idea.
Kurt	Don't speak for me.
Tracy	But you have to go along with it.
Kurt	It's a complicated issue. I don't believe in it. I don't believe in adoption.
Tracy	Why not?
Kurt	Because they never get over it, being adopted. That's one thing.
Tracy	You don't know.
Kurt	And the other thing is, you shouldn't give it up.
Tracy	Easy for you to say.
Kurt	That's how I feel.
Tracy	You don't know how you feel.
Kurt	Do you?
Tracy	How can I? It's too much for me! The whole thing!
Kurt	I'm sorry. Shit. It's not all my fault. Is it?
Tracy	You're a guy.
Kurt	Who is that talking? That's Jamie.
Tracy	She's a big help to me. What would I do without Jamie? I'd be in a lot of trouble. My mother and father won't help me. They won't do anything. Jamie is all I have.
Kurt	No, she isn't.
Tracy	I don't have you.
Kurt	No, she isn't, Trace.
Tracy	Do I have to give everything up? Is this the end?
Kurt	Why?
Tracy	You're so stupid.

Kurt	It's not the end of the world.
Tracy	Yes, it is. It's the end.
Kurt	That's the Adventists.
Tracy	It's so fucking weird. Kurt! I feel horrible!

Blackout.

*

5. (Tracy, Joan & Rick)

Tracy	I talked to a guy, he works for this company, they do adoptions.
Rick	They charge for that?
Tracy	It's a company. It's a business.
Rick	How much?
Tracy	Not me. Them, the adopters. They're the ones.
Rick	They pay for it?
Tracy	Yes.
Rick	Well, that's right. That's how it should be.
Tracy	Anyway, so I'm on there.
Joan	What does that mean?
Tracy	I'm on his list. Mr. Webster. Jim. He'll match me with a couple.
Joan	Is that what you're thinking now?
Tracy	I think that's an option. Don't you think that's an option? That's a reasonable option, it seems to me.
Joan	I don't think you have any idea.
Tracy	I'm trying to deal with this.

Joan	I don't think you know what you're doing for one single minute.
Tracy	I can't help it if I'm pregnant.
Joan	No, now you can't. Now it's too late.
Tracy	Right.
Joan	So make the best of it.
Tracy	I think this is the best of it.
Joan	You think you are a special person. And you're not.
Tracy	I'm not. Great.
Joan	No. You're like everyone else. You have to pay. For your actions. You have to pay.
Rick	Reap what you sow, Trace.
Tracy	Great.
Joan	And earn your way.
Rick	What about school?
Tracy	I'm going to school.
Rick	You're going to classes?
Tracy	I can go to classes.
Joan	Are you going to your classes?
Tracy	I go to most of my classes.
Rick	Because you may not get another chance.
Tracy	I need a place to stay. But I can't stay in the dorm.
Joan	You're starting to show.
Rick	You need to get yourself straightened out. And fast.
Tracy	I can't have an abortion.
Rick	I don't mean with an abortion. Abortion is another sin.
Tracy	I wouldn't have one.
Rick	Don't even think it.
Tracy	You know I wouldn't. We've been over this.
Rick	It is against the Christian temperament, the Christian

	ideal, and it has to stop, nationwide!
Joan	All right, dear. She knows. What about Kurt?
Tracy	What about him?
Joan	Do you have a relationship?
Tracy	We're friends. But we're not together.
Joan	How can that happen? He is the father!
Tracy	We don't want to be together.
Joan	Why not?
Rick	That's one end of the stick. Promiscuity and abortion. And the other one is, we've got all this infertility rampant, which is a clear sign, it seems to me.
Tracy	*(To JOAN)* We just don't.
Joan	You need to straighten that out.
Tracy	No, that's it.
Rick	We've got unwed children having children, widespread infertility, and legalized abortion! Does that not all mean something?
Joan	*(To TRACY)* You can't stay here.
Rick	Marry him and get on with it.
Tracy	I don't want to.
Rick	Why not?
Tracy	He's with someone else.
Rick	Who?
Tracy	Yvonne. I'm working on it, Dad.
Rick	How are you working on it?
Tracy	I'm trying to tell you.
Rick	And in the meantime?
Tracy	I'm working on it with Jamie.
Joan	I knew it. I knew you were getting guidance somewhere.
Tracy	I'll get some money out of it to keep me going.

	And then we'll see.
Rick	Money for what?
Tracy	For the adoption. I'm meeting with a couple. Through Mr. Webster. Jim. It's his business. We'll come to an agreement, and they'll pay my expenses.
Rick	How do you know?
Tracy	I know they will.
Joan	Because they want a child, dear. So they'll pay. They'll pay a lot.
Rick	I don't know about this. Adoption is a tricky business.
Tracy	This is just a measure, Dad, this is a common thing.
Rick	Common?
Tracy	Yes. Jamie says. And, you know, if I'm going to have the baby...
Joan	You're going to have the baby.
Tracy	I'll have to be prepared, you know, with the parents.
Joan	Well, if they pay. If that's what you want to do, you and Kurt.
Tracy	Not Kurt.
Joan	As a temporary measure. (*Exchanges a look with* RICK)
Rick	You'd better be careful. You'd better watch out for your rights. This is your flesh and blood here.
Joan	Don't sign anything.
Tracy	It doesn't matter what I sign.
Joan	It doesn't?
Tracy	No. I don't have to sign, and even if I did, it doesn't matter, because I can change my mind.
Rick	What about them? Don't they have rights? This couple?
Tracy	No. They don't have any rights at all. None. I checked.
Rick	With who?

Tracy	Mr. Webster, the consultant.

Blackout.

*

6. (Tracy and Jamie)

Jamie	Did you hear Rush?
Tracy	No, I didn't.
Jamie	He was saying like, you know, "How is it my fault?"
Tracy	I love that guy.
Jamie	"I'm not responsible for people who are maniacs."
Tracy	Of course not.
Jamie	He advises people, "Watch out for your rights, but don't break the law."
Tracy	Like my Dad.
Jamie	"Don't take the law into your own hands."
Tracy	He says you can say things, but there's a difference.
Jamie	Someone has to say it, or there'll be nothing left of this country.
Tracy	The thing is, I'll have to deal with an agency, and a lawyer, and a doctor. Besides like, the couple. I don't know. It's a lot. You know, these people. Like I was saying.
Jamie	You just do one thing at a time, Trace.
Tracy	It's a challenge.
Jamie	Are you worried?
Tracy	Well, it's a lot.
Jamie	You get some checks, we'll go to the mall, we'll have fun.

	It's not all work.
Tracy	I have to believe I'm giving it up.
Jamie	You're giving it up.
Tracy	I'm giving it up.
Jamie	There you go.
Tracy	While I was talking to them, the couple—
Jamie	Oh, right!
Tracy	You know, I felt like I would.
Jamie	You went to Chili's?
Tracy	I believed.
Jamie	How was it?
Tracy	Nice. You know. Chili's.
Jamie	What'd you have?
Tracy	What did I have? Nothing. I couldn't eat. I ordered something, who remembers? I was nauseous.
Jamie	But, so, you did it, right?
Tracy	"I don't want to be a mother, not really. I'm only twenty years old. I want to go to school and travel and what0not."
Jamie	Is that what you said?
Tracy	"I'm not prepared for this, and like Kurt, you know, forget about it."
Jamie	That's rational.
Tracy	And they were very nice.
Jamie	I'm sure.
Tracy	They were. They were so nice.
Jamie	Older?
Tracy	Yeah, older, and like, you know, trying to please.
Jamie	They like you?
Tracy	I think so.

Jamie	How could they not?
Tracy	They asked those questions. You predicted it. Why do you want to give up your child? Etcetera, etcetera.
Jamie	How much older?
Tracy	Late forties maybe?
Jamie	That's it. Last chance.
Tracy	I did the religion thing, you know, values.
Jamie	You believe that, don't you?
Tracy	"I want it to grow up in an environment with religious values."
Jamie	So of course they agreed with that.
Tracy	I thought so.
Jamie	What religion?
Tracy	You know my religion.
Jamie	Obviously, I mean theirs. Their religion, Trace. Like, I hope it wasn't something weird.
Tracy	No. Very straight. Very straight people. I don't know what. Some kind of Christian.
Jamie	That's good.
Tracy	At one point she asks, "Do you read?" I said, "Well, I read Rush, I read Nancy's autobiography." And then I couldn't think.
Jamie	They don't care.
Tracy	I don't think that was a mistake.
Jamie	So do you go with them?
Tracy	I'd just as soon stick with them. What's the point in looking, wasting time? They're fine, they're perfect. I got to get this thing rolling.

Blackout.

*

7. (Tracy, Joan & Rick)

Rick	The government of the United States is not obligated to pay anything, arrange anything, or do anything for anybody.
Joan	Tracy?
Tracy	It's Medi-Cal, Mom. That's the usual. That's the lawyer.
Joan	The lawyer?
Tracy	What she said.
Joan	You don't make sense, Tracy.
Rick	She's dissociated, honey, or this thing wouldn't have happened in the first place.
Joan	Dissociated?
Rick	When a person is in one place and their body is in another.
Tracy	If you can get on Medi-Cal, then you have to, Dad.
Rick	And a child is the result. Incredible.
Joan	They should pay for it, the ones adopting.
Tracy	They will pay.
Rick	How much?
Tracy	All expenses, plus everything above the Medi-Cal.
Rick	That's nothing. For a child? Peanuts.
Tracy	It's the law. You're not allowed to buy a child. She explained.
Joan	Who explained?
Tracy	The lawyer.
Rick	You'd better be careful, that's all I can say.
Joan	Where are you living now?
Tracy	I live everywhere. I stay with Jamie. I go over to her mother's. Once in a while I come home. Like now. I spend a lot of time in the mall.
Joan	How do all these people keep in touch with you?
Tracy	I have a beeper, I have voicemail.

Rick	And you don't have a car!
Tracy	I get rides. I take the bus. I'll pull this off. Give me some credit.
Rick	What are you doing, sleeping in the mall?
Tracy	You can't sleep in a mall.
Rick	Homeless expect the government to pay for housing. I can't afford to live in certain places either.
Tracy	No, I'm staying with Jamie and her mother. I told you.
Rick	Oh. Okay.
Tracy	I moved out of the dorm. Is that all right?
Rick	I suppose so. They're trash, but I suppose it's all right.
Tracy	Don't say trash.
Rick	Trash. I'll tell you about adoption, how it used to be in this country. Back in Oklahoma, in the Depression. I'll tell you what "put up for adoption" means. There'd be certain trains coming through, they were called orphan trains. And on those trains there'd be people in open cars with babies. The train would come in and stop, the people would raise their babies, put them up, and the farmers would bid on the babies. That's how they'd adopt, and get help on the farm, eventually. So you keep that in mind. That's real Americana, right there.
Joan	That Jamie is very smart, dear.
Tracy	Anyway, I had a meeting.
Rick	Don't sign anything.
Tracy	You have to sign certain things. Why would they give you money if they don't believe you?
Joan	You're a good little actress, aren't you?
Rick	Just be careful you don't get tricked into something.
Tracy	There's a lawyer and an agency, they look out for my interests.

Joan	They should look out for your interests.
Tracy	They do look out for the, uh, adoptive parents, but mainly it's me. It's my baby.
Joan	That's right.
Rick	Who are they?
Tracy	They're a couple from L.A.
Rick	Where in L.A.?
Tracy	Encino, maybe. Or Sherman Oaks. I'm not sure.
Rick	So they have money?
Tracy	They look like they have money. I don't know how rich they are. I mean, they seem willing to pay.
Joan	It's not enough money.
Rick	What do they do?
Tracy	I think they do real estate. I think they're in real estate.
Rick	Oh.
Tracy	They're like, efficient, you know?
Rick	Great.
Joan	What's the name?
Tracy	Goodman. The Goodmans.
Rick	Is that a Jewish name?
Joan	Sounds Jewish.
Tracy	I don't know, actually.
Joan	Oh, come on Tracy.
Tracy	I can't tell.
Rick	Watch out, that's all I can say. Don't let them take advantage of you.
Joan	Let them pay you, but be careful.

Blackout.

*

172

8. (Tracy & Kurt)

Tracy	My parents, they're so full of shit, you know? It's like, so hard.
Kurt	You'd think they would help you out.
Tracy	Help me?
Kurt	Someone in your situation.
Tracy	Just me?
Kurt	You know.
Tracy	It's you too, Kurt.
Kurt	You know what I mean.
Tracy	So don't give me any of that shit.
Kurt	I have my own problems.
Tracy	Don't tell me.
Kurt	What do you want from me?
Tracy	I want some cooperation, is what I want.
Kurt	How can you act like you want to give up the child?
Tracy	Because a part of me does want to.
Kurt	What if they take it away?
Tracy	Don't be immature. They won't take it away unless I give permission.
Kurt	Will you?
Tracy	Maybe I will.
Kurt	Why?
Tracy	Part of the reason is you.
Kurt	That's what I figured.
Tracy	You don't have your shit together.
Kurt	Do you?
Tracy	No. So what am I supposed to do, leave it in a dumpster?
Kurt	Yeah, that's Jamie. That's how she talks.

Tracy	You can make any kind of a deal and they still can't take the kid.
Kurt	Are you sure?
Tracy	It's becoming popular.
Kurt	Says who?
Tracy	Jamie.
Kurt	How does she know?
Tracy	Her friend Mary, in Agoura.
Kurt	Really?
Tracy	Yeah, only if you do it with more than one couple, it's illegal. Otherwise, that's it.
Kurt	Obviously, that's illegal. Jesus.
Tracy	But that's not what we're doing. We're staying with one couple, the Goodmans. And she, especially, she wants to know everything. Background, everything. Yours, included.
Kurt	I'm not telling them.
Tracy	Okay, we'll make it up. It doesn't matter.
Kurt	I won't tell them anything.
Tracy	I'm sorry I mentioned it. I knew you'd be a jerk about this.
Kurt	Who are these people?
Tracy	I told you already.
Kurt	They give you any money yet?
Tracy	Yes.
Kurt	How much?
Tracy	Five hundred dollars. And they want to meet you. And you have to come with me to the lawyer's.
Kurt	Why do they have to meet me?
Tracy	It's normal. And they're so like, you know, greedy for information.
Kurt	Why?

Tracy	Oh, Kurt. Because they think it's going to be their kid, and they're excited. And maybe it is.
Kurt	No. I don't want to get involved.
Tracy	And you have to meet them.
Kurt	I told you, Tracy.
Tracy	I have to go with them for a checkup, and you have to come, too.
Kurt	I'm not going. I'm not ready for this.
Tracy	And at the lawyer's you'll have to sign.
Kurt	Sign what?
Tracy	Papers.
Kurt	What papers?
Tracy	Waiving your rights.
Kurt	Waiving my rights?
Tracy	To the child.
Kurt	Why would I necessarily do that?
Tracy	Otherwise, they won't go forward. They won't go forward unless they're sure about you. The lawyer and the Goodmans. You have to sign, Kurt.
Kurt	I'll sign, but it don't mean shit.
Tracy	Just sign. And be nice.

Blackout.

*

9. (Tracy & Jamie)

Tracy   We're sitting there in the lobby and Kurt does not speak.

Jamie   The Goodmans?

Tracy   They're sitting across from him.

Jamie   Oh, God.

Tracy   And he will not speak. He is staring out at the rain, stiff, like a dummy, it was so strange. It was intense. Like, what is going on here? Is this my life? Because he will not acknowledge, you know, the adoption.

Jamie   He's a guy.

Tracy   He's a dumb guy. He is not charming. In those situations, with people. But with them? The Goodmans? And I'm having this eerie feeling of like, something or someone is coming into this world, and they're coming through me, and there is Kurt, Mr. Wordless, the speechless wonder, and he is the father, so-called, and there are the Goodmans being very nice as they can be, and tense, they want this life from me, and Kurt, and the Mexicans are coming and going all around happily like there is no problem—

Jamie   It's common. It's very common. To give up a child, and to make arrangements. It happens. Because there's a line—

Tracy   No problem—

Jamie   —for babies. Because that generation, you know, those women, the liberal, upper-class ones of the sixties? They fucked up. They had abortions, they had nine husbands, they took drugs. One day they woke up and the clock ran out, game's over.

Tracy   I know. I saw that.

Jamie	And now they're lined up and they'll pay. What happened, besides Kurt?
Tracy	You could see it and hear its heartbeat, Jame.
Jamie	That's exciting. You were all in there?
Tracy	Yeah. Me and the nurse and the Goodmans and Kurt. You could see the baby in the machine like a ghost and it had a face. It was so weird.
Jamie	It?
Tracy	They think it's a she.
Jamie	Oh, that's so exciting.
Tracy	They can't see the genitals. But it had like a face. Breathing and pumping. It's so weird. It was like, yawning.
Jamie	Who'd it look like?
Tracy	Oh, Jamie, you can't tell!
Jamie	I hope it's you, I hope it looks like you, though Kurt is not bad-looking, actually, per se.
Tracy	No, he's not.
Jamie	Geeky, though. And not charming.
Tracy	Ha! Jamie!
Jamie	Hey, let's be honest.
Tracy	He's having problems. I shouldn't tell you.
Jamie	Tell me.
Tracy	With Yvonne. It's like with the husband. He barges in, you know. The husband. They're supposed to be like separated, and he apppears. He walks in. It's bad, you know. Or he calls her on the phone. They're such jerks.
Jamie	I can't fuckin' believe it. They never fuckin' grow up.
Tracy	So Kurt is in it.
Jamie	But he showed for the appointment.
Tracy	For the ultrasound. What a scene, you should have been

there. With Kurt standing and the Goodmans, in shock, looking at the picture and with me under a sheet? God, what could they be feeling? I mean, Jame, about looking at this shadow of a kid on the screen that could be theirs, but is really mine? In a medical building? In the Valley? And with Kurt?

Jamie   Really. Well, you know, they're hoping it's healthy.

Tracy   I know. Especially her. She's the one.

Jamie   The missus.

Tracy   Right.

Jamie   Can you get rent? From them? The couple? The Goodmans? You think you can get rent?

Blackout.

*

10. (Tracy & Kurt)

Tracy   I'm so tired, I just hate this. And I have to meet with this counselor, at the agency? I wish they'd all, you know, drop dead basically.

Kurt   The counselor?

Tracy   At the agency, like I told you. You're not stupid.

Kurt   Why?

Tracy   Why?

Kurt   Do you have to.

Tracy   I have to because of them, the couple, the Goodmans. Otherwise, I don't have to.

Kurt	Why?
Tracy	So they'll have confidence. A certain amount of hours, so I'm supposed to meet with her for counseling.
Kurt	Then don't do it.
Tracy	You're not helping.
Kurt	Don't do it.
Tracy	No confidence, no checks, Kurt. You're no help at all. You don't do shit, and you're grim.
Kurt	What am I supposed to do?
Tracy	Support me?
Kurt	I don't have any money.
Tracy	It's not just money! It's moral! Moral support! Emotional support! Okay?
Kurt	Okay, okay, who are all these people?
Tracy	You know who they are. It's the counselor, it's the lawyer, it's them, the couple, and it's the consultant, Webster, who calls me every fucking day.
Kurt	It's a lot.
Tracy	I feel like they've all got their fucking hooks into me and I don't want to do it. I don't want to see this woman. I procrastinate. Which comes first, Kurt? Should I give up my life? And I can't deal with my fucking parents at all. Not one iota. I can talk to Mrs. Goodman better than my own mother. Rachel. Do you realize? But she's so eager I can't stand it. She's so nice and so eager. It's pathetic. And she wants to know. She wants to know everything. All of them. They all want to know. I can't stand it anymore, this question of information, constantly. *(Pause)* Anyway, the kid would be one-eighth Cherokee.
Kurt	Indian?

Tracy	Cherokee is Indian, Kurt. My grandfather. My father's father. It almost put a wrench into it. It was a close call.
Kurt	Why didn't you tell me?
Tracy	You weren't around to ask.
Kurt	Ask?
Tracy	Your opinions.
Kurt	What opinions?
Tracy	Your background and views.
Kurt	What for?
Tracy	For them, the social workers and so on. They're so vague.
Kurt	So are you.
Tracy	They keep it vague, and play both sides.
Kurt	So do you.
Tracy	Are you acting smart?
Kurt	What is this about?
Tracy	It's over, it's all fixed. You have to get permission from the tribe.
Kurt	Why?
Tracy	It's a law. The Indians have to give permission. It almost queered it. But he wasn't registered. He wasn't registered with either of the Cherokee nations, so it didn't matter. The Goodmans didn't care. They liked it. They liked the Indian part.
Kurt	It ain't gonna happen.
Tracy	Because the tribes won't give up their kids.
Kurt	Neither will you.
Tracy	It's yours, too.
Kurt	I know it is.
Tracy	You don't care? If there's Indian?
Kurt	What do I care? I could be anything.

Tracy	You're English. You're a Bradford.
Kurt	Yeah, but it got all mixed up. There's French and God knows what else in there. My Dad talked Creole when he was drunk. It don't matter. I liked my stepfather best anyway. We're American.
Tracy	Anybody can be American. They just walk in. They make money on it. It's our money. We give them the money.
Kurt	You're getting money.
Tracy	Why are you so hard on me? They can afford it. That's the standard procedure. The liberals want to give away their money, then let them. It's expensive to have a baby. It's very expensive.
Kurt	That's fine with me.
Tracy	Then what's your problem? *(Silence)* Kurt?
Kurt	I have rights.
Tracy	You have no rights.
Kurt	I can give you some money now, maybe, set up an apartment or something.
Tracy	Oh, sure.
Kurt	Why not?
Tracy	I don't want to take any money from you.
Kurt	Why not?
Tracy	Because then it gives you rights. You think I want to have a family? Be a single mother? The answer is *no* to both. I'm sorry.
Kurt	Okay, Trace, I have to tell you.
Tracy	What, Kurt?
Kurt	He beat her up. Yvonne. Her husband, Warren. He went over there. To her apartment.
Tracy	When?

| Kurt | Last night. She's in a coma. |

Blackout.

*

11. (Tracy, Joan & Rick)

Rick	It's girls like you who keep these people in business. The lawyers. The social workers. So of course they're nice to you.
Joan	In the old days, a girl would disappear, before she started to show, and the relatives would make up a story, and that was it. And nobody knew anything.
Rick	It was all done privately, under the table.
Joan	The mother would leave the baby, period. And nobody knew, not the adopted, not the parents, nobody.
Rick	I'm not so sure that was so bad.
Joan	Of course not. It's practical.
Rick	It's changed nowadays, like everything.
Joan	If that's what you wanted to do. Girls made mistakes. Girls slipped on the path.
Rick	There are different laws now. But it's still blood that counts. They can't change that.
Joan	No complications, and the girl went back to her life, if she had a life.
Rick	There were certain doctors and lawyers and they made arrangements on the side.
Joan	We may not know the answers, or the reason for the

	test, or the meaning of the test, at the time. But there is a lesson to be learned.
Tracy	Was Jesus a person?
Rick	What do you mean, Tracy?
Joan	Of course, he was a person.
Rick	And he was also God.
Tracy	So he had to go to the bathroom and stuff?
Joan	You know he did, Tracy.
Tracy	Because I heard you say, on the radio, that Jesus was a Herald and the son of God, come to announce the end of time as we know it.
Rick	As we know it, that's the key.
Tracy	And he did that in the form of a human being?
Joan	Yes. But he was also God.
Rick	And the trumpet of God, the clarion. The Calling.
Tracy	I see. Because I have this life inside me. I don't know what it means, or what I'm supposed to do with it.
Rick	Responsibility.
Tracy	I don't want it.
Joan	You should have thought about that earlier.
Rick	What I say on the air, daily, personal responsibility. You can tell Kurt, if he doesn't marry you, I'll have him shot.
Tracy	I don't want him.
Rick	I have friends. Riflemen.
Tracy	We don't get along.
Rick	And Christians.
Tracy	So you don't need to shoot him.
Rick	I'm only kidding, Tracy.
Tracy	We won't be hearing from Kurt for awhile.

Joan	Why not?
Tracy	His girlfriend, Yvonne, her husband attacked her.
Joan	What is going on here?
Tracy	She might die.
Joan	This is incredible. I don't understand it. I don't understand any of it. It's beyond me.
Tracy	So I'm really concerned.
Joan	I'll bet you are.
Rick	None of this could have happened in a Christian country.
Tracy	I can't count on Kurt.
Joan	So you're going to give this child away?
Tracy	The Virgin Mary did it.
Joan	Don't say stupid, blasphemous things, Tracy.
Tracy	I mean, she was a friend of Jamie's. Mary, of Agoura. They called her Virgin Mary. I guess because she...I don't know why.
Joan	You'll never be able to give it away.
Tracy	Actually, she was going to, and she changed her mind.
Joan	She was planning to change her mind. And so are you.
Tracy	I don't know if I am.
Joan	Believe me.
Rick	I get kids calling in all the time in sexual trouble. It's the way this country is going. The white kids marry and work it out.
Joan	You're getting big, Tracy.
Rick	Are you paying rent over there? With Jamie?
Tracy	The Goodmans are paying Jamie.
Joan	The Goodmans?
Tracy	I told you.
Joan	What do they do?

184

Tracy	I think they're like in real estate or something.
Joan	These are smart people?
Tracy	I think they're smart.
Joan	They must really like you.
Tracy	She does. I know she does.
Joan	To go along with this.
Tracy	Oh! Oh! I just felt a kick!

Blackout.

*

12. (Tracy & Jamie)

Tracy	She's calling all the time now. They're all calling. I don't know whose side they're on.
Jamie	You mean like the woman?
Tracy	Mrs. Goodman! Rachel Goodman!
Jamie	Rachel. That's Jewish.
Tracy	She like can't help herself, you know? She leaves a message, you know, on the voice mail, on the beeper, and then I have to call her back, eventually. They don't know there's no phone, okay? I try to let it slide, and she'll call. A few days and she'll call again.
Jamie	Well, it's the clock.
Tracy	She wants what's in my body.
Jamie	That's what happened with Mary. She had a relationship.
Tracy	It's so stressful. Because it's a relationship.
Jamie	She talked to the woman all the time. They became like

friends. It's only natural.

Tracy We talk about intimate things. She trusts me.

Jamie She must trust you.

Tracy At one point she goes, "How are you feeling?" She always asks that question. Because it has a double meaning. And I go, "Do you doubt me?"

Jamie Very excellent, Trace.

Tracy Oh, no! Oh, no! She says. And she goes on. Because it's all very ambivalent.

Jamie On your part, of course.

Tracy Not only mine, not only mine, because she hates me, because it's in my body, and she can't, you know? She's very dependent. On what's going on in my body. So I don't know what to do.

Jamie You have to think of yourself.

Tracy She loves me and she hates me, both.

Jamie That's the main thing, Trace.

Tracy And if I don't keep an appointment.

Jamie Otherwise it's so confusing.

Tracy Then she panics.

Jamie You can't be distracted by that.

Tracy And I have to reassure her. And there's this whole thing spiritually, you know?

Jamie Spiritually?

Tracy About the spirit of the child, waiting to be born, and it's choosing its parents.

Jamie Oh, wow.

Tracy Did I? Did you? Is everybody that's alive today everybody that's ever been alive?

Jamie What?

Tracy	The child is coming back because it has to learn something. He's coming back from a former life and he's waiting somewhere—actually, in my body—to choose its parents?
Jamie	It's a girl, right?
Tracy	Whatever. To learn something it needs to know?
Jamie	That's what she says?
Tracy	Rachel Goodman.
Jamie	We don't believe in that.
Tracy	But there is a soul. Do we believe in a soul?
Jamie	We believe in a soul.
Tracy	What is that? According to you?
Jamie	Well, it's us. I don't know.
Tracy	And so in the end-time we go as us?
Jamie	I don't know, Trace. What else could we be?
Tracy	And where do we go?
Jamie	Good question. We go up into the sky?
Tracy	Jesus was God.
Jamie	We have to stick to practical.
Tracy	Because of Yvonne.
Jamie	I know.
Tracy	She never woke up yet.
Jamie	That sonofabitch. Whoever the fuck he is. The husband jerk. He'll rot in jail.
Tracy	She could die. *(Pause)* I don't understand any of it, and I don't care.
Jamie	I want to get through the week. I want to get through the day.
Tracy	I wouldn't have chosen my parents.
Jamie	I'm not worried about the Apocalypse at the moment.

Tracy	Ha, Jamie! Let's go out to the mall!
Jamie	Are you up to it?
Tracy	I want to go!
Jamie	Let's go to the mall!
Tracy	Let's go!

Blackout.

*

13. (Tracy & Joan)

Joan	You're ready with the doctor and the hospital?
Tracy	I had to change them. I changed the doctor and the hospital. I did it with Rachel Goodman.
Joan	Did you?
Tracy	Because she has to approve, because it's an adoptive situation.
Joan	I see.
Tracy	I like him, though, I think he's better. The new doctor. Brownstone. He's the obstetrician. They're like mechanics. But he isn't a wiseass, at least.
Joan	So who's going to be there?
Tracy	At the birth?
Joan	At the birth.
Tracy	I don't know.
Joan	You better start thinking about it.
Tracy	They'll have to be there.
Joan	Who?

Tracy	The Goodmans.
Joan	Think about it.
Tracy	I don't know who else. Jamie?
Joan	And Kurt?
Tracy	Kurt. God.
Joan	And his family.
Tracy	Oh, no.
Joan	And what about us?
Tracy	You want to be there?
Joan	Of course we want to be there, Trace, on such a special occasion.
Tracy	I don't know.
Joan	What don't you know?
Tracy	I don't know if we can do all that.
Joan	Your father and I will be there.
Tracy	Oh, shit, Mom.
Joan	I wish you wouldn't talk like that. I wish you would purify your mouth before it's too late. That's what it all means, Tracy. Do you never think? Purification. A birth can do that for you. It's a new beginning.
Tracy	Well, you've sure changed your tune.
Joan	A clean slate, Tracy.
Tracy	Now you want to be at the birth.
Joan	It's an important occasion for all of us.
Tracy	I don't know what to do. I'm not prepared.
Joan	Are you going to your classes?
Tracy	No.
Joan	I mean the Lamaze.
Tracy	No. But I'm walking.
Joan	At the mall?

| Tracy | Yeah, I walk the mall. |
| Joan | Well, that's something. |

Blackout.

*

14. (Tracy & Jamie)

Tracy	We got a problem here?
Jamie	What is it?
Tracy	At the birth?
Jamie	Uh, huh? *(Pause)* Trace?
Tracy	Everybody's coming.
Jamie	Exciting!
Tracy	Like my mom and dad. Like Kurt's mom and his sister from Albuquerque.
Jamie	Like me and my mom.
Tracy	It's a lot.
Jamie	Oh, it's a celebration, Trace! It's a party!
Tracy	What about the Goodmans?
Jamie	Oh. Shit.
Tracy	Yeah.
Jamie	They can't come to it.
Tracy	I told them. I agreed. I said she could be at the birth. Mrs. Goodman. Rachel. I said she could be there.
Jamie	You have to tell her no.
Tracy	She really wants to. She wants to see it. She thinks it's hers!
Jamie	I don't think that's right. It's in your body. It's in you.

Tracy	I know.
Jamie	We're talking basic family here. Not them.
Tracy	I'll have to call her.
Jamie	Call.
Tracy	What should I say?
Jamie	Tell her you'll phone her as soon as it's born. First thing it's born, it's arrived, you'll call, they'll come and take the baby. She'll do it. She'll go for it. She'll sit there by the phone.
Tracy	I think she will, Jamie. Okay. God.
Jamie	I know! The ultrasound, the checkup? Let them come to that.
Tracy	Good idea. That'll make 'em feel—
Jamie	Involved.
Tracy	Can you be there with your mom? At the checkup? Jamie?
Jamie	Okay, I'll take off school.
Tracy	I can't face it. I really need some support on this.
Jamie	They'll look at the baby? Through the ultrasound?
Tracy	Yeah.
Jamie	It's so exciting!
Tracy	And remember, at the ultra sound, the Goodmans? Your mom can't call you Jamie. She has to remember to call you Nicole. Because remember the rent checks? They went to you. You're supposed to be the landlady.
Jamie	Right. Jesus. And when you call, tell them, you know, you want the check. The rent check. Because the first is Monday. Tell them you want the check before the first. Okay, Trace? Tell them you want the rent. In the mail.

Tracy	Oh! She kicks! She really kicks!
Jamie	I'm so excited!

Blackout.

*

15. (Tracy & Jamie)

Tracy	I was freezing in there. It was awful.
Jamie	They had the air-conditioning on.
Tracy	It was so cold.
Jamie	What a day!
Tracy	I was due a week ago! Maybe more!
Jamie	That happens, the first time. Like my mother said.
Tracy	She won't come out!
Jamie	It's very common.
Tracy	I hate them!
Jamie	The Goodmans?
Tracy	I hate them!
Jamie	What an awful experience.
Tracy	And your mother called you Nicole.
Jamie	Nicole?
Tracy	I mean, Jamie! Right in front of them!
Jamie	I don't think they noticed.
Tracy	You don't?
Jamie	No. She's beside herself with anticipation. And him, Mr. Goodman, I think he's weird.
Tracy	He went and got me that apple juice.

Jamie	Otherwise he was frozen stiff. He was so tense I wanted to kick him.
Tracy	You shouldn't have started in on men.
Jamie	Oh, who cares.
Tracy	You think he smelled a rat?
Jamie	No. You did very well, I thought.
Tracy	It took so long!
Jamie	You did great.
Tracy	He thought the apple juice would induce labor, which I wish he was right.
Jamie	What we have to do is walk around the mall a few hundred times.
Tracy	Right, Jamie!
Jamie	Get your water to break.
Tracy	I don't know what took them doctors so long to let us in for our appointment. You know, it's like the Third World or something, America in the Valley.
Jamie	If it doesn't come by Monday, they induce?
Tracy	Yeah. I feel sorry for them.
Jamie	Who?
Tracy	The Goodmans. They don't know what's going to happen. They're waiting, and they don't know what's going to happen.
Jamie	Do you know what's going to happen?
Tracy	No.
Jamie	You don't know what's going to happen, either. So don't feel sorry for them.
Tracy	What did you think of them?
Jamie	I don't feel sorry for them. They're not like us at all. They're older. They have money, obviously. They're educated. Why should I feel sorry for them?

Tracy	They can't have children.
Jamie	Doesn't mean they're entitled to yours. That's the thing, they're outside the law. Natural law. Infertility, that's not right. And giving up your children, that's not right either. They're going against two natural laws there, so I don't feel sorry for them.
Tracy	Kurt won't do it, give up his flesh and blood. No way. No way Kurt'll do it, even though.
Jamie	Even though?
Tracy	Even though we're not together.
Jamie	They know they're not coming to the birth, right?
Tracy	How can they? We've got a huge crowd already. It's like an event.
Jamie	But you told her?
Tracy	Yeah.
Jamie	And she sent the check?
Tracy	I told that to the lawyer, not her. I told the lawyer I wanted the check, for the rent.
Jamie	I'm excited, Trace. *(Long silence.* TRACY *groans)*
Tracy	Oh, God. I can't stand it anymore. Jamie.
Jamie	Let's go to the mall. Let's walk around. Buy a blanket for the baby? Okay? Come on.
Tracy	I'm freezing.
Jamie	Put a coat on and we'll go, Trace.

Blackout.

*

16. (Tracy and Kurt coming out of the hospital)

Tracy, exhausted, is in a wheelchair with the newborn wrapped in a pink bundle. Multicolored balloons are tied to the wheelchair. Kurt is beaming happily, triumphantly. Tracy looks off.

Tracy   Kurt!

Kurt   Yeah?

Tracy   I thought...

Kurt   What are you looking at?

Tracy   I thought I saw...

Kurt   What?

Tracy   Her.

Kurt   Who?

Tracy   No. It couldn't be. Never mind.

She continues to look back as we dim out.

*

17. (Tracy on phone)

Off, baby crying. Tracy on the phone. Radio in background.

Tracy   Jamie? Are you there? Okay, you're not there, you're not there. So. I'll call back. I'll call you later. Or you call me. Okay. I just wanted to tell you—I saw her again today— Mrs. Goodman. I saw her, I'm sure of it. Across the park.

Watching us. I'm not being paranoid. So can we talk? Bye. *(Hangs up. Dials, waits)* Kurt? Answer the phone, asshole. I think we have to share responsibility here, Kurt. I'd like to go out and go shopping. I'd like to have this house protected. This apartment. I think we need protection. I'm not seeing things. I'm not imagining it. They may want vengeance, Kurt, and I'm not staying here alone. *(Hangs up. Changes radio station. Voice of* RICK *comes on)*

Voice of Rick   KVIC Christian talk radio, you're on the air.

TRACY *dials.*

Voice of Sara   Dr. Dressen?

Rick   Yes, Ma'am.

Sara   Am I on the air?

Rick   You're on the air.

Sara   I just wanted to say...

Rick   Feel at ease to speak before the Lord, ma'am. Say your say. This is still a free country. What's your name?

Sara   Moseby. Sara Moseby.

Rick   Say what you have to say, Sara. Bear witness.

Sara   I feel that the End Time is near, Doctor.

Rick   Many do, Sara. Many do.

Sara   Because of the bombing, and the peace in Israel.

Rick   There is no peace in Israel, Sara.

Sara   I mean, just the idea, just the plan it seems to me.

Rick   Why?

Sara   Because if the Jews make peace, then Jesus will come, as it was foretold in scripture.

Rick   Where is that foretold, Sara?

Sara	Well, I thought. Well.
Rick	Never mind. And the bombing?
Sara	In Oklahoma? Would you say it was a sign?
Rick	I would.
Sara	A portent?
Rick	I would say that. I would. Thank you for witnessing. Thank you, Sara. Hello? KVIC Christian talk radio, you're on the air.
Tracy	Hi, Dad.
Rick	Tracy?
Tracy	Is today's theme, uh, signs?
Rick	Yes it is, child.
Tracy	Can I say something?
Rick	Of course. This is my beautiful daughter, Tracy Dressen, ladies and gentlemen, and she has something to share with us. Turn down your radio, dear.

She does so.

Tracy	Well, I just wanted to mention AIDS? And those viruses, you know? Coming out of Africa? And infertility? And promiscuity? Rampant? *(Turns up volume on radio)*
Rick	Thank you, dear. Thank you for that. My daughter, Tracy Dressen.

TRACY turns down volume.

Tracy	I would like to also mention ice?
Rick	Ice?
Tracy	I think there's ice. There's a wall of ice. Coming down.

(Turns up volume)

Rick   Yes, dear?

Tracy   You know, like frozen.

Rick   Thank you, Tracy. Thanks for your call. I'll see you soon, dear. Now it's time to move on, on to the next caller. Hello? KVIC Christian talk radio...

TRACY turns the radio off. A pause. The phone rings. She lets it ring. We hear her happy message: "Hi! This is Tracy! A real phone! Leave a message for me or the little one? When you hear the beep?" *The beep, a pause, a hang up. Blackout.*

*

18. (Tracy & Kurt)

Kurt   That's two funerals I've been to already in a year.

Tracy   I know. Poor Kurt. That's a lot of losses.

Kurt   She never did speak again. Yvonne.

Tracy   I hope they electrocute him, or inject him. Warren what's his face.

Kurt   So do I. Davis. But they won't.

Tracy   Maybe they will. We have a voice now. Now it's our turn.

Kurt   That's your dad.

Tracy   Every time I say something you say it's somebody else talking.

Kurt   I do?

Tracy   Yeah. Who are you, I wonder?

Kurt   Not my father.

Tracy	More like your stepfather. You do him. And your mother.
Kurt	Really?
Tracy	Yeah. The same little expression, like, "What happened?"
Kurt	Why doesn't Jamie come over?
Tracy	She's too busy now. She has finals.
Kurt	You know I'm going to school too, Trace, on top of a full-time job.
Tracy	What are you learning?
Kurt	Investment. I need it. Investment in a global economy. You have to be quick. You have to learn a lot. Things are changing fast.
Tracy	You just better fucking stick around, that's all I can say.
Kurt	Why?
Tracy	Now that you have your fucking kid.
Kurt	It's your kid, too.
Tracy	I know whose kid it is.
Kurt	What's the problem?
Tracy	I feel like I'm being stalked.
Kurt	Stalked?
Tracy	Okay?
Kurt	Who is stalking you?
Tracy	Mrs. Goodman. Rachel.
Kurt	Oh, come on Trace.
Tracy	She calls on the telephone.
Kurt	How do you know it's not the telephone company?
Tracy	She calls and hangs up.
Kurt	How do you know?
Tracy	I see her everywhere. In the park. In the mall. She wears disguises. She's very good at it. But I recognize her right away. I know her.

Kurt	They're calling to sell you shit.
Tracy	I know her well. I'm not fooled by those disguises.
Kurt	Then call the police.
Tracy	I seen him around, too.
Kurt	Who?
Tracy	Him. Mr. Goodman.
Kurt	Call the police next time.
Tracy	I'm afraid to.
Kurt	Why?
Tracy	I don't know why. I'm sorry about Yvonne. I'm really sorry about her. I'm so emotional. I'm sorry about everything, including Yvonne and you.
Kurt	That lady at the hospital? She was Hispanic.
Tracy	It was her, disguised.
Kurt	That was an older lady, Hispanic.
Tracy	Fuck off, Kurt.
Kurt	Well, I never liked those people, the Goodmans.
Tracy	Just fuck off.
Kurt	So I wouldn't be totally surprised.
Tracy	They didn't like you either, Kurt.
Kurt	Because I was a threat.
Tracy	No, because you're stupid compared to them.
Kurt	I don't care what they think.
Tracy	She'd better leave me alone.
Kurt	That's all over with now.
Tracy	Or I'll scratch her.
Kurt	And there's nothing they can do.
Tracy	But haunt me.
Kurt	Put it out of your mind.
Tracy	Let them get their own, those people. *(Baby cries, off)*

Your flesh and blood, Kurt.

Kurt   I hear it.

Tracy   There are too many demands. There are just too many demands, Kurt.

Kurt   You think I want to work for $4.75 an hour? My stepfather straightened me out on that, believe me. There are going to be two classes of people, just two. The ones on top, with investments, and the hourly workers. That's what's coming down. Global. *(Exits)*

Tracy   Ice. That's what's coming down, Kurt. Ice. A wall of ice. A glacier. You can see it in the air, like crystals.

Blackout.

The End

The Chemistry of Change

by Marlane Meyer

The Chemistry of Change *was first presented at the 15th Annual Padua Hills Playwrights Festival, U.S.C., Los Angeles, California, in 1995. The play was directed by the author with the following cast:*

Lee: Kathleen Cramer
Corlis: Dendrie Taylor
Smokey: Ryan Cutrona
Shep: Mark Fite
Baron: Van Quattro
Farley: Steve Keyes

Characters

Lee *Fifty-five, a determined matriarch, glamorous, vain, generous, bright and sexy.*

Corlis *Thirty-nine, Lee's daughter, quietly attractive but dresses down to be plain, vigilant, critical, practical.*

Dixon *Forty-nine, Lee's younger sister, witty, criminal, attractive, bookish.*

Shep *Eighteen, Lee's son, innocent, direct, open.*

Farley *Thirty-five, Lee's son, lazy, shiftless, bright, irritable.*

Baron *Forty, Lee's son, handsome, charming, bright, critical, strong-willed, alcoholic.*

Smokey *The catalyst.*

The Scene

The time is 1956, the place is Long Beach, California.

Act 1

Scene 1

*The back of an old, two-story house in a non-naturalistic
backyard. Up left, a couple of trees with a clothesline strung
between them. A man's shirt, yellow, hangs on the line.
Down right, an old sundial, cracked with age. Down center,
some ratty bamboo lawn furniture on its last legs; a couch,
two chairs, an ottoman. Up right is a huge boulder coming
out of the ground, big enough to climb upon.*

*DIXON is reading a racing form, she wears half-glasses, her
hair is stuck up with chopsticks. She's attractive but wears
men's clothes, à la Katherine Hepburn. She makes no
attempt to beautify herself.*

*CORLIS enters wearing a bloody apron. She's dressed down
to be plain. She wears men's clothes as well. She pulls a
cigarette from behind her ear and lights it with a wooden
kitchen match using her fingernail.*

Corlis	*(Shakes her head, disgusted)* God.
Dixon	*(Absently)* What.
Corlis	That girl? Lying about how far along she was...? *(Beat)*

	Man, you shoulda heard Ma give it to that boyfriend when he came to pick her up, I thought he was gonna start crying.
Dixon	You got any money?
Corlis	I can't let you have any money.
Dixon	There's a beautiful long shot in the fifth at Del Mar.
Corlis	I can't let you have any money.

LEE enters wearing a beautiful white dress and hat, she looks like a movie star. She carries a small suitcase.

.

Lee	*(Indignant)* You know, I don't mind helping a girl out of trouble, but when they lie...? Brother, that's it...
Corlis	What are you wearing?
Lee	Because it's my butt in the big house...
Corlis	Ma?
Lee	And for what? Performing a public service. I should be getting a plaque from the city. Instead, I get a trip up the river...
Dixon	*(Pointedly)* Lee, why are you all dressed up?
Lee	Well, why do you think?
Dixon	Oh God...!
Corlis	*(Afraid)* Not getting married...?
Lee	I can't do *this* anymore...it's too dangerous, what if that girl goes to the hospital? She's not the stand-up type, she could cave in and then what? Prison, that's what! Ever see the inside of a jail cell?
Dixon	No, and neither have you.
Lee	I saw *I Want to Live*, the story of Barbara Graham, it made a big impression, it let me know, let us all know, that being a woman does not preclude death at the hands of the state.

Corlis	I would rather you die than get married again.
Lee	That's because you're too young to know what death is, I'm the one who knows...
Corlis	I know what death is...!
Dixon	So you're gonna marry Gerald?
Corlis	He is such a creep.
Lee	He's very rich, he's a scrap metal king.
Corlis	He has little tiny hands. I don't remember seeing finger-nails his hands are so small.
Lee	That's the mark of the upper class, they marry amongst themselves and develop these genetic novelties. But except for his hands...
Dixon	And his eye...
Corlis	And his very short torso!
Lee	He's quite a catch.
Corlis	Is he going to live with us?
Lee	I was thinking we could live with him.
Corlis	In the junkyard?
Lee	He's got a beautiful big white house behind that junkyard...
Dixon	I'm not moving...
Lee	Well, we can't let him move in here...
Dixon	I'm too old to move anymore, I can't move.
Lee	It's an awfully pretty house.
Dixon	I've seen it, I won't have my own room, I'll have to share with Corlis.
Corlis	I'm not sharing a room.
Lee	It's only temporary.
Dixon	That's what you said last time and it took you almost eight months to get us out of that stinky mansion in Hancock Park with all those goddamn cats urinating on

the furniture, toadstools growing in the dumbwaiter...

Corlis I didn't have my own room there either.

Dixon Those creepy kids from previous marriages living in the cellar like something out of H.P. Lovecraft.

Corlis I just have to have my own room, Mother.

Dixon Why can't he move in here?

Lee I'd have to sleep with him if he moves in here.

Dixon It takes longer to get rid of them if you sleep in separate bedrooms. All that romance and false modesty is Big Sexy and you know it.

Lee Then we'll have to get rid of him quick.

Dixon Too bad Baron's not here.

Lee *(False)* Oh what a good idea.

Corlis No it's now...

Dixon I was joking, it's a joke.

Lee *(Reluctantly)* No. Actually, I've already made the arrangements.

Dixon Lee?

Lee What?

Corlis You can't bring Baron home!

Lee Baron is your brother, Corlis, home is where he belongs.

Corlis He's not my brother, he's demon spawn.

Dixon He's only been in there for six weeks.

Lee Six weeks is a long time to a housefly, besides, Baron hates new husbands.

Dixon He's supposed to stay in detox for six months.

Lee You don't stay in detox for six months and let's try not to say detox in front of Gerald, okay? Baron has been in the Veteran's Hospital and he has mustard gas poisoning from the war.

Corlis	What happens when he drinks Gerald's aftershave and starts screaming about the utter darkness stealing the souls of murdered children?
Lee	It's all grist for the mill.
Dixon	Lee, Baron is a serious drunk.
Lee	He's not a drunk, he's Swedish, if we lived in Europe he'd be the life of the party.
Corlis	Look, Ma, if you marry Gerald and Baron comes home and then there's Shep and Farley...? We'll have too many men in the house. Think about it. All that testosterone and cigarette smoke, the air full of all that sweaty smell, they start pretending things that never happened, lying about where they get money, what you look like and staring at your breasts, grabbing their crotch every ten seconds, nice when they want something, mercenary when you want something, jail and bail and lots of loud talking and drinking all night and singing stupid songs about sex! God! I hate being around a lot of men, it changes things, it shifts the axis, the Axis powers, Hitler, Tojo and Mussolini were all men, mother, you marry bugs but you end up the cockroach...!
Lee	Corlis!
Corlis	What?
Lee	It's only temporary.
Corlis	How do you know?!
Lee	How many times have we been through this?
Dixon	Seven.
Lee	Is it? So this is...
Dixon	Eight.
Lee	A few weeks of living with Baron will send Gerald straight to Reno where he'll make a nice settlement and we'll be in

the clear for awhile.

Corlis   That money never lasts.

Dixon   And it's so goddamned calculating.

Lee   Yeah, well, everybody's got an opinion, fine...we could all get jobs? How about that?

Dixon   What about my system?

Lee   What system?

Dixon   I have a system for picking the horses that involves converting your name to numbers, all you have to do is be able to add.

Lee   And you want to support us with this system?

Dixon   It doesn't work, but I could sell it for a buck in the back of *Field and Stream* magazine? The way I sold Farley's poker secrets?

Lee   That worked great till the bunco squad came calling.

Dixon   *(Fondly)* You know, I haven't seen those guys in a long time. One of them had a crush on me...

Corlis   Tim.

Dixon   Maybe I could get married?

Lee   He was only making up to you to get next to me.

Dixon   Maybe at first, but not after I slept with him.

Lee   You slept with a policeman?

Dixon   And I made him wear his gun when we did it.

Lee   You'll never be successful with men as long as you enjoy sex.

Corlis   What's wrong with the idea of us all getting jobs?

Dixon   Corlis, please...

Corlis   Well, why not? We could work at something! Like a hospital or a nursing home?

Lee   Doing what, emptying bedpans? Is that what you want to be doing for the rest of your life because I'll tell you something, it's these little impulsive gestures that send you straight to the gutter.

Dixon   Remember Opal? Taking a job in that candy factory till she could save enough to open the hat store...? Remember how much she weighed when she died? No hat store! A single room over a butcher shop, the smell of rotting meat and stale cigarettes and something burned on the hot plate from the night before...? What happened to Opal can happen to anybody.

Corlis   It didn't happen to you guys.

Lee   Do you know what genetics are?

Corlis   It's the branch of biology that deals with heredity.

Lee   Dixon and I come from a good family. Whose child are you?

Corlis   Yours!

Lee   And who else?

Corlis   I don't know.

Lee   I gave you a picture.

Corlis   I threw it away, I mean who was this guy...? Some architect.

Lee   *(Correcting)* Archetype! Men come in archetypes. He was a *(Quotes in the air)* good looking drunk, looked like Baron, he was clever like Baron, he could speak several languages...

Corlis   Baron can speak pig Latin.

Lee   Her father, *(To DIXON)* you remember Frank, he could speak five languages including Swedish...

Dixon   He could say, "where's your bed" and "what's for dinner."

Lee   Well, he could talk to me...!

Dixon   He could sing dirty Swedish songs...

Lee   He had a beautiful voice and I was fresh off the boat. All the way out in Ogden, Utah. Surrounded by Mormons. Living with your Uncle Larry, my favorite brother. Yes...there

I was, fourteen years old, and fully developed and this good-looking guy was talking me into having sex, which is why you and Baron were born which at the time seemed like a curse from God...Christ, I hope you never know what it's like to be lonely in Utah...

Dixon   How lonely could you have been? You were Miss Salt Lake City.

Lee   That was later and I was disqualified for being too young...

Dixon   No, for lying about being married.

Lee   The point is I could have gone to Hollywood and been a big star...

Dixon   You did go to Hollywood.

Lee   I know but not with the same cachet I'd have gone with if I were...

Dixon   Miss Salt Lake...

Lee   Yes! Instead I end up with a drunken husband and these two colicky babies and fights and dirt and all that silence at night, that's the worst of it, how quiet men get when they give up. I hate them when they get like that, it's so draining.

Corlis   I'm never getting married.

Lee   Yes, it's lucky you were born plain.

Dixon   She's not plain...she's had opportunities.

Lee   You mean that drunken mailman...

Dixon   Oh Lee, honestly...

Lee   He was a worm.

Dixon   He was a very nice guy.

Lee   *(To Corlis)* Do you ever think about him? Corlis?

Corlis   What? No.

Lee   What was his name?

Corlis   Fred.

Lee	I've always hated men named Fred.
Dixon	Let it go.
Lee	All I'm saying is that if Fred is who Corlis might have married then I'm glad she's a spinster.
Corlis	I want to go to school and be a nurse, a clean white nurse in the middle of the night, writing on an old man's chart, do not resuscitate.
Lee	Euthanasia is a noble ambition, but Corlis, somebody needs to be here for the boys. Especially now that I'll be queen to the scrap metal king. He's very successful in society.
Dixon	They're not boys anymore, Lee, they're grown men.
Lee	Men never grow up they just get bigger.
Corlis	Mother, why not let *me* get a job?
Lee	Corlis, do you think I *like* getting married?
Dixon	Yes.
Lee	I *don't* like it, I never *liked* it, men are *dirty*, this marriage business of mine is just that, *business*.
Corlis	You tell the boys you're in love.
Lee	The boys are sentimental. If they became privy to our motivation it would make them cynical, that's why we create two worlds.
Dixon	Don't you think they can feel that?
Lee	They think it's part of our mystery.
Dixon	This is the crap that keeps the sexes *en garde*.
Corlis	But if you don't like men, how can you sleep with them?
Lee	Who says I sleep with them?
Corlis	You go in the same room and close the door.
Lee	That does not mean I am sleeping.
Dixon	It doesn't sound like you're sleeping.
Lee	How do you know what it sounds like?

Dixon	Everybody can hear you having sex!
Lee	I am most certainly not having sex, whatever that is, is that what you think?!
Corlis	It sounds like sex.
Lee	How would you know?
Corlis	From inside myself.
Lee	What does that mean?
Corlis	It's a biological intuition.
Lee	Have you been having sex?
Corlis	Just with myself.
Lee	Then what do you know about it?
Corlis	*(A defiant lie)* Baron fucked me.
Dixon	He fucked me, too.
Lee	That's not funny, it's sickening and don't ever say fuck in front of Gerald, we're ladies, we're not even supposed to know that word, in fact, I *don't* know it. *(A horn honks outside. She waves gaily, annoyed)* There he is...that's Gerald. *(Teeth clenched)* Right on time! Did I tell you he's buying me a fur? *(LEE gathers her belongings)*
Dixon	For California...?
Lee	A fox fur for the track. *(LEE starts downstage towards GERALD)*
Corlis	What about Baron?
Lee	Don't give him any money, he has to get a job...
Corlis	But what if he disappears again...?
Lee	Then I'll know who's responsible, won't I?
Corlis	Not everything around here is my fault!
Lee	*(Stops, turns)* Do you know what a matriarchy is? You do, don't you? You *know* what it is. A matriarchy!
Corlis	Yes.

Lee   *(Screaming)* THEN QUIT FIGHTING ME!

Lights.

*

Scene 2

The backyard. BARON *appears, he carries a box of books
and suitcase. He's dressed in good clothes, well worn. He
lights a cigarette. Speaks out.*

Baron   My mother tells people I have mustard gas poisoning. But
that's not true. That's an excuse she's invented because
she's ashamed of how I turned out.

She's got these archetypes. My brother Farley is a "ma-
lingerer." My sister Corlis is "her good right hand." My
brother Shep is "sensitive" and I'm a "good-looking drunk."
This is how you keep from seeing the truth. She looks at
me and sees this archetype. But the truth is, I pass in the
world as a monster. Or maybe I should say, minister?

My ministry is lost women. Very intelligent, very lost
women will find me, like the virgin finds the volcano, and
we will begin this conversation that takes us straight to hell;
home to hell where we can talk frankly about our mistakes,
talk endlessly about what went wrong, all the different
ways life has disappointed us. I've cultivated this way of
listening to them talk, just the right measure of fascination

and detachment. Of course, the truth is I am not listening at all. I am waiting for my turn to speak, and when I do, I don't shut up. I can make a sentence last for two or three hours. That's the kind of sadist I am. And if the woman tries to interrupt, which she will because she's drunk, I become *enraged*. And, of course, this is the point. This is what I am saying when I say let's go someplace and have a drink. They think it's the prelude to intimacy. But what I'm really saying is, I need to become enraged, I need to become a monster. Because when I am this monster, I believe, that whoever I am with represents the chaos in my life and that if I can fix them, then I myself can become healed. From my perspective I am making a loving gesture. From their perspective I am a vicious nag, an unrelenting scold that will not let them sleep until I have wounded them in ways I myself feel wounded. *(Beat)* You don't know what a comfort it is to pass in the world as a monster.

CORLIS enters with a load of washed-out bloody rags, she hangs them on the line. She works with dispatch. BARON watches her.

Corlis.

CORLIS screams.

Corlis   God, you scared me! I wasn't expecting you till tomorrow. *(Sniffs)* What's that smell? Smells like vomit. *(She follows her nose to his box of books and smells them)* You should get rid of these books.

Baron	So, Corlis, how've you been?
Corlis	What did you say?
Baron	How've you been?
Corlis	What are you doing?
Baron	Practicing conversational openers.
Corlis	I can't let you have any money, you have to get a job.
Baron	Oh, I know...sure. That's part of it. Working is the uh...secret of something.
Corlis	You know what would happen if I just gave you money?
Baron	That depends on how much you give me.
Corlis	You'd go to hell and not give a shit.
Baron	That's one option but Corlis, I just asked how you are to see how you are. How are you?
Corlis	Quit saying my name.
Baron	How are you?
Corlis	We're all the same as when you left. We stay the same so you can change into and out of that which possesses you.
Baron	And that would be what?
Corlis	A demon, some kind of shape-changing entity.
Baron	*(Innocent)* So, are you seeing anybody?
Corlis	Am I seeing anybody?
Baron	Like dating anyone?
Corlis	*Am I seeing anybody. (Amazed)* What kind of shitty question is that?
Baron	*(Struggling to remember)* Well, like what ever happened to Merle, the barn swallow, or the incredible tenor, Phil, or Fred the mailman, I liked Fred, Fred was the real deal, whatever happened to Fred?
Corlis	You were there the night Fred *died*, I blame you for Fred's death. If it weren't for you Fred would never have been

	drinking and if he hadn't been drinking he would never have started to fight because he couldn't fight, he wasn't a fighter like you are.
Baron	*(Beat, remembering)* Oh...God, yeah, that's right, that was Fred.
Corlis	I have the police report if you want to see it.
Baron	The police report.
Corlis	All there in black-and-white in a birch frame next to my dresser.
Baron	Isn't that a little grim?
Corlis	What?
Baron	The black-and-white version of your lover's murder, Corlis, is grim.
Corlis	Quit talking like you know me. You don't know me.
Baron	I know you should get some kind of a life.
Corlis	I have a life.
Baron	Just like the Brontës, they lived in a cemetery.
Corlis	I read quite a bit and I write letters!
Baron	To whom do you write letters? Imaginary friends?
Corlis	Never mind I just do, and I clip cooking recipes and shop and help Ma with the business which was going pretty good till yesterday, then Ma got scared and she brings you home and now we're looking at six weeks of covert warfare.
Baron	What are you talking about?
Corlis	None of your beeswax.
Baron	Is Ma getting married again?
Corlis	That's for me to know and for you...

BARON grabs her hand and pushes it back, she falls to her knees, screams.

Yes!

He drops his hold.

Baron   *(Tired)* She told me she couldn't stand the thought of my being locked up like an animal...that I belonged home.

Corlis   But you're not really home, you're living with your mother, a man your age should have a home but all you have is a cardboard suitcase and a box of books and everything you own smells like vomit. I told Ma there was *no way* for a person like you to come home, because when you come home we lose that which is our home, because you change everything by looking at it, by witnessing it, you change it and it destabilizes like chemicals...I hate this feeling you bring with you because of what's inside you that makes you so much like a man.

Baron   I have a job interview and I need a shirt pressed.

Corlis   Bring it downstairs in plenty of time, you don't want to be late and make a big depression.

Baron   *(Correcting)* Bad impression.

Corlis   What did you call me?

Baron   Stoic.

Corlis   That's not what you said.

He walks inside, she follows him. Lights.

*

222

Scene 3

A large drop falls, a carnival attraction called the "Hell Hole" appears. It's an entrance, the mouth of Satan, practical. An amplified voice speaking in a Dracula accent is heard.

Smokey   Von't you...come een?

LEE appears, she stands looking around...she's waiting.

Come...come...do not be afraid, I vill not hurt you...

She turns self-consciously and looks at the devil head.

Lee   I thought this place was closed.

Smokey   Vee never close.

Lee   Things like this don't scare me.

Smokey   I'm sure you vill be...unpleasantly surprised.

Lee   I'm waiting for my fiancé to park the car. We're getting married up the street at city hall.

Smokey   How vonderful...to be...a bride.

Lee   I've been married before, that's why we're not having a church wedding. I told him I'd meet him here.

Smokey   There ees no charge for...brides.

Lee   No, that's okay. I mean, it's...you know, stupid.

Smokey   *(Drops the accent)* It's not stupid, it's scary.

Lee   I don't get scared.

SMOKEY appears. He's dressed in a tuxedo, he has devil horns and hands like claws. He screams at her, she screams.

Smokey	You were scared just then.
Lee	Yeah 'cause you screamed.
Smokey	Well?
Lee	Well that's not really scaring me...!
Smokey	If you come in here, I'll scare you.
Lee	No, that's okay.
Smokey	See, it's not just this...walking around in this outfit, I really scare people.
Lee	It's a living.
Smokey	*(Annoyed)* Well, it's more than that! Okay? I *am* a scary guy.
Lee	Yeah, but you're not going to scare me, I know you.
Smokey	Oh really, you know me?
Lee	I mean I know you here.
Smokey	Maybe I know you, too? Is your name Betty?
Lee	My name isn't Betty.
Smokey	What if I called you Betty?
Lee	It wouldn't be my name.
Smokey	Well, Betty! That's just like telling someone you know them when you don't!
Lee	I don't want to talk anymore.
Smokey	Oh now you're mad...
Lee	No, not really...
Smokey	What's your name?
Lee	*(A moment)* Lee.
Smokey	Like Pinkie Lee?
Lee	Like Peggy Lee.
Smokey	Why do you think you're here, Pinkie?
Lee	I made the *mistake* of telling my fiancé I'd meet him here.
Smokey	Why did you pick this place?

Lee	Because it's visible from the street.
Smokey	So is the roller coaster.
Lee	I said I made a mistake.
Smokey	It's that big devil head...? It attracted you. You wanted to meet me. You wanted to meet the devil. You've always thought men were devils, but you wanted to meet the real devil, and here you are. You think you're ready for me?
Lee	No.
Smokey	Are you in love with this guy...?
Lee	Is it any of your business?
Smokey	Everything about you is my business. I'm the devil. This guy, what's his name?
Lee	Gerald.
Smokey	Does he know what you do for a living?
Lee	I'm a midwife.
Smokey	Does he know that?
Lee	He doesn't know anything.
Smokey	Does he know you help girls out of trouble? Isn't that what midwives do?
Lee	During the Depression my ex-husband, a doctor, taught me to perform this relatively simple surgery so I'd never run short of cash if anything were to happen to him, unfortunately...
Smokey	He wasn't your husband, he was your lover. And he showed you how to perform this relatively simple surgery because he couldn't marry you when he found out you were pregnant because he was already married. So, in addition to the cash settlement, he taught you this procedure so you could be self-supporting.
Lee	God, he was a bastard. You know, he never said it was illegal?

Smokey   Not that it would have mattered.

Lee   Well, it's an awfully stupid law. I mean, men are so very sentimental about motherhood as long as it's their wife and not their secretary. *(Beat)* You know what kind of woman comes to see me? I get a few smarty-pants college girls just starting out in life, I get a few older women, scared to have a baby with problems. But mostly, I help poor women with too many kids, responsible for families, who know what it is to be up all night for a week running with a new baby. Maybe he's sick and can't stop crying and she can't get him to stop and so she has to put him down and let him cry because she's afraid she'll lose her temper if she picks him up. She's afraid something terrible will happen. Because in addition to no sleep and no help, she can't pay the bills and she can't feed her kids and she's taking in wash and giving the landlord a quick feel to keep him from asking her for the back rent. And the next thing you know the baby has grown into a man who can't get started in life, a good-looking drunk who can't get married, can't find a job once he's out of the service. And then he begins to disappear at night. And then he's gone for days on end because he's lost. He's missing something that should have been given to him in the first few years of his life, a sense of his own importance, but instead he was looked upon as one more mouth to feed. If we lived in an agrarian society we could use all the children we can make and they'd all have a place and they'd all have jobs. But nowadays they just get in trouble and you get scared every time the phone rings.

Smokey   Is this what happened to you?

Lee	I don't want to talk to you anymore.
Smokey	Have you ever met a man you can talk to?
Lee	I'm not going to start with you.
Smokey	You already have.
Lee	*(Points at him)* No.
Smokey	Oh. Why? 'Cause I work here? I'm too...what? Seedy? Weird. Goofy. Poor. From the carnival? Carnal, I'm too carnal...
Lee	I could call the cops on this kind of talking...it's called mashing.
Smokey	You don't like the police.
Lee	I can still call them.
Smokey	Why are you getting married?
Lee	To secure my future.
Smokey	What if you don't have a future? What if you have three more...no wait, five more hours of...no, no, two more days, yes, two more days of life, wouldn't you rather spend it shacked up with me? I sleep here, right back here in a trailer...ooh! *(He grimaces)* A guy who sleeps in a trailer! A trailer? Uck! He is so ucky, why won't he stop talking to me...!
Lee	*(Giggles)* You are ucky!
Smokey	Why do you think I have the Hell Hole?
Lee	To make money.
Smokey	To scare people. That's my talent. Remember the parable of the talents...? What's your talent?

LEE *looks into the distance for* GERALD.

Lee	Oh God, where is Gerald?
Smokey	The scrap metal king.

Lee	How did you know that?
Smokey	You met him at the track. He was at the rail and you were in a box. You spotted him through your binoculars and said to yourself, I'm going to marry that man. Then you cocked your big picture hat and slinked like the queen of the snakes down through this crowd of men, they parted like the sea before Moses! Gerald was a little put off by how boldly you came up to him, but then you made a joke and he dropped his guard thinking that a woman who could make him laugh was harmless.
Lee	You know, you wouldn't like it very much if someone tried to pick up your fiancée the day of your wedding.
Smokey	If someone tried to pick up my fiancée, it would be about my fiancée's not really wanting to be my fiancée otherwise she wouldn't attract guys to pick her up, I'm the outpicturing of your secret desire for a marriage of equals.
Lee	I don't think I've ever met a man like you.
Smokey	You know, I have a picture of you in here.
Lee	You do not.
Smokey	I painted it from memory.
Lee	You don't know me.
Smokey	Sure I do. I've always known you. Look. I'll bet you. If this picture doesn't look like you, I'll give you one hundred dollars cash American. Come on, we'll shake on it... *(He offers his hand, she looks at it, starts, he pulls it back, embarrassed. Shyly)* It used to be a hoof now it's a claw, I can get real hands next time if I can make a woman love me.

A long moment, she offers her hand, he takes it. They disappear inside the big devil mouth, a moment later, spooky

sounds of hell can be heard. Souls in torment. Fiery death.
Diabolical laughing. Lights.

*

Scene 4

Early evening. The backyard. FARLEY is on the couch, he
wears pajamas. He plays cards with DIXON. SHEP is atop the
giant rock. BARON sits reading the want ads.

Dixon	*(Impatient)* It's your turn.
Shep	Miss Hazelbaum says pregnancy is a concept to men but not to women.
Dixon	Shepherd, don't you think you should call her Phoebe instead of Miss Hazelbaum.
Farley	Gin.
Dixon	How did you do that?
Farley	You let me deal, I can do it every time.
Shep	Okay. Phoebe says that once a woman becomes pregnant there is nothing conceptual about her life. She is getting bigger. She is getting sick, and this birth will cause her pain no man will ever know.

CORLIS appears upstage with a huge bag of groceries. She
stumbles under the weight, dropping things.

Farley	*(Frowns)* I don't understand why you want a baby. They're very noisy and quite demanding. I remember when you arrived, unannounced, you were a terrible nuisance.

Dixon	Shep wasn't noisy. We used to call him Mouse because you'd forget he was there.
Farley	I never forgot. He was in my room! He still is. The baby, the babykins wants a baby, for God's sakes, it's repulsive.

CORLIS drops the bags.

Shep	You're jealous, jealous of my baby...
Farley	It's not really a baby yet, it's a spot of blood no bigger than a hen's eye.
Corlis	*(Amazed)* Who is having a baby?
Farley	You have something black on your tooth.
Corlis	*(To FARLEY)* It can't be you... *(To SHEP)* Not you?!
Shep	Oh Spymaster, thy wicked eye has beheld my secret.
Corlis	*(Disgusted)* Ooooewwww!
Dixon	Corlis, it's the miracle of life.
Corlis	You better get rid of it, Shep, Ma says it's easy with young girls.
Farley	She's not that young.
Shep	Childbirth is a defining moment for a man.
Corlis	Men don't have babies, women do, if men had to give birth we'd be extinct.
Farley	But more to the point, Phoebe is dwarven, your children will be trolls.
Shep	She is not dwarven, she's small boned.
Farley	That is dwarven.
Corlis	*(As if seeing him for the first time)* Baron! You've come home just in time for a big family disaster that will bring us all closer together.

Shep	I'm going to be a father.
Baron	Congratulations, why don't we break out the champagne and celebrate?
Corlis	What are we celebrating? Some midget tricking Shep into fatherhood?
Shep	Nobody tricked me...
Corlis	She knew what was happening with her body, Shep. Women know when they're making an egg. Like I know when I'm making an egg, I get a sharp pain...
Farley	That's because you make one pterodactyl egg every ice age.
Shep	She didn't trick me, we planned it, scientifically.
Corlis	It doesn't matter, it has to go away.
Baron	What if it's part of a larger plan?
Corlis	You mean like Armageddon?
Baron	Like what if this is God's idea?
Corlis	God doesn't want to have a baby with Shep.
Shep	What's wrong with me?
Corlis	What are you gonna teach it, how to be you?
Baron	He could teach it how to be you.
Corlis	You know, you're getting mean.
Baron	What's mean about that?
Corlis	BECAUSE I AM MISERABLE!
Farley	Because you hate everybody.
Corlis	I don't hate everybody, I just hate men, and I don't really hate men, I feel sorry for them, but he's not a man, he's a Shep and he shouldn't have a baby, he didn't even talk till he was five years old.
Baron	*(Reminiscing)* Remember what he said?
Farley	*(Smiling)* I want to go to school.
Corlis	We weren't going to send him, we thought he was, well,

	you know...
Shep	Look, everybody has an identity but I'm just Shep, like one of the stooges. I want to be the family man.
Corlis	You don't even know what that is.
Shep	Sure I do...I get a lot of useful information from the television, about how dinner is supposed to be...talking, calmly about the events of the day...and the kids take a bath, and every night after work father reads a story, that's me, and I can read so...
Farley	And he's got a job...
Corlis	Working? You're *working*?
Farley	*(Disgusted)* He likes to work.
Baron	There's nothing wrong with work.
Corlis	How would you know?
Baron	I read a book about a man who worked.
Shep	I like it and I'm moving out after graduation and getting married.
Corlis	*Moving out*? I'm telling Ma.
Shep	Tell her you big fat ratty mole of a man-hating shrewsberry.
Corlis	*(She chases him)* TAKE IT BACK!
Shep	BARON! If you name a thing, does it give it power?
Baron	No, naming a thing gives us power *over* it.
Shep	Old maid, old maid...
Farley, Baron and Shep	
	Old maid, old maid...*(etcetera)*
Corlis	Take it back, take it back...! *(Sees LEE offstage)* It's Ma...Ma's home. Now you're gonna get it!
	LEE enters. She looks bedraggled. Her dress is soiled. Her hat is askew. Her suitcase is missing its handle; she has to

carry it. One of her shoes is missing its heel. She limps in,
glares at them, defying anybody to question her, nobody
says a word.

Lee	*(She looks at* BARON*)* Who's been smoking?
Everyone	Baron.
Lee	*(She looks at Baron)* I wish you wouldn't smoke.
Baron	Oh! I thought you *liked* me to smoke. *(Tsk)* Oh I'd never have smoked this much if I'd known you didn't like it.

She settles into a chair, center. CORLIS *helps her off with her shoes.*

Lee	I don't understand why they couldn't break you of one more bad habit while you were in the hospital. Like when they did my lift, they got rid of that mole on my shoulder and those keloids on my neck.
Baron	It's not good to rob a man of all his vices.
Lee	I hope I don't smell liquor?

Everyone sniffs the air.

	(To Baron) Has somebody been drinking?
Farley	Well, Mother, we all have. I mean we all drink everyday, it's the Swedish way to have drinks in the evening and wine with dinner, brandy after, and it just evaporates through our skin and we all reek of booze that's why it's so impossible to understand how Baron is supposed to improve surrounded as he is by big stinky boozebags.
Lee	I was talking to Baron, and now I'll be talking to Corlis,

	but I'm not talking to you, comprende? Corlis, has Baron been drinking?
Corlis	I put alcohol on those rum spots on his legs, that's probably what you smell.
Lee	Where did you get alcohol?
Corlis	I kept a little back in case of emergencies, but I locked it in my desk...
Lee	I told you, no alcohol, no sterno, no paint thinner, no acetone...
Baron	What about shoe polish? Shoe polish has the kick.
Corlis	It's not funny, Baron, it's sad.
Lee	Did you go to the employment office, like we talked about?
Baron	Yes I did.
Lee	You have to make an effort.
Shep	He knows that.
Lee	I'M TALKING TO BARON...!
Baron	I've had two interviews in two days.
Lee	What jobs?
Baron	The jobs? Okay. Yeah. One was selling something. Door to door. It's a one syllable word, like blood or soap. Brooms. That was it. Selling brooms.
Lee	Oh Baron, you can't sell. Selling requires a certain warmth, a bonhomie...and what happens when a customer invites you out for a drink?
Farley	After selling them a broom.
Baron	I'll wake up in an alley, soaked in vomit, a rat in one hand a cockroach in the other.
Lee	It's not a joke. Now, what about the other job?
Baron	Bookmaking. I ran into Benny the Book and we talked, he said you'd have to front me a bankroll.

Lee	*(To Dixon)* What were you doing at the track?
Dixon	Eating lunch.
Lee	At the track...
Dixon	We made seventeen dollars.
Lee	*You* did?
Dixon	No, not me, I lost twelve bucks but Farley...
Farley	I played a long shot named Fido...
Shep	He always bets on horses named after dogs.
Farley	And I always win, Ma.
Lee	Don't start with that dog business!

Farley and Shep exchange looks.

	It amazes me how everyone grew up and nobody knows what to do.
Baron	I grew up at the track, I know what to do.
Lee	Bookmaking is illegal, Baron.
Baron	So is helping girls out of trouble, Mother.
Lee	I'm not discussing this with you.
Dixon	You know...I used to go down to T.J. and get a scrape every couple months. Nice clean hospital. Go in the morning, shop in the afternoon. Never thought a thing about it. But now that I'm a "woman of a certain age," living with my sister and her children...I wish I'd gone one time less, isn't that funny?
Lee	*(To Baron)* See what you're doing, you're making your Aunt Dixon wistful.
Baron	Every couple of months?
Lee	She's misremembering.
Baron	Your uterus must be made of cast iron.

Lee	Don't say uterus to your Auntie Dixon.
Dixon	Oh come on, let's talk dirty, testicles!
Baron	Ovaries!
Farley	Scrotum!
Shep	Fallopian tubes!
Baron	Penis, gonads...labia major.
Lee	STOP IT!
Corlis	I told you what would happen if he came home.
Lee	Baron, it's this kind of devil-may-care attitude that got you lost last time and it took us twenty-two months and three private detectives to find you.
Baron	I wasn't lost I was right downtown at the Midnight Mission.
Lee	You need to have a plan, that's the trouble with you people, nobody has a plan.
Baron	I had a plan, I was going to drink myself to death.
Lee	How can you joke about something as serious as suicide?
Baron	I have a wonderful sense of humor.
Lee	You know I could sign papers and have you committed. All alone in a padded cell for the rest of your life watching the bats fly in and out of the light socket...
Baron	Do it, I love the comfort and security of a straightjacket because I never know what to do with my hands.
Shep	You know, I read a story in the Bible that reminds me of what she's doing to Baron.
Farley	The one about the goat.
Corlis	It's just that Ma doesn't want Baron to slip through the cracks.
Baron	Depends on whose crack it is.
Lee	You know I can't tolerate that kind of smuttiness!
Baron	Oh, sorry, I meant, it depends on *what* crack it is. Who

knows what might be down there? The beginning of some kind of...revolution, revelation, a marriage of true minds... maybe I'll meet somebody, Ma, maybe I'll get lucky and meet somebody in the cracks that will change my life?

Lee You can't expect salvation to swim up out of the gutter and resurrect you.

Farley Actually from what I've read it happens all the time.

Shep It's called divine intervention.

Lee *(To the boys)* You're not helping.

DIXON sees SMOKEY offstage.

Dixon Lee. I think someone is here.

Lee It's probably the police! *(She turns and sees him, touches her hair, self-consciously)* Oh...

Smokey Hello.

Lee Hello.

He has a bandage on his head, a cut on his cheek. He wears a sharkskin suit, a bright red shirt. He looks sharp. He still has the horns. He looks around.

Smokey Hi. Hi. Hello.

Baron Who is that?

Corlis I don't know.

Smokey *(To the group)* I wonder if you could all excuse us?

Lee Nobody move, just stay where you are.

Smokey *(Warning)* It's a personal conversation.

FARLEY starts off.

Lee	Stay!

FARLEY stops.

Smokey	So, there I was, asleep in the trailer. I wake up, the bed is empty, my wallet is gone, I have a lump on my head. I didn't know if you were a dream or some kind of hallucination but then I smelled your sex on my hands.
Lee	Okay, everybody get out, get out now...!

They start out, DIXON dawdles.

Dixon	*(Interested)* Do you want me to talk to him?
Lee	No I do not...
Dixon	I can if you want me to...
Lee	Go in the house. Take Corlis.
Corlis	I'm not leaving you alone.
Lee	I won't be alone, I'll be with him.
Corlis	Who is he?
Lee	I'll tell you later.

CORLIS moves upstage and watches.

	(To SMOKEY) I want an annulment.
Corlis	Married?
Lee	Go in the house!
Smokey	What's an annulment?
Corlis	It's like a divorce but it's less money.

LEE turns and waves her away, CORLIS exits.

Smokey	I don't believe in divorce. I'm a Catholic.
Lee	But this is not going to work.
Smokey	Why not?
Lee	Because it's not, okay?
Smokey	Why not?
Lee	Okay look...the woman is the one who knows about feelings.
Smokey	Uh-huh.
Lee	And what happens in life, for her, is based on or about these feelings.
Smokey	Okay.
Lee	And these feelings, they flow from...deep within.
Smokey	Like intuition?
Lee	It's more than that, intuition is like a hunch, but this is knowledge, a very deep knowledge of herself and her circumstances, what is possible and what is not. It operates somewhat like instinct, it's like an instinct for the future.
Smokey	Okay but what about *my* instinct for the future.
Lee	Well, see, you...your...gender, doesn't happen to possess these levels of awareness.
Smokey	Excuse me?
Lee	You might have instincts, the way animals have instincts, but you don't have this deeper inner knowing.
Smokey	What about intuition?
Lee	No, you definitely do not have intuition.
Smokey	And these other, whatever, levels of awareness. I don't have those either?
Lee	Correct.
Smokey	So...men and women don't have the same feelings.
Lee	I know.
Smokey	We don't have the same feelings about each other?

Lee	I know that.
Smokey	We don't?
Lee	God, you are like so impossible to talk to.
Smokey	Maybe, but I love to listen to you talk, I love this new information, you're like this Nazi goddess spewing crazy propaganda...it's another world...come here and give daddy a big kiss!

She moves away from him.

Lee	You're going to have to stop talking to me like that.
Smokey	You better kiss me or I'm going to start screaming.
Lee	I'm not that big a deal.

He starts to scream, she kisses him, and moves back.

Smokey	Yes you are, you are my little liar and I *love* a woman who lies to me like I'm some kind of a moron...! It's just the cutest thing...
Lee	I'm not lying!
Smokey	Sure you are, you're saying that your feelings are real and my feelings are transcendental...
Lee	Transient.
Smokey	Sure, sure, you're scared...
Lee	Scared of what? You? Hah!
Smokey	You let your guard down, you were intimate and now you feel vulnerable, so you're going to try and get rid of me.
Lee	Oh God, that is so...typically...no! Okay? Besides which, making assumptions about my...whatever you call it...based on this...sexy business is just...! well, it's not that big a deal.

Smokey	Good sex with someone you can talk to is no big deal for you?
Lee	I was faking it.
Smokey	The body never lies.
Lee	Oh grow up and quit talking like a dime novel. I have commitments, people depend on me, I can't be married to someone like you...
Smokey	It was your idea to get married.
Lee	It was not!
Smokey	Well, I certainly don't care to get married just to have sex, would I? I went along with it, it was very romantic...and well, frankly, I like it. And look at my hands? They're beautiful. You must love me.

She looks at his hands, they're normal.

Lee	I'm calling the cops.
Smokey	Call them let's see what happens. We're married, this is my home. Everything you have is mine. House, cars, furniture...all mine. Not that I want that crap...Maybe I'll sell it! Sell it all off! Get our life down to one suitcase and take a trip to Lake Havasu, I'll teach you to water ski.
Lee	*(Alarmed)* EVERYBODY COME BACK NOW!

CORLIS *rushes in, the rest straggle on.*

Corlis	I saw you kiss him...
Lee	I did not kiss him...
Smokey	Hello, hello...I'm Smokey...and you are?
Corlis	Don't say your name. Nobody say your name.

Shep	My name is Shep, this is my sister Corlis and my Aunt Dixon, my brothers, Farley and Baron.
Smokey	Lee, you led me to believe your children were much younger and your sister much older.
Lee	I did not...
Dixon	Where'd you get a name like Smokey?
Smokey	I like to smoke.
Dixon	Me, too.
Lee	*(To DIXON)* Knock it off.
Corlis	Is he staying here?
Smokey	We're married.
Baron	As if that means anything.
Smokey	*(Teasing)* So she's been married before?
Baron	Numerous times.
Lee	I was married once, very young.
Baron	And then once again every ten minutes.
Corlis	She may be your wife for a couple of days but she'll always be our mother.
Smokey	Well, dear, you're too old to have a mother, okay?
Corlis	*(To LEE)* Mother?
Smokey	She's a grown up person who got married.
Corlis	And we're not supposed to be concerned, you come in here, drop in, all of a sudden like this is what, destiny?
Smokey	Evolution.
Corlis	I'm a scientist so don't run a science game on me like I don't know what evolution means...
Smokey	You need to be touched...
Corlis	*(Aghast)* What...?
Smokey	*(To LEE)* Do all these people live here?
Lee	Of course they do. This is my sister and these are my children.

Now they're your children. They come with the house,
the cars and the furniture. Welcome home, Papa!
(She moves off)

Corlis	Did you hear what he just said to me?
Lee	Come on...
Corlis	He said the "f" word.
Lee	He did not...
Corlis	Where are you going?
Lee	I'm going inside so the boys can talk to Smokey. You come, too.
Corlis	The bus stops at the corner, Mr. Smokey.

LEE exits, CORLIS follows and FARLEY tries to leave as well.

Corlis	No, she wants you guys to run him off.
Farley	I'm not going to do this.
Corlis	Yes!
Farley	I'm not good at this kind of thing.
Lee	Just do it! Get rid of him!

The women exit, SMOKEY stares after them, longingly.

Baron	So. Mr. Smokey. When did you get out of prison?
Smokey	Oh Farley, you've got a good eye.
Shep	That's Baron, he's been in jail a few times...This is Farley, he's been in jail as well.
Farley	Just for loitering.
Shep	I visited prison to see my father before he was executed. We didn't have much to say to each other but I was better for having made the trip. We talked a little about the safety

	of the cage and I got a lot out of that.
Farley	And the award for Miss Congeniality goes to Shepherd the spaz.
Shep	I can talk to guests, it's a courtesy and I'm practicing socialization. *(To SMOKEY, brightly)* You know, there's a minimum security prison right near here that I've heard is a lot like a country club. I wouldn't mind being in prison myself if it had a swimming pool.
Baron	Did your prison have a swimming pool, Mr. Smokey?
Smokey	No.
Baron	What about a bowling alley? You bowl? No, I don't think bowling is your sport. I bet you're a golfer, a scratch golfer. What's your handicap? Or don't you have one?
Smokey	You know what I like about being in a society of men is how men respect each other's privacy and they don't pry. They don't try and trick each other into personal revelation. They keep secrets so they have secrets because it's these secrets that give us gravity. That give us shadow and depth. It's these secrets we trade to establish friendship. Refining and enhancing a relationship with these personal revelations. My secrets are like a dowry to my beloved. And when I find someone who loves me as God does, and you can feel that, it's called empathy, I will spill my guts. But till then, don't ask me to reveal myself in small talk. It's not small to me. It's my confidence and my strength.
Shep	*(To FARLEY)* I didn't catch it.
Farley	Doesn't like to talk about himself.
Baron	So, in addition to being a jailbird are you also the scrap metal king?
Shep	He doesn't want to talk.

Baron	Ma wants us to get rid of him.
Farley	If she wants to get rid of him why doesn't she do it herself?
Baron	She's asked him to go but he won't go, isn't that right?
Smokey	She doesn't really want me to go any more than she wants you to stay.
Baron	She wants me here.
Smokey	But not for the right reasons.
Baron	Did you get married for the right reasons?
Smokey	*(Firmly)* I'm not discussing your mother with you.
Baron	Do you love her?
Smokey	I just said…
Baron	I just asked if you love her? Is that a difficult question, I wouldn't think a new bridegroom would have trouble answering that…
Farley	I'm terribly uncomfortable with this business…I feel like it's always something, you know? Everyday. Some fresh horror. Baron is coming home, Shep is having a baby with a dwarf…
Shep	She's not a dwarf.
Farley	And now we have to share a bathroom with two extra men and it's going to smell like the rest room at the Greyhound station in a couple of days and guess who's room is right next to the can?
Baron	Why don't you go inside and fix yourself something to eat?
Farley	I think that when somebody says they don't like to talk about themselves, that they shouldn't be pressed.
Baron	*(Patiently)* Farley?
Farley	And I don't understand why nobody in this family respects boundaries.
Shep	What are boundaries?

Farley	They limit your accessibility.
Shep	Accessibility in what sense?
Farley	*(Impatient)* Where you stop and someone else begins.
Shep	Like skin, emotional skin?
Farley	It's like a feeling, of safety, a safe space inside ourselves that needs to be kept safe...and everybody needs it and nobody has it because *she* won't let us keep anything in ourselves for ourselves, it all gets used up in the pursuit of something, I don't even know what it is!
Smokey	Nobody gives it to you, she's not going to give it to you...
Farley	Oh screw off, what do you know about it?
Smokey	I know you have to leave home to get that, whatever it is you're talking about...
Shep	I don't think that's what Ma wants.
Smokey	You guys are going to have to move out anyway.
Farley	That's how I got arrested for loitering is moving out.
Smokey	You have to have someplace to go.
Farley	*(Beat)* Well, yeah, I know that now...I mean, at the time it was a spur of the moment decision but it was a bad idea, it still is...
Shep	I'm moving out.
Farley	Baron moves out all the time and here he is again. And Corlis tried to move out with this guy, mail guy...man, something...she never did that again. She gave up!
Shep	Why does Baron keep moving back?
Farley	Because he can't stop drinking and he can't keep a job...
Baron	I'm right here.
Farley	He gets thrown out of his rooms and has to live on the street and then he gets sick and ends up at the V.A. Hospital where Ma fishes him out and he begins the life cycle of the

worm all over again...

Shep   Baron is a poet, he's not just some drunk.

Farley   Oh I know, I'm sorry, it's just I find it all so...distressing.

Baron   You're distressing my brother.

Smokey   I don't think it's me.

Baron   So, what exactly is it that you do?

Smokey   It's none of your business. I'm not telling you anything that I don't want you to know so you can use it against me and I'm not going to confide in you unless I feel some kind of respect. I mean, that's just what it is, okay?

Shep   Have you ever been married before?

Farley   He just said...

Shep   I want to get married and I want to talk to men who have been married! Okay?!

Smokey   *(Beat)* I was married to the mayor of Gardena. Briefly. I helped her decide to legalize gambling in that town.

Farley   You can gamble in Gardena?

Shep   Farley can really play cards.

Farley   It's a gift.

Shep   What happened to your wife, the mayor, if I may ask?

Smokey   She rules in the Kingdom of Regret. You ever regret anything?

Shep   Sometimes.

Smokey   Then you know what it was like to be married to my ex-wife.

SHEP *laughs a beat late.*

Shep   Oh that was good, did you see how he did that...?

Farley   It's a setup. Professional comics use that device all the time.

Baron   How come you didn't stay married?

Smokey   The day-to-day intimacy of marriage to the wrong woman can bring forth the lesser nature. It can make some men think terrible thoughts.

Baron Does it make *you* think terrible thoughts?

Smokey I am terrible thoughts.

Baron Are you a terrible thought right now?

Smokey Getting there.

Shep I love stories about couples, how did you meet your wife?

Smokey We met on a tour of a maximum security prison where I was taking a vacation. I asked if we might correspond.

Baron You must write a very good letter.

Smokey Will you stop judging me? I mean...the deal is, this...whatever it is, it's not about me.

Baron What's it about?

Smokey It's about *you*. It's about you and your mother and your jealousy and self-hatred and your secret love.

Baron *(Laughs)* My what...?

Farley Your jealousy and your secret love.

Shep Remember that psychic in Hollywood that said you were married to Ma in another lifetime?

Baron No, I don't...

Farley But it would explain a lot.

Smokey Let me tell you something, poodle...

Shep *(Sadly)* He said poodle. *(He looks at FARLEY)*

Farley *(Clenched teeth)* Damnit!

Shep *(Referring to FARLEY)* Ma won't let him have a dog.

Smokey It's hard for strong women to find men they can respect. A strong woman has had to become much stronger to survive. Stronger than most men. Stronger than you are. But now I am a *man*. I have done *terrible* things and paid a *terrible* price and I am here to tell the tale. I am a survivor. Your

248

	mother has kept you like children and it shames you and so you attack me trying to prove you're a man but you're children with children's problems...Does anyone know what I'm talking about?
Shep	*(Raises his hand)* I do.
Baron	My mother doesn't want to be with you. She wants you to leave.
Smokey	But I'm not leaving, you're leaving.
Baron	I'm not leaving.
Shep	He's talking about getting away from Ma so we can be men.
Baron	I don't think that's what he's talking about.

SMOKEY fishes in his pocket and pulls out a roll of bills, he pulls off several and holds them out to BARON.

Smokey	There's a beautiful slick dark night waiting for you to slide into it and be gone.
Baron	*(Firmly)* I'm not leaving.
Smokey	Sure you are...

He stuffs the money into BARON's pocket. BARON slaps his hand away.

Farley	Hey, Baron relax...
Baron	How can I relax, my pulse is racing, my skin is crawling and the hair on the back of my neck is standing straight up at attention.
Smokey	Your female is getting polarized by my male, arming herself with language, she's a chatty bitch.
Baron	What the hell is up with you...?

Shep	Hey you guys...?
Smokey	You want to go all tense on me, let's go for it...come on, Baron...
Shep	No...!
Baron	I think Mr. Prison Smokey wants to fuck me.

BARON moves toward SMOKEY, FARLEY and SHEP brace him.

Shep	Baron's just out of the hospital he really shouldn't be fucking anyone.
Farley	Please, Mr. Smokey...we're not of your world...
Baron	Shut up...
Farley	We're not! We're hopelessly outmatched here! C'mon you guys...this is embarrassing. Baron...?
Baron	Just get out of the way!
Smokey	No, he's right, this is stupid. I'm sorry. It's my fault. Whenever I get with a group of men, all I want to do is fight. That's what I liked about prison, all the fighting. *(Smiles, extends his hand)* No hard feelings, Baron, just a little man talk.
Shep	Come on, Baron.

BARON watches his brother, looks at the hand, he takes it reluctantly, SMOKEY abruptly pulls him close and kisses him...he pulls back, then lunges but SHEP and FARLEY grab him, Shep holds on to him...

	(Calling out) MA...?
Smokey	*(Gleefully)* Let him go...!
Baron	LET ME GO!

Shep and Farley force him to the ground and hold him down.

Farley	Mother...?
Smokey	Let him fight, let him go!
Farley	*Mother*!
Baron	Let go...!
Shep	No!
Baron	Shepherd!
Farley	Ma!

Lee and Corlis come running. Lee is in a nightgown and kimono. Her hair is down.

Lee	What happened?
Farley	What do you think?!
Shep	He kissed him!
Corlis	*(Starting off)* I'm calling the cops...
Lee	No, Corlis...no cops!
Corlis	Get rid of him right noooooow!
Smokey	*(To Lee)* Nothing happened.
Lee	Now everybody just calm down...nothing happened.
Smokey	*(To Lee)* Everything is fine, we'll talk in the morning.
Lee	Look we'll all go to bed and talk in the morning.
Baron	Where's he going to sleep?
Lee	What do you mean?
Baron	Where's he sleeping tonight, here? Is he sleeping here?
Lee	Baron...
Baron	Just tell me if he's sleeping here!
Lee	*(Beat)* No, he's coming in the house for a cup of coffee

and then he's going home. Alright? Come on, Smokey, you come with me. *(LEE exits)*

Smokey Nice meeting you all. Goodnight, Baron. *(He follows her. CORLIS follows them a few steps, stops)*

Corlis *(Amazed)* What is going on?

DIXON comes out in a green dress, wearing a turban, fully made up.

Dixon She's in love.

Corlis How could she be?

Dixon Love isn't something you plan.

Farley Whatever it is it'll keep us awake all night. Talking, laughing, fighting, then quiet, then the bang bang banging of the bed hitting the wall, the groaning and panting and the yes yes yes daddy...I hate these guys, the way they throw their weight around, life lessons they want to teach you, learning from their mighty failures, surrogate sonship, then abandonment, one more alpha dog in a long line of alpha dogs, woof woof.

Shep Why don't you move out if you're so miserable?

Farley Maybe I will.

Corlis NO! This is our home! He can't run us out of our home. Don't you see what he's trying to do...?

Farley Yes but how do we get rid of him?

Corlis First we have to get a good night's sleep. *(Moving off)* I'm going to sleep in the car.

Farley Where am I supposed to sleep?

Dixon Sleep in the back seat you whiney windbag.

Farley Why are you picking on me?

Dixon I don't know.

Farley	I'll tell you why, for the same reason you're wearing that outfit, that's why.
Dixon	I felt like getting dressed up and going down to the corner bar and letting a gentleman buy me a drink, that's why.
Farley	It's that guy in there with Ma.
Dixon	If she's met someone special, I'm happy for her.
Farley	You're not happy...
Dixon	Oh, shut up.

She exits. FARLEY watches her leave, shakes his head, disgusted.

Farley	All dressed up going out for a drink...
Shep	Maybe she's going out to find her place in nature.
Farley	What in the douche does that mean?
Shep	Mr. Smokey said that if you find your place in nature, the earth will make you a witness to miracles.
Farley	*(Beat)* When did he say that?
Shep	When I was talking about how good you were at cards.
Farley	I never heard him say that.
Baron	He doesn't exactly say it. It comes up in your head while he's talking. Some version of your own thinking taken one step further.

A beat. FARLEY gets the creeps.

Farley	I'm going to go sleep in the car and stay sleeping in the car till that man is out of here. *(Exits)*
Baron	Too bad we don't have another car.
Shep	We used to have one. You crashed it.

Baron	You know, everybody thinks Corlis is the rock, but you know who the rock is?
Shep	The doctor said you were lucky to be alive.
Baron	It's me, I'm the rock.
Shep	You told him, "God won't kill me yet, she's waiting for me to start having a good time."
Baron	Oh, hell, I've had plenty of good times. She's had plenty of chances.
Shep	Tell me just one. One good time.
Baron	Okay. Sure. That's easy. When I first got out of the Navy. I was down at the civic center waiting for a bus to bring me here. I was a little anxious, I wanted a drink, I thought one couldn't hurt. I went into a bar and had one, then I had another, then another...after awhile I decided to buy a bottle, you know, to save money. So I was out on the street with my bottle, walking around the Pike and I saw the roller coaster, decided to take a ride. I bought a ticket, took a seat in the back and we started off. As we neared the top of the first descent I noticed the safety bar was broken, there was nothing to hang on to, and as we roared into the first turn my body slammed into the rail and I broke my new bottle of scotch and it soaked my clothes. So, there I was, whipping around in this little car, losing gravity, floating on this rich smell of booze, hurtling through space...and suddenly I had this...tremendous epiphany... and I knew...I was in the right place at the right time doing exactly what I'd been intended for. *(Beat)*
Shep	Going straight to hell and really not giving a shit.

A moment. BARON looks at SHEP. Long beat.

Baron	Think I'll take a walk. *(BARON moves off)*
Shep	Want me to leave the light on for you?
Baron	*(Stops)* If it makes you feel better.

They watch each other. Lights.

End of Act 1

Act 2

Scene 1

The house is being painted. SHEP paints, FARLEY sits watching, they're both covered with paint.

Shep	*(He stops, watches him)* What're you doing?
Farley	Thinking.
Shep	About what?
Farley	The future.
Shep	What's that?
Farley	It's what's going to happen. The future.
Shep	Oh. Right.
Farley	When I was in the past I never thought about the future and here it is. And it's totally unacceptable. And you have to wonder, should I have made a plan?
Shep	Phoebe says you're fatalistic and not in the good way.
Farley	She would say that, Miss Premeditation.
Shep	You have options, Farley. You could play cards for money. You're not like Aunt Dixon, you're lucky.
Farley	Luck, insofar as it extends to you, causes envy in others. Creates bounty, therefore, responsibility. One day a box of things, a favorite clock, a book of lies, two shoes. The next day a car filled with newspapers and old clothes and

	soon, a warehouse filled with car parts and toys from the turn of the century.
Shep	What's wrong with that?
Farley	What's wrong with it, well, it's obvious.
Shep	Those are things you like.
Farley	So what?
Shep	Well?
Farley	Quit hounding me.
Shep	I'm trying to help.
Farley	*(Beat)* One thing. If I play cards for money, I won't lack for feminine companionship.
Shep	Women?
Farley	What am I? A toad in a hole.
Shep	No, it's just...I mean...do you want to get married?
Farley	I would only do it once.
Shep	Oh, yeah, me too.
Farley	And if it didn't work out...? A life of solitary pleasure; cigars, old books, reading till late in the night...
Shep	Eating dinner in your underwear...
Farley	The memory of love. A bachelor's delight.
Shep	You don't sound convinced.
Farley	No. It's just that, lately, being around a certain amount of domestic bliss, I've started to imagine certain...scenarios.
Shep	Scenarios?
Farley	Picture this. A small, but perfectly formed, little pixie queen in an Airstream trailer, parked at the edge of the sea, waiting up for me at night with a bottle of beer and an egg sandwich and a brood of yapping mongrel dogs anxious to take a long walk in the cool night air and relieve themselves against an old tree built just for that purpose.

Shep	A well-articulated revery.
Farley	It's just a notion.

CORLIS enters, shower cap, paint splattered.

Corlis	Where is Dixon, she's supposed to help me scrape the paint on the eaves.
Farley	Registered with an employment office. Tired of working on the house for no money. Smokey cracking the whip.
Corlis	You're lying.
Farley	She doesn't feel comfortable around Ma and Smokey. She wants out.
Corlis	She never said it.
Farley	Why should she?
Corlis	I thought she liked him.
Farley	Sure, she likes him...
Shep	All women like him. Wherever we go, women pay a lot of attention to Smokey.
Farley	Even when Ma is right there.
Corlis	Of course, he makes it happen with the way he is with us, so smooth and easygoing. An answer for everything.
Shep	He says women still pay attention to him because he's not used to being married.
Corlis	He said that?
Farley	We heard them fighting about it and that's what he said.
Corlis	What did she say?
Shep	She said she understood...
Corlis	She did not!
Farley	She did.
Corlis	God, isn't it sickening what sex does to you, I hate it.

Farley	You've never had it...
Corlis	I have so, sort of...
Shep	When?
Corlis	Never mind!
Farley	Aren't you supposed to be working?
Corlis	*(Resentful)* I was supposed to get the paintbrushes out of the freezer. Smokey and his handy painting tips. I liked this place better when it was falling apart. *(CORLIS goes back inside. Lights)*

*

Scene 2

It's evening. LEE is in a kimono, smoking. CORLIS comes out.

Corlis	So now you're gonna have to get a real job.
Lee	Not necessarily.
Corlis	We were supposed to be rich.
Lee	We've been rich, that money never lasts.
Corlis	Gerald called.
Lee	He did not...
Corlis	Yes. He wanted to let you know he understands and that if you still want that mink coat, he has it.
Lee	You're lying. It was a fox fur.
Corlis	Maybe you should call him. Maybe he'll take you back.
Lee	I don't want to go back.
Corlis	So what's going to happen with this guy?
Lee	What are you talking about?
Corlis	He's been here one week and he's just...God, so under-

mining, everybody's talking about getting jobs and moving out, and Farley is getting phone calls from dog breeders and pamphlets on pet supplies! And Baron...he hardly ever comes home and when he does he smells like he's been sleeping with animals, his odor is so strong.

Lee   He's been stealing the silverware.

Corlis   Well, what's going to happen?

Lee   We'll have to eat with our fingers.

Corlis   That's not what I mean...

Lee   I can always get it back, it's down at the pawnshop.

Corlis   I mean, with this guy!

Lee   Oh. Well. *(Smiles)* We'll have to see about him.

Corlis   See what?

Lee   I don't know, see how it works out.

Corlis   *(Beat)* Okay, what's going on here?

Lee   What do you mean?

Corlis   He's not rich.

Lee   He always has money.

Corlis   He won't say what he does for a living. Do you know?

Lee   I might.

Corlis   What?

Lee   I don't want to say.

Corlis   I could follow him and find out if I wanted to get dressed that early in the morning. Is that what you want me to do? Sneak around in the morning? Like some kind of water beetle?

Lee   *(A moment)* He works at the Pike.

Corlis   *(Horrified)* The Pike? You met him at the Pike? The Pike...? OooooooooHHHH!

Lee   So what?

Corlis   He works at the Pike...!

Lee	So what?
Corlis	He's like some kind of...*(Grimace)* carney?
Lee	He owns a ride he designed himself!
Corlis	What ride does he own?
Lee	Hell Hole.
Corlis	He owns a ride called Hell Hole...
Lee	I don't want to discuss this.
Corlis	What is that?
Lee	It's like, you know, scary.
Corlis	I bet he knows all about it.
Lee	You know it's quite a popular attraction!
Corlis	At the Pike!
Lee	It's none of your business, you've never worked...
Corlis	*(Overlapping)* I worked washing your bloody rags...
Lee	You don't know what it's like...
Corlis	Getting blood up from the cracks in the table...
Lee	To try and find a job and get no help...
Corlis	God'll never let me have a baby...
Lee	To come up with some idea and put it together and paint the whole thing yourself?
Corlis	Maybe he practiced painting in prison, he seems to know a lot about it....
Lee	I don't even know if that prison stuff is true, I think he was kidding you guys, you're all so gullible.
Corlis	He is weird!
Lee	He's a little different, that's all.
Corlis	I think you should get rid of him now...it's just crazy to keep him here, it won't last...whatever this is, this, this...he's too young for you!
Lee	He loves me.

Corlis	They don't love you, they don't even know you.
Lee	He does.
Corlis	He knows all about you...what you do and how many times you've been married.
Lee	Yes.
Corlis	*(Aghast)* You told him?
Lee	Yes.
Corlis	You did not.
Lee	He knows everything about everybody and it felt right to tell him things. I like talking to him...
Corlis	Don't you see what it was that felt right? Don't you see?
Lee	I don't know. Something about the way he is with me and I don't think he's been that way before with other women, I mean, at least, that's what he says...
Corlis	I can't believe you're talking like this, do you know how stupid you sound?
Lee	I trust him!
Corlis	You are pathetic...
Lee	Oh be quiet...
Corlis	He's turned you...
Lee	He has not...
Corlis	Satan only has to turn you one degree...
Lee	He's not like Satan!
Corlis	Remember "Invasion from Mars," where the evil martian puts a little martian transmitter in your head and then you're an alien. That movie is a metaphor for going to hell! He is the evil martian and you are going to hell and taking us all with you.
Lee	It's not like that...
Corlis	Mother, you hate men. That's what we all have in common,

	our common hatred of men.
Lee	I don't really hate men.
Corlis	Yes you do, we all do!
Lee	No. I've been thinking about this. See, I got into the habit of saying I hated men because it relieved the tension I'd feel when I was younger and I would be dependent on them and they would disappoint me. Hating them was much easier than confronting them and fighting it. Talking to them was nearly impossible so I made them the enemy. And well, frankly, they can be so dense, some of them. And I had you and Dixon to talk to about how men were so awful. And it was so much fun, remember? But then Mr. Farley, you remember Farley's father Mr. Farley...? *(Confessing)* I really liked him.
Corlis	Oh, how could you? He was so fat and he gambled all your money and as soon as he found out you were pregnant he stole your jewelry and ran off with that dumb slut Coco.
Lee	Well, I know and after that I swore next time would be different and it was. I steeled myself against my emotions. But then I found myself lying in bed at night wishing these poor jerks, my husbands, would die. Not just leave but die. Fortunately they never did, I would have felt awful. No, they'd leave, sometimes with a speech, sometimes with a note in the middle of the night...but what a relief, remember the parties we used to have? How drunk we'd all get. But now all that's changed. I think about this Smokey all the time. I look forward to the end of the day when we can be alone, when everyone goes to sleep and it's our time to be with each other...Smokey says that night is the oyster and sex is the pearl and this is the treasure of love. If any other man would have said this to me I'd have puked on their

shoes. But now, I get this queer feeling like I'm growing a flower from the center of my heart.

Corlis	Do you love him more than you do this family?
Lee	I love him differently.
Corlis	That's because it's not really love...
Lee	Yes it is. It's true love.
Corlis	I DON'T WANT HIM IN OUR HOUSE!
Lee	My house, this is *my* house. If you don't like how things are run in *my* house, you can get the hell out.
Corlis	*(Beat)* Shep's pregnant.
Lee	What?
Corlis	Shep got some girl from school pregnant.
Lee	Shep? Our Shep? How could he?
Corlis	He has a penis...
Lee	Well I know that but I haven't seen it in a long time, have you?
Corlis	No but apparently he has one. And it's all your fault!
Lee	Shep having sex...what's next?

SHEP walks out, senses something, tries to get away.

Corlis	There he is...!
Lee	You! Come here!
Shep	I can't, I'm late.
Lee	Come here I said!
Shep	What?
Lee	Sit down.
Shep	I have to go...
Lee	Sit!

He sits. She studies him.

	Somebody is having sex with you?
Corlis	Phoebe.
Shep	Corlis, you are such an asshole...
Lee	Do you like having sex?
Shep	Corlis, I am going to kill you.
Lee	Answer me.
Shep	I don't know what you want me to say.
Lee	Just answer.
Shep	Yes. I like it.
Lee	Replicating your species, is that what you want? More little Sheps.
Shep	I don't like talking about sex with you but when I'm doing it, I think it's pretty great.
Lee	Did you notice any...change?
Shep	No. Well. No. Like how do you mean?
Lee	Did you begin to imagine...for instance...your own death?
Shep	Why would I?
Lee	You would if you were doing it right.
Shep	Is this a trick?
Lee	Never mind. Now. This Phoebe...is that her real name?
Shep	No.
Lee	Okay, good. She is how old?
Shep	Thirty-eight.

Lee looks at Shep.

Corlis	I thought she was a friend from school?
Shep	She's my biology teacher.

Lee	Thirty-eight. She's so old...
Shep	I don't think of her like that.
Corlis	Farley said she was some kind of midget.
Shep	Farley is a body Nazi.
Lee	There's nothing physically wrong with this biology teacher?
Shep	*(Firmly)* She's small-boned.
Lee	Are you lying? I'll kill you if you lie to me.
Shep	You're just nervous about being with this guy.
Lee	What did you say?
Shep	Paying attention to me...it's too unusual.
Lee	I care about you.
Shep	Oh, Ma...
Lee	Who's been telling you things?
Corlis	It's that man.
Lee	What did he say?
Shep	*(Beat)* He said that doing what I felt was right, whether it was what other people felt was right, was the only way I was ever going to build character. It was the only way I was ever going to learn to be a man. Men make mistakes and recover, that's what being a man is all about. Making mistakes. And recovering.
Lee	*(Beat)* Well, that's not so bad is it...?
Corlis	Mother...! *(To SHEP)* Why would you want to be a man? What have men ever done for you? If this were the Middle Ages you'd have been left out on a rock to die, to have your eyes eaten by eagles, that's what would have happened to you at the hands of men.
Shep	But I was not incarnated into the Middle Ages, was I?
Lee	Corlis, I don't know how you expect to get married with an attitude like that...

Corlis	*(Beat, stunned)* Get married...?
Shep	*(Starting out)* I have to go.
Corlis	Get *married*?!

CORLIS *holds her head and shakes all over.*

Lee	Shep, you bring that woman here, I want to talk to her.
Shep	No!
Lee	It's not right for somebody that old to have a baby.
Shep	You did!
Lee	I'm Swedish!
Shep	No!
Lee	I just want to meet her.
Shep	*No! (Exits)*
Corlis	I could have gotten married.
Lee	Did you see that?
Corlis	Three times, but you turned them away, you wanted me here with the boys.
Lee	He stood right up to me, Shep stood right up to me! I've done a good job with Shep!
Corlis	WHAT HAS HAPPENED TO YOU?
Lee	You know, you should stop yelling, it draws attention to your mouth, my older sister had a mouth like yours, but wider, and when she laughed it looked as if her head were going to split in two, my mother used to slap her when she laughed and eventually she stopped it altogether and made a very good marriage, married royalty...
Corlis	The Potato King...
Lee	He's still a king and my point is that if you keep yelling to a minimum you might still get married...

Corlis	I'd rather have my potato skin peeled.
Lee	I had a peel once, my skin turned bright red. How would you like to learn my old job?
Corlis	No!
Lee	Helping girls out of trouble, I could set you up in a small apartment somewhere?
Corlis	I don't want to help girls, I *hate* girls.
Lee	Hating people comes from sitting around the house all the time. You should get out, meet people, have a life.
Corlis	Sitting around the house is my life!
Lee	Well, I'm selling the house. Smokey wants to take a trip to the Salton Sea.
Corlis	Selling the house? *selling* the *house*? What about us?
Lee	You know, Corlis, sometimes you just have to stop living your life for other people. You'll understand that when you fall in love. It's a miracle.

She exits. CORLIS *calls after her.*

Corlis	It's not love, it's RUTTING ANIMAL INSTINCT.
Lee	*(Off)* Integrating our animal nature is the next step in our spiritual development.
Corlis	*(Screaming)* OH THAT'S THAT STUPID GUY TALKING NOW, IT'S NOT WHAT YOU THINK IT'S NOT WHAT ANYBODY THINKS...YOU HEAR ME? IT'S JUST SEX TALK MAKING ITSELF OUT TO BE MORE THAN IT IS!

BARON appears from behind the big rock. He scrounges a cigarette butt from the ground. He's a wreck.

Baron	You'll never know the black sucking peace of surrendering to the inevitable unless you do it once in awhile, Corlis.
Corlis	Nothing is inevitable just because you want it to happen because of a feeling, feelings don't matter when a way of life has been established, to go against that is to go against nature, what is natural. *He* is against nature, this guy... if that's what he is, manimal, animal, cannibal, Hannibal riding over the mountains on a goddamned elephant...I rode on an elephant one time and it wasn't that hard! This guy is just one more creature to be mastered and removed like a tree stump.
Baron	*(Amazed)* God, you sound like Ma.
Corlis	Do not.
Baron	Yes, yes...remember the time she talked you out of eloping with Freddy...?
Corlis	I wish everyone would quit saying his name.
Baron	You had all your bags packed, a ladder against the house, Freddy was outside on the ground and you were climbing out the window and Ma laid a hand on your shoulder and pulled you back...
Corlis	My head is about to explode and when it does the brains and blood are going to fly out all over you.
Baron	Do you remember what she said to you that night?
Corlis	*(Beat)* She said, he's not one of us, he's a creature.
Baron	Creature, see? Ma calls people creatures.
Corlis	*(Remembering)* She likened him to a worm that glows in the dark because he was losing his hair and he was so very self-conscious he smiled all the time and he had such big teeth. I just closed the window and turned off the light. I remember him crying. It was a windy night and I could hear

him crying up to me. You went down and took him away and I never saw him again. He's made me hate the sound of wind and I used to love all nature. I saw in it this beautiful pattern of life, flowing, give and take, like the rising and falling of Freddy's breath when he would fall asleep reading to me. There was randomness and within it, human complement, Freddy and I, finding each other, in the bones of our bones, kindredness, destiny, coming right to our house delivering the mail...the male, see? The man, making me the woman...Now why is it I couldn't be the woman?

Baron   You can be.

Corlis   No, I'm not because she couldn't believe that anyone would love me because I wasn't perfect. And she wouldn't let me love him because he wasn't perfect either. She made me feel ashamed to have loved him. Ashamed of loving. But now...I don't even know what I look like anymore. My female face and hands, breasts and legs, nobody has said anything about these things in such a long time, Baron.

Baron   Maybe if you wore a dress once in awhile...?

Corlis   I have a dress I made. From the old curtains Dr. Shepherd sent us from the Philippines. I sewed it by hand so I would get a good fit in the bodice.

Baron   Why don't you put it on?

Corlis   *(Thoughtfully)* Yes, why don't I?

Baron   Do it and we'll go out.

Corlis   I have a woman's body, I could use it for a woman's purpose.

Baron   What's that?

Corlis   Sacrifice.

Baron   Corlis? Have you ever thought about going and meeting somebody and just having a good time...no purpose,

	just...fun.
Corlis	What for?
Baron	I'll show you. I'll get cleaned up, and we'll have some fun. Okay...be right back. *(He starts off)*
Corlis	Don't you think I know what you're doing?
Baron	I'm saying let's go out to dinner. My treat.
Corlis	With what?
Baron	Money...I borrow...from you.
Corlis	You just want to get drunk and disappear.
Baron	You know, there's a beautiful slick dark night waiting out the end of the world, and when it appears I'll slide away into it and be gone forever, but not tonight, tonight I just want to go out with my sister and have a nice dinner. Just a nice dinner...talking, trying to be...kind to each other, can't we please just have dinner?
Corlis	Really?

He watches her a long beat and looks away.

Baron	No. I'm just trying to get out of here. The minute we got someplace, like a restaurant, and you left your purse in the booth when you went to the rest room, I'd be gone.
Corlis	Oh Baron.
Baron	I just need bus fare and cigarette money.
Corlis	God, I get so tired of having to push the donkey up the hill. I need your help to get rid of this guy.
Baron	Why? She's happy...she's in love.
Corlis	You know why...!
Baron	Sure, it's revenge for Freddy.
Corlis	*(Furious)* You know, you don't know shit about keeping a

family together, you big queer, you're the reason Rome was sacked by the Goths, all the men were too busy humping each other to pay attention to defending the city!

Baron   Is that Ma's theory about me or yours?

Corlis   Well, you never got married, did you? Never brought a girl around!

Baron   I brought girls around, you and Ma scared 'em off.

Corlis   Oh, those tramps! They just liked to have a good time.

Baron   *(Beat)* Ma's hid the rest of the silver, do you know where it is?

Corlis   Ma didn't hide it, I did. It's locked up in the pantry and I have the only key.

He grabs her and throws her down, rifles her clothes looking for the key.

Stop it, stop it...you, goddamnit, Baron?! Stop it you...Damnit, you're hurting me...Goddamnit! QUIT IT!

He rolls her over and finds her wallet, takes the money. He pockets it.

Baron   If you sorry sonsabitches could ever figure out how to have a good time, maybe I wouldn't have to kill myself being the life of the party. *(He drops the wallet and goes inside)*

Corlis   BARON!

FARLEY enters, sits down, dejected. He's dressed in a sharp suit.

Baron stole my money and I think he's going to disappear.

Farley	I'm sure of it.
Corlis	He'll get lost again.
Farley	Let him.

DIXON enters, she's all dressed up, carrying a newspaper, jaunty.

Corlis	Where have you been, Baron beat me up.
Dixon	I just got the greatest job. This bedridden old lady smoking Raleigh filters in a bed jacket likes to play the horses, right? So, my job is to go to the track to place her bets. Then I come home, the maid cooks dinner, we watch a little TV and turn in. She's a good conversationalist, she was one of the founding members of the Girl Scouts of America so she's traveled all over, I get my own room and thirty-five bucks a week and ten percent of what she clears on the ponies *and* she's got a system that works. What about you?
Farley	I won so much money at the Bicycle Club they gave me a job playing poker. But I don't know if I want a job. As soon as I got some money, I went and put a couple of bucks down on a car. Got some clothes, rented a trailer out in Palos Verdes.
Dixon	We should have a party?
Farley	I don't remember ever going to a party.
Dixon	It'll be fun.
Corlis	You guys...You're just about the worst bunch of traitors...! *(Runs inside. Lights)*

*

Scene 3

The Hell Hole. SMOKEY *is making a mummy out of rags and muslin wrapping.* CORLIS *teeters in on high heels, she is wearing a purple dress.*

Smokey	Jesus, you scared me.
Corlis	It's because I'm wearing a dress.
Smokey	How come you're so tall?
Corlis	High heels.
Smokey	What're you doin' here?
Corlis	I had to renew my bicycle registration at city hall.
Smokey	In a dress?
Corlis	And perfume.
Smokey	Where did you get that...
Corlis	It's a dress.
Smokey	Did you make it? It looks homemade.
Corlis	Did you make this? *(HELL HOLE)*
Smokey	Yes.
Corlis	Well, it looks homemade, too.
Smokey	It's supposed to look scary.
Corlis	So is this. It's supposed to take advantage of the imagination 'cause it's open at the bottom. Dresses have that effect on men. That's why you got scared.
Smokey	I wasn't scared like that, I was more startled than anything.
Corlis	You were scared. Something went through your mind that had to do with this dress, now what was it?
Smokey	I can't say, it's not polite.
Corlis	See?
Smokey	*(Beat)* You know, we've met but we've never really talked.
Corlis	You want to have a talk about dreams?

Smokey	Okay.
Corlis	I don't dream.
Smokey	Never?
Corlis	Nope.
Smokey	Every woman has a dream.
Corlis	Like what?
Smokey	They don't like to say but it has something to do with the domination of the world.
Corlis	I'd like to be a nurse.
Smokey	That's not a dream, that's a goal.
Corlis	It's a dream for me.
Smokey	Nursing just takes training.
Corlis	Don't you think I know that?
Smokey	You're not getting any younger, Corlis.
Corlis	I never liked being young. In school they mocked me.
Smokey	Did you make your own clothes?
Corlis	Ma made me wear her clothes, I looked like a librarian which was fine since I loved to read. But I had a difficult time studying, worrying about what people were going to say next. At one point Ma made me invite a few girls over for Cokes, but the boys were so mean to them they never came back. They're all married now. They didn't invite me to their weddings. They say weddings are a good place to meet new people, but who wants to meet new people? Of course if I could be a nurse and help people it would be okay. But I'm not comfortable with people, which is why I sent for the Dale Carnegie course but it has all this stuff about positive thinking which is hard for me because I can hear Ma talking in my head as I make my list of goals and I never get very far past "new clothes" when I hear her

quote Emerson who said, "beware of endeavors that require new clothes," but I can't go through life wearing Baron's old clothes especially to nursing school.

Smokey	In nursing school they wear uniforms.
Corlis	They do not.
Smokey	Yes they do. Nobody stands out. Everybody fits in. (*He fishes in his pocket and takes out some money, he counts it, he thinks, he hands her the wad*)
Corlis	What is this?
Smokey	Get a uniform, go to school.
Corlis	Ma says uniforms encourage conformity.
Smokey	It's difficult enough to be you without walkin' around in some nutty getup.
Corlis	You mean like what I'm wearing?
Smokey	You look like the Virgin of Guadalupe.
Corlis	I'm not a virgin.
Smokey	You act like one.
Corlis	I've had three boyfriends.
Smokey	Is that a fact?
Corlis	Yes and one of them put his hands inside me, so I don't think I'm intact. I guess that's good in way, but if I died tomorrow I wouldn't know what it was to be a woman.
Smokey	(*Checks his watch*) Oops. Look at the time. I have to take your mother to the blood donor's dinner dance at the Elks club, I never would have imagined your mother would be a lady Elk, it's quite a bonanza...
Corlis	Smokey?
Smokey	Yes.
Corlis	(*With difficulty*) I have always thought it was important to keep yourself like a present for somebody special.

Smokey	Well, everybody is special, Corlis, once you learn that you'll have the secret of making friends. (SMOKEY *closes up shop for the night*)
Corlis	Smokey?
Smokey	I'm still right here.
Corlis	I'm not wearing anything underneath this dress.
Smokey	*(Sigh)* I know.
Corlis	Do you know what that means?
Smokey	You must be cold, take my coat.
Corlis	No.
Smokey	Okay, what does it mean?
Corlis	*(Hurriedly)* I'm making myself available for sexual intercourse, okay? *(Stands)* Okay, so where do we go, in here...?
Smokey	No.
Corlis	Oh, right, you have that trailer thing...?
Smokey	Corlis, I'm not going to have sex with you.
Corlis	Why not?
Smokey	Because.
Corlis	Men sleep with anybody.
Smokey	No they don't. Well, some men do. I don't.
Corlis	Are you too old?
Smokey	No!
Corlis	I won't tell anyone if that's what you're worried about because that is what I intended was to tell Ma, but then while we were talking and I was telling you about myself? And you gave me all that money and wanted to help me? Nobody has ever tried to help me and now I feel towards you as a woman does towards a man. A kind of opening up in myself. I assume this is the beginning of sexual feelings.

Smokey	It can be.
Corlis	*(Beat)* But you prefer my mother.
Smokey	I love her. It's not that I prefer her, in fact, there are times I wish I'd never met her. But, in fact, I love her and it makes a difference.
Corlis	Oh yeah, well, Ma really changes around men, she's all glittering eyes and wet lips, Freddy used to call her piranha fish right to her face. My other two boyfriends preferred her to me. She'd laugh at everything they said and make fun of me in front of them and then tell me that they were no good if they could be had so easily by another woman.
Smokey	She was wrong to do that.
Corlis	She wouldn't like to know you had a bad opinion of her.
Smokey	You want to tell her, go ahead. She's wrong about all kinds of things.
Corlis	But you still love her.
Smokey	I love her more when she's wrong, especially when she admits it. That's when it's a marriage of equals.
Corlis	Okay. Guess I'll be going.
Smokey	See you later.
Corlis	You know I wasn't really going to let you do anything.
Smokey	I know.
Corlis	That was a joke. Baron's not the only one with a wonderful sense of humor. *(Starts off, stops)* I would appreciate it if you didn't tell Ma I came down here, dressed like this. I mean, you can, I'm not asking you to lie but it would be less embarrassing if...
Smokey	I have a bad memory.

She exits. Lights.

*

Scene 4

Evening. DIXON is in the backyard. She's got a rickety barbecue she can't get started. SHEP and FARLEY are stringing Chinese lanterns. They all wear different devil costumes. LEE comes out, she's in a robe.

Lee	Where is everybody?
Dixon	We're right here.

LEE looks at them, frowns.

Lee	Did Baron come home?
Dixon	Yes.
Lee	At least he's coming home. *(Irritated)* Where is Corlis? It's her turn to clean the bathroom, it smells like a urinal up there.
Farley	I predicted this.
Lee	So where is she?
Dixon	We're having a costume party and we all came as the same thing. Isn't that funny?
Lee	It's funny peculiar, not funny ha-ha. *(Everybody gets busy, they don't answer)* Shep, have you seen Corlis?
Shep	*(Looks at DIXON, DIXON looks away)* She went out.
Lee	Out where?
Shep	I don't know, maybe she went visiting. Isn't that what people do when they get older, visit each other...?

Lee	She doesn't have any friends.
Shep	She gets letters.

DIXON slaps her forehead in disbelief, LEE looks at her.

Dixon	*(Making an excuse)* Mosquitos...
Lee	*(To SHEP)* What do you mean she gets letters? What letters?

DIXON waves at him, "no," LEE looks at her, she swats at the air for imaginary bugs.

Shep	I don't know.
Lee	How do you know she gets letters?
Shep	I don't know.
Lee	You've seen these letters.
Shep	I've seen her writing. And well...she got a letter.
Lee	What did it say?
Shep	I don't know.
Lee	Did you read it?
Shep	I couldn't quite make it out.
Lee	Why not?
Shep	Because it was not ordinary talking.
Lee	How do you mean?
Shep	I mean, I have never heard talking exactly like what was written in this letter she got from this guy.

DIXON draws her finger across her throat.

Lee	What guy?

He sees her repeat the gesture, nods.

Shep   He's dead.

DIXON shakes her head "no."

Lee   Some dead guy has been writing letters to your sister.

Shep   No, he's not dead! *(He looks at DIXON)* He's...

LEE steps between them, blocks his view of DIXON.

Look, I'm no snooper. Damnit.

Lee   You've snooped.

Shep   Accidentally finding it in the bathroom is not exactly snooping.

Lee   You read it.

Shep   I tried to read it...

Lee   Go get it.

Shep   It's not there now.

Lee   I have a right to know what goes on with Corlis. This is a matriarchy and she is the only girl. I have expectations of her I don't have of anybody else. You see?

Shep   No.

Lee   I'm asking you. Politely. To cooperate.

Shep   I know that.

Lee   She would never protect you.

Shep   I know that, too.

Lee   You might be helping her.

Farley   You always say that but it never helps any of us for you to know things about us.

Lee	What if these letters are from the Devil himself, writing letters to your dear sister. She is innocent. She wouldn't know if someone were trying to steal her soul.
Farley	Well, I think she would...
Lee	I'm talking to Shep...
Farley	From everything I've read, the Devil comes right up to you and offers you a deal. And what would Corlis have traded for her soul if *this* is what she's getting?
Lee	*(Frowns)* Have you ever met the Devil?
Farley	Well, we all have, that guy you brought home, what is he?
Lee	Don't be so ridiculous...
Farley	He's something, if not a devil, a lesser demon. A minion.
Dixon	Shep you were not raised a Christian so these ideas will not scare you.
Shep	They shouldn't but they do.
Lee	That's because your sister has been receiving letters from Satan, written in the blood of children.
Farley	A letter like that would be worth a lot of money.
Shep	*(Beat, remembering)* When I read what was written in this one letter, the hair went up on the back of my neck. And I felt a strange tingling in my body.
Lee	Get it! *(Beat, firmly)* Get the letter!

He exits.

Dixon	Are you sure you know what you're doing?
Lee	You're just as curious as I am.
Dixon	It's an invasion of privacy.
Lee	Oh it is not, it's Corlis, what could she have that's so private.
Dixon	It's none of our business, that's the point. She needs to

have a personal, private life, we all do.

Lee	We don't have any secrets from each other.
Dixon	Of course we do.
Lee	Like what?
Dixon	Like I have a job.
Lee	You do not.
Dixon	Yes I do.
Lee	You don't need to work...
Dixon	I want to work.
Lee	You'll work for awhile and then you'll get lazy and think of a scheme that will land you in jail.
Dixon	If I go to jail, it's my own damn fault.
Lee	I'd blame myself. I'm the firstborn, you're the baby.
Dixon	We're not kids anymore.
Lee	*(Reminiscing)* You know it's funny, I know we get older, but I don't feel any different than I did when I was ten years old and I won my first beauty pageant. I still feel very, very lucky.
Dixon	And I think about killing myself everyday.
Lee	Oh, you do not.
Dixon	I have no life.
Lee	Is that my fault?
Dixon	Yes.
Lee	I don't want to talk about this now...here's Shep.

SHEP comes back with a box of letters, he hands her the one he's read.

Shep	I don't feel good about this.
Lee	You shouldn't. You've betrayed her. *(She reads, frowns)*

Good grief...it's pornography.

DIXON looks on with great interest.

Dixon   Really...? *(She rifles the box)*

Lee   From some convict.

Dixon   This one isn't pornographic, let me see yours.

Shep   Let me see...

Lee   No! *(Slaps his hand away, continues reading)*

Dixon   *(Reading)* I don't see where it says they're in prison...

Lee   They sign with their prison I.D.'s...

Dixon   Oh! Okay. I've read about this. Prison pen pals...women getting addresses from places like Dear Abby and writing to these men. Seems safe enough. Sometimes they get married. Happy marriages. You'd like to see Corlis happy, wouldn't you?

Lee   Happy with some skeevy lowlife, I certainly would not...*(To SHEP)* Okay, where is she?

Farley   She went out.

Lee   Out *where*?

Farley   She said something about wanting to renew her bicycle registration.

Lee   Bicycle registration? She never rides a bicycle. Did you see her go? Shep?

Shep   Well...not precisely watching her through the door, no.

Lee   You're hiding something.

Farley   Of course he is, but have you ever thought that maybe it's your fault, I mean, all these questions, it's like you don't trust us.

Lee   Why should I trust you, everybody lies.

BARON enters, he's cleaned up, suit, clean shirt.

Baron	Baron never lies and you trust him least of all.
Lee	You tell the truth to spite me. *(To SHEP)* Now, tell me how your sister looked when she left the house?
Shep	An ordinary girl.
Lee	See? You're lying.
Shep	I guess she might have been wearing some kind of an outfit.
Baron	Oh, for God's sake, she was wearing a dress.
Lee	*(Aghast)* A DRESS?!
Baron	So what's wrong with a dress?
Lee	There's only one reason to wear a dress and you know it.
Dixon	*You* wear a dress.
Lee	I have to wear a dress, I support our family by wearing a dress but why would Corlis be wearing a dress to the police station?
Baron	She didn't go to the police station, she went to visit Smokey.
Lee	Why would she visit Smokey?
Baron	Have you ever seen Corlis dressed up? She's a very pretty girl.
Farley	Corlis and Smokey don't even like each other.
Baron	You didn't like him when she first met him, did you, Ma?
Lee	You know, Smokey has been in prison.
Shep	That's true.
Baron	So?
Farley	Corlis has been corresponding with convicts.
Baron	Ah, and some of Corlis's letters are from Smokey.
Dixon	I sincerely doubt it...
Lee	Wouldn't that be a coincidence? That's why he's so nice.

	So accommodating. It's a mother-daughter act. Am I stupid or what?
Dixon	Yes, but not for the reason you think.
Lee	*(To DIXON)* Did you know about this?
Dixon	There's nothing to know.
Shep	Ma, it seems to be working out really well between you and Smokey.
Lee	Yes, a little too well.
Baron	And maybe that's the problem.
Lee	What do you mean?
Baron	Things are going a little too smooth between you two and it's feeling a little uncomfortable?
Lee	And now I know why.
Baron	Well, you know...it's a brand-new thing, this love thing, right?
Lee	Love is my business.
Baron	But you've never really been in love.
Lee	I've been in love dozens of times...
Baron	Not really. I mean, being dependent on a man, other than me, scares you, doesn't it?
Lee	I'm not dependent on you.
Baron	Why did you bring me home? I was doing okay in the hospital.
Shep	Maybe you could go back.
Lee	No.
Baron	No, you need me here.
Dixon	Smokey's home.
Lee	Here he comes, just keep quiet now.

SMOKEY enters.

Dixon	We were just talking about you.
Lee	*(To SMOKEY)* How was your day?
Smokey	Lousy. The gear assembly went out on the mummy, you know that mummy that swings out at you as you ride past the Carnival of Death, well, it swung out and fell on this woman and her fiancé, and she started screaming, and she runs out with a piece of the mummy wrapping caught in her zipper, I don't know what they were doing back there, but anyway when she runs out she completely unwrapped the mummy and what do you think was in there? A little dwarf skeleton. So she sees this and starts screaming, her boyfriend calls the cops, they come and I have to go spend the morning in the station. I told the police I bought the mummy from the guy who had the haunted house, 'course he croaked himself last summer and in the meantime they're gonna run some kind of test on this skeleton and the cops don't want me to leave town. So, half days work, had about forty-five customers. Found about eight dollars in the barrel walk...but it's all yours, Sunshine.

He goes to kiss her, she avoids him, moves away.

Lee	Did you see Corlis?
Smokey	Isn't she here?
Lee	She said she was going to see you.
Smokey	*(Alert)* She did come by briefly.
Lee	*(Looks at DIXON, triumphant)* How did she like the Hell Hole?
Smokey	She never went inside. I had it closed down.

Lee	Was she scared?
Smokey	I said she never went in.
Lee	You didn't go inside with her?
Smokey	Why would I?
Lee	How come you didn't kiss me hello?
Smokey	I tried to kiss you but you pulled away.
Lee	Maybe I don't want to kiss you.
Smokey	*(To SHEP)* What's going on?
Shep	If I tell you, you'll get mad.

CORLIS enters. She's wearing white nurse's shoes and a uniform and carrying a suitcase.

Lee	What in God's name are you wearing?
Shep	It's a uniform.
Lee	I can see that.
Dixon	It's a costume party. Corlis has come as a nurse.
Corlis	No. I have something to say.
Lee	Where's your big purple dress, Lolita?
Corlis	My purple dress...? *(Casually)* Who said I was wearing a dress?
Lee	Don't *Gaslight* me, okay? I'm Swedish...!
Smokey	What is *Gaslight*?
Dixon	It's a movie with Ingamar Bergman...
Shep	Inger Bergan...
Corlis	Ingrid Bergman.
Lee	What were you doing at the Pike? Picking up sailors?
Shep	I haven't been to too many parties, is this what they're like?
Farley	I don't know.

Corlis sees the box of letters.

Corlis	GOOD GOD! *(Picks up the letter box, aghast)* WHAT IS THIS DOING HERE?!
Lee	What is it doing anywhere is a better question.
Shep	She made me get it.
Corlis	*(To LEE)* How could you do this?
Smokey	What the hell is it?
Corlis	It's my collection of personal correspondence to the outcasts of society.
Lee	Sex letters to convicts.
Corlis	They're not all sex letters, that's not always what they need, sometimes all they need is reassurance.
Lee	You can't get a normal man, so you find some desperate, incarcerated half-mad animal and write them a letter.
Corlis	That's not why I write to them...
Lee	Don't you see how you've put us all in danger. What if one of these creeps finds his way here?
Farley	Maybe he'll turn out to be someone you were married to at one time.
Baron	It may not have been the ideal choice for a pen pal...
Lee	It's nothing that electroshock therapy can't cure.
Dixon	Lee, every time one of the kids does something you don't like you threaten them with shock therapy, but it never helped Baron. If anything, it's made him more inclined to sit in the dark and brood. The lonely way it makes you feel? Just to see him sitting and smoking and staring into space.
Baron	I never had shock therapy.
Dixon	You haven't?

Baron	No!
Smokey	What could have possessed you to read someone else's mail?
Lee	This is none of your business.
Baron	Corlis, why don't you tell us what happened between you and Smokey today?
Corlis	Nothing happened. I went down there, we talked, he gave me some money for nursing school and I went and bought a uniform.
Lee	He gave you money and what did you do for him?
Corlis	I practiced my conversation so that when I move I can have some kind of social life and not feel so awkward.
Lee	You don't have to move as long as you tell me the truth.
Corlis	Nothing happened.
Lee	Corlis, I'm going to give you one more chance.
Corlis	I just told you.
Baron	She wants to hear how Smokey has seduced you.
Corlis	Why does she want to hear that?
Farley	She's trying to get rid of him.

SMOKEY *looks at* LEE.

Smokey	Is that right?
Lee	I won't be a fool for a man.
Smokey	*(Beat)* Okay. If this is what you want. Go ahead Corlis.
Corlis	I don't know what to say.
Smokey	Tell her what she wants to hear. Exactly what she wants to hear.
Corlis	*(Beat)* This morning, at breakfast Smokey asked if I ever wore a dress, he wondered what my legs looked like. I don't

	know why, but I told him I'd come down to the Pike later on and show him. Show him my legs.
Shep	I never heard this...
Lee	SHHHH!
Corlis	So I went down there. We made small talk. But you could feel this...tension. Chemistry I think it's called. After some verbal sparring, we began to talk in earnest. I found him remarkably easy to talk to, it was almost as if he was reading my mind.
Lee	I don't need to hear anymore...
Smokey	No, tell her everything.
Corlis	He asked me if I'd ever been scared before, I said I supposed I had but I couldn't remember when. But by then he was standing so close to me, my knees were shaking...I thought I was going to faint.
Dixon	Did you? Did he carry you inside?
Corlis	He was so strong, so masculine...so...
Dixon	Virile?
Corlis	YES, YES, YES! It was wonderful and after...I felt like singing as I caught the bus home, in fact I did sing, *(Singing)* "Some enchanted evening..." Oh mother, is this what it is to fall in love?
Lee	Don't be ridiculous.
Corlis	Tell her, Smokey, tell her it's true love.
Smokey	Corlis, you're a nice kid but I'm a carnivore, I need fresh meat daily.
Corlis	I guess that makes me an old maid with an old maid's shame.
Farley	Don't we want to hear his side of it?
Lee	I suppose if he had anything to say, he'd say it. Do you have anything to say?

Smokey	Yes. Trust is a key ingredient of love, without it...there's just no way to be in love, it's too scary. So, I'll just put my things together and be on my merry way.

He turns and goes into the house. Everyone stares after him.

Lee	*(Disappointed)* He didn't say one word in his defense. Did you notice? I have to admit, I admire that.
Shep	Well, then maybe it's worth giving him another chance.
Baron	Shep, it was a lie.
Shep	What was?
Baron	The story about Corlis and Smokey.
Lee	Corlis never lies to me. She is my good right hand.
Corlis	I'm not a hand, I'm a person.
Lee	What's going on?
Baron	A spinster's revenge on her domineering mother.
Dixon	It's your own fault, if you'd let her go when she wanted to maybe she'd be a grown woman, happy for her mother's September romance.
Lee	Are you saying you made this whole thing up?
Corlis	Yes! No! Well, I did go down there with the intention of seducing him...
Lee	You were the aggressor...?
Corlis	Yes. But he said he loved you.
Lee	*(Thoughtfully)* I don't get it, why would you lie?
Baron	She did it for Freddy.
Lee	Freddy? Who's...*(Grimace)* Oh that Fred? Him? He was such a nothing...
Corlis	We loved each other! But because you'd never been in love

you didn't think it was real. You didn't know what it was to be part of each other, because all you could think of was how you needed me here to watch the boys so you could go to the track and marry these men you didn't give two shits about. When Freddy and I got serious you set your mind against us and then he was gone and I have never been okay since then and it's all because you didn't believe in love! And you still don't!

Lee   Well, gee, I just thought you could do better...

Dixon   They were in love.

Lee   Well, they were awfully young to be so wild about each other...

Corlis   You broke my heart.

Lee   Well, technically, you broke your own heart.

Dixon   Lee?

Lee   IT'S TRUE!

Corlis   I felt for him as you feel for Smokey.

Lee   I'm not the one who shut the window...

Baron   You owe Corlis an apology.

Lee   Look, I'm not apologizing to anyone about anything. Okay? Now, Corlis, I want you to go inside and straighten out this mess with Smokey.

Corlis   Me?

Lee   NOW!

CORLIS *looks at the house.*
Goddamnit, Corlis, you get in there right now!

CORLIS *starts toward the house.*

Baron	Corlis? You've imagined yourself eloping with Freddy, going down that ladder instead of closing the window. You've imagined it a hundred times. Isn't there something you'd like to tell Ma, something you should have told her that night? Standing in that window? Isn't there something you should have said?
Corlis	*(Stops, turns, looks at LEE)* Yes. *(Beat)* I'm never doing one damn thing you say!
Lee	*(Beat, she stares at her)* Okay, *Okay*! Look, you want an apology. I'm sorry.
Corlis	You're not sorry.
Lee	Yes I am, but I don't like to think you've been suffering and that I'm responsible. I know now that men are not inter-changeable. That losing someone you love means you'll never find that particular love again. You may find a different love, but never that same love. For that I am sorry. Because thinking back to that time, I'm certain that Freddy really loved you, Corlis. That is why you must go into that house right now and fix this thing for me or I swear to God...
Baron	Corlis...?
Corlis	I'm not going.
Baron	Good for you.
Lee	Damn it, Baron, this is your fault, you're the one who should go in there...
Baron	Nope, I have a bus to catch. I can just make dinner at the hospital. It's chicken cacciatore night.

He picks up his bag, waves, and he exits.

| Lee | Go on, get lost again, see if I come and find you. |

Dixon	He's never really lost, he's always right downtown at the Midnight Mission.
Lee	Dixon, why don't you go in and talk to Smokey?
Dixon	Why don't you?
Lee	Because he'll leverage me now that he knows I'm jealous.
Dixon	I'm not helping you when I help you.

LEE *looks at the boys, decides that's useless.*

Lee	Okay, fine. Who needs him. Who needs any of them? Right? This is better, all of us together, just like it's always been. One big happy family. I know. We'll go to the desert. Corlis and I will give a Swedish massage and make a good living, just like Aunt Rose! Palm Springs. Yucca Valley. Retirees! Bet they'd like a massage...these old men, out in the desert. Needing to be touched! Corlis, let's start packing, we'll have to get the boxes out of storage and call the movers...
Corlis	I want to live on my own.
Lee	And how do you plan to do that?
Corlis	*(Hesitates)* Well, I don't know right now but...
Farley	She's going to the YWCA where they rent cheap rooms with meals and I can help her out till she gets going.
Corlis	I'm going to the YWCA. *(Picks up her suitcase)*
Lee	What about me? Does anybody care what happens to me? After all I've sacrificed to keep this family together? This is the thanks I get?
Corlis	That's what it is to be a woman. Sacrifice is all in a day's work. You work at holding it all together with the power of your mind. Even when the earth tilts and tries to shake you free, you just keep clinging to it...clinging to how it's

all going to work out one of these days, and the days turn into nights, and every night tomorrow will be a better day, but it never is. The sun comes up and goes down and every-day you're all alone at the end of the day listening to the wind and thinking about all those nights where all you did was sleep. Is that what you want to look forward to at the end of the day? An empty bed and a good night's sleep? Not me.

CORLIS exits, LEE stares after her a long moment, she turns.

Lee	*(Laughs)* You see that? She stood right up to me. She stood up for *herself*. I did a good job with Corlis. Corlis is finally going to be okay. *(To SHEP)* What are you gaping at, go help your brother pack.
Shep	You're gonna let him move?
Lee	You think I raised you guys to live here for the rest of your sorry lives? What kind of monster do you think I am? Go get your crap together, you little cheese-eater, before I change my mind.

SHEP and FARLEY exit.

Dixon	You're still going to have to apologize to Smokey.
Lee	*(Thoughtfully)* Maybe I can make him apologize to me.
Dixon	For what?
Lee	For letting me get so wound up. He's supposed to see through my defenses and not let me go off half crocked.
Dixon	Cocked.
Lee	He's supposed to balance me. That's what men are for.

Dixon	How are you going to get him to apologize for that?
Lee	If I could be wearing my new black dress with the low-cut front when we have this conversation...?
Dixon	I never thought I'd live to see the day when you would use cleavage to win an argument.
Lee	I can do it because I know he loves *me* and not my boobs.
Dixon	I hope he makes you beg like a dog.
Lee	He's not that kind of man.
Dixon	You never know...he could turn.
Lee	Dixon, you can't go through life imagining the worst about people. Look at me. I've always been fair and open-minded in my dealings with the opposite sex...
Dixon	When?
Lee	And see how it's worked out?
Dixon	When were you fair and open-minded?
Lee	Always. I just kept it to myself. A wise woman keeps her own counsel. Now, go keep him busy while I wiggle into that dress...

They walk inside. The sky turns into a thousand stars, the moon appears and we can just barely discern a woman's face. She smiles. Lights.

The End

The Tight Fit

by Susan Mosakowski

The Tight Fit *was first presented at the 13th Annual Padua Hills Playwrights Festival, Cal State, Northridge, Los Angeles, California, in 1991. The play was directed by the author with the following cast:*

Sibyl: Tina Preston
Simon: Lee Kissman
Willy: Bert Hinchman
Lucy: Molly Cleator

Characters

Simon *A short-order cook and a shrink on the side.*

His Customers:

Sibyl *An actress afflicted with Tourette's syndrome.*
Willy *A historian without a memory.*
Lucy *A mystery writer with autistic tendencies.*

The Scene

The Orbit Diner. An elliptical white countertop orbits the entire stage, floating like a ring in space. The counter features three seats on the upstage side. SIMON works in the center of the ellipse at a free-standing stove. The backside of the stove has an elevated shelf area which doubles as a podium. A pedestal cake dish sits on the downstage curve of the counter, featuring one slice of chocolate cake with a candle. The downstage portion of the counter puts the audience in the fourth seat.

Scene 1

Simon's Story

Sibyl   *(Calls out)* Lights!

Lights up. Willy, Lucy and Sibyl sit absolutely still around the counter. Simon is at the stove.

Sibyl   *(Breaking the tableau she turns to the audience and announces)* "Simon's Story."

Simon grabs the coffeepot and passing from one to another, refills their coffee cups. Willy begins reading from Simon's journal.

Willy   *(Reading)* When I first met them, they were filthy—absolutely filthy. All of their money couldn't buy them someone to take care of them the way that I could. I could give them what they needed.

Simon   Give me that! *(Grabs the book and places it on the podium)*

Willy   *(Continues by rote)* They needed everything; they had to be told what to do and when to do it.

Simon   *(Cuts him off)* Put a lid on it!

Willy   You were writing about me.

Simon   I was writing about my experience.

Willy   You were writing about your experience of me. Half of it belongs to me.

Simon   *(At the chopping block)* Half is nothing.

Willy   I'm hungry. So hungry that I don't mind eating leftovers. Chew up those words and spit 'em out. I want to eat those

	little time bombs and watch my memory explode. Give me another taste Simon. MORE.
Simon	Willy, I'd rather you take a bite out of my arm because then we'd have something real to talk about.
Willy	HEAT IT UP!
Simon	*(To SIBYL)* What'll it be? I've got a pork chop special today with mashed potatoes and baby peas.
Sibyl	Don't rush me.

SIMON returns to his chopping. WILLY advances toward SIMON, SIBYL prods him on.

Sibyl	Go ahead Willy. Don't let him pull the curtain on you. You gotta act or die. Acting is the most important thing in my life and I've been doing it all my life that it's worth talking about. You can see that I've had excellent training, but where I've really had it, is right here. *(Points to her heart)*
Simon	I'm doing a liver special, too. "The Prometheus," $5.95.
Sibyl	Go Willy, cause he's out to get ya. You can tell. He never talks about himself. Never puts up his half. He knows about moving scenery. *(To SIMON)* I bet you're not even a doctor. QUACK! The only liver you can fix is in the frying pan. *Quack, quack.*

WILLY continues to advance.

Simon	*(Chopping away)* Cooking's my calling.
Sibyl	Do you do baptisms or bar mitzvahs?
Simon	Pork chops or liver?

Sibyl	You're a control freak! Isn't that right Lucy? Tap one for yes, two for no.
Lucy	*(Taps one for yes)*
Sibyl	Damn right.

WILLY leaps from behind the counter, grabs SIMON's arm and struggles to bring it to his open jaws. SIMON reels around, yanks his arm from WILLY's grip and faces WILLY.

Simon	Another cup of coffee, Willy?
Willy	*(Disoriented)* Yes, I will.

WILLY hops over the counter into his seat. SIMON pours him a coffee.

Simon	Stay out of the kitchen, it's too hot.
Sibyl	Don't worry, Willy, you have plenty of time, the arm'll still be there the next time.

WILLY hurls the contents of his coffee cup over his shoulder. The liquid splatters behind him. He presents the empty cup to SIMON.

Willy	How about a cup a java?

SIMON pours him a coffee.

Simon	*(To LUCY)* What about you, Miss Marple?

LUCY glares at him.

	Only kidding. A mystery writer needs a sense of humor in the midst of all that death.
Sibyl	*(Interjects)* She needs an agent that's what she needs. Fuck the humor. Give her a cup of coffee.
Lucy	*(Taps one for yes)*
Sibyl	*(Shouts)* TAKE MY ORDER!
Simon	I'm coming.
Willy	How about a cup of java?
Simon	It's in the cup.

SIMON grabs his dupe pad.

Sibyl	*(Dictating to SIMON)* There's a bunch of dildo-heads out there. Smooth fucks crapping up the sidewalks. Prick dicks trailing the ground with their wick dicks, igniting the earth. Scorched balls telling their son of a bitch'n, witching, cocksucking lies. Felicitous mouths, cunningly they lie—big wicks lick the bigger wick—Go pogo stick go, dish out the shtick! Tic tic tic.
Simon	*(Interrupting)* Is that all?
Sibyl	That's all. Get out of my sight and eat the nearest dog turd you can find—puckhole, bumcrawler, fuckersucker pogo pucker found a chicken and tried to pluck her; when she was plucked, without any hair, she grabbed her merkin and placed it right there.

SIBYL, LUCY and WILLY break out into loud laughter. SIMON raises the meat cleaver in the air, they abruptly stop. WILLY hurls the coffee over his shoulder. The liquid splatters.

Willy	I'll have another cup of java.
Sibyl	*(To SIMON)* Give him the damn pot. *(To WILLY)* You've got a short circuit buddy. *(To SIMON)* Gimme a Haldol, water back. Hit me.

SIMON takes aim and pitches pills into her mouth. WILLY returns to the podium and reads SIMON's journal aloud.

Willy	In 1969, I gave my first Tourette patient Haldol. Driven to frenzy by an excess of dopamine in the brain, Tourettic patients must have their dopamine lowered by the drug, halo halo…

SIBYL passes out and slips off the stool, disappearing behind the counter.

Simon	*(Cutting WILLY off)* HALOPERIDOL! STAY OUT OF MY KITCHEN!
Willy	I need memory. I already know a great deal about you. I'll have you down soon.
Simon	WILLY! GET YOURSELF DOWN! Name?

WILLY jumps on top of the counter and comes to attention.

Willy	WILLY!
Simon	Profession?
Willy	Historian.
Simon	Address?
Willy	Willy's.
Simon	Goodnite Willy.
	WILLY abruptly turns on his heel and steps off the

counter—plunging from sight—followed by LUCY *dropping from sight.* SIMON *steps to the podium and edits* SIBYL'*s recent Tourettic tirade into more fluid passages.*

Simon   *(Transcribing from memory)* There's a bunch of dildoheads out there. Smooth fucks (smooth fucks is alright) crapping up the sidewalks, prick dicks (cut prick dicks, insert slick dicks) trailing the ground with their wick dicks, igniting the earth, (this works) scorched balls…

WILLY *pops up from behind the counter.*

Willy   *(Interrupting)* Simon? Simon? I'd like to talk to you about your arm.

Simon   Lie down.

WILLY *lies on the downstage curve of the ellipse, clutching a briefcase.* LUCY *surfaces and inches her way toward him.*

Simon   When were you born?

Willy   January 4th 2003.

     (Note: use date prior to the day of performance.)

Simon   That was yesterday.

Willy   That's close enough.

Simon   Don't waste my time.

Willy   This is all about time. Yesterday is yesterday is forty years ago, it's all the same pot.

Simon   Do you remember anything before yesterday?

Willy   No.

Simon   How do you know you're a historian?

Willy   It's in the bag. *(Displays his briefcase)* My lectures are in here. My name's on every page. I describe people and places; cultures and ancient worlds. I travel through time on these pages. I'm going to give these lectures again, and I'm going to write new ones.

SIMON grabs the briefcase from WILLY and is about to hack it open with a meat cleaver but is intercepted by LUCY. LUCY grabs the case and gives it back to WILLY.

Simon   *(To LUCY)* What's up?

LUCY takes SIMON's dupe pad and writes her response.

Willy   *(Still lying on the counter)* Last time she talked was January 4th, 2003.

SIBYL pops up from behind the counter.

Sibyl   Don't give him the other half Lucy, he'll eat it up. He'll lick the bowl clean, then you'll be a goner.

LUCY stops writing and tosses the pad—SIBYL swings her legs over the side of the counter.

There was an old buck who did it with shoes, who especially liked spats, and high-heeled shoes. One day while diddling a wing tip or two, he found a lass who wanted to screw and get screwed. He went out to buy some fuck-me pumps for the occasion and wore out his sole while shopping.

(Pause) Oh, fuck fuck fuck that's not the way it goes—oh, fuck shit fuck fuck—he wore out his soles while pounding the pavement. *(Pause)* I'm hungry.

SIMON *gives her a Haldol and water.*

Simon   *(To* LUCY*)* Point to something on the menu and I'll make it for you.

She points beyond the menu to the lying figure of WILLY.

Simon   Are you sure you want the meat loaf?

Lucy   *(Taps one for yes)*

Simon   I once tasted an unusual and hidden Japanese delicacy. The Japanese call it *Saru No No Miso* which translates as live monkey brains. Young monkeys are prepared for this dish while they are still alive. A special vice is brought to the table, there, the skull is cracked and the brains are scooped right out of the living skull. The monkey often remains alive in the vice lingering for moments after the meal is finished. When I had my first taste, it produced a myriad of sensations, transporting me in virtual space through my taste organs. I ate and ate, and I ran and ran, through open grasslands until I vomited. My mouth was on fire and I roamed the caves. I went back for more, but the head chef had disappeared and his recipe had vanished with him. His sous-chef told me he was lying with the gibbons. I'd do anything to duplicate that taste.

WILLY *rises from the counter.*

Willy	Do you have anything in your notes about me being baptized?
Simon	No.
Willy	Nothing?
Simon	Nothing.
Willy	You have nothing?
Simon	I have nothing.
Willy	*(Looking back over his shoulder at the audience)* It's a terrible thing to look back, over your shoulder, and not see a single person or place behind you. *(Beat)* Could I have a glass of water?

SIMON *gets one and offers it to him.*

	No! Pour it over my forehead.
Simon	OH FOR CHRISSAKES!
Willy	Those words could work. Use 'em.
Simon	I can't do this.
Willy	You're right. You don't have *It*!
Sibyl	*(Pipes up)* You need an actress. You need someone with presence. I'll do it Willy.
Simon	Tomorrow Willy.
Willy	Tomorrow never comes.
Simon	Then yesterday never was.
Willy	Yesterday was my birthday or have you forgotten?
Simon	Tomorrow then.
Sibyl	*(To WILLY)* Let's find a cab and we can watch the meter run.

LUCY, SIBYL, *and* WILLY *jump on the counter and assume the static representation of running—as in a Eadweard Muybridge study.*

SIMON steps up to the podium to make his entries in his journal.

Simon   *(Writing his thoughts)* I compressed their experiences into words. I composed cogent, thoughtful sentences. I created paragraphs, architectonic brain transmissions exceeding all time and space. I have given them order. They know what to expect when they come here. I smooth out the bumps. I make them fit. I make them bacon and eggs.

SIMON makes a phone call and places his meat order.

Hi, this is Simon at *The Orbit*. Fifteen pounds of ground beef, twenty double-cut pork chops, ten prime ribs, how's the porterhouse? Okay, fifteen twelve-ouncers, and a shoulder of veal. *(Pause)* Do you have any monkey?

WILLY, SIBYL and LUCY break their Muybridge tableau and leap from the counter, dropping from sight. SIMON returns to his chopping.

WILLY reappears at his seat.

Willy   *(Reciting the menu)* "The Greenwich Village"! Grilled American cheese with crisp bacon, tomato, sauteed onions on a toasted roll—served with our famous french fries: $5.65.

Wipes his mouth with a napkin as if he had completed a meal and then continues:

"The Rhode Island!" Fresh tunafish salad, melted Swiss, sauteed onions, tomato on rye: $5.95.

Wipes his mouth again and continues to savor the menu with gusto:

"The Indiana!" Broiled sausages, melted American cheese, tomato, sauteed…

Simon *(Interrupts) What do you want?*

Willy Just a check.

Simon Willy?

Willy *(Protests)* No really, I'm stuffed. Nothing else. Just a check.

SIMON rips off a check and flings it at him — WILLY drops from sight.

SIMON begins to clear WILLY's spot — suddenly he starts sniffing around. He grabs WILLY's napkin with his teeth and shakes his head violently, growling like an animal with wild prey in his mouth. He finally wrenches the napkin from his mouth, then wipes his mouth as if he had finished a meal and exits.

WILLY pops up from behind the counter.

Willy *(As if he were lecturing a class)* Today we're focusing on the collective experience. In other words we are examining the idea of history. The question we must ask ourselves is: Who prints up the big calendar? The collective experience recorded over time is a compilation by those who are at the top, whose eyes gaze upon the human battlement in search of the big picture. I have forgotten the names and dates. *(Beat)* It doesn't matter, they have all been changed by the editors, nobody cares about precision. All that anyone agrees upon, is that there is a calendar. This is critical. *(Tries to unlock his briefcase)* The question we must ask ourselves is: *Where* is this calendar? Who has got the big watch? *(Slams his briefcase against the counter trying to bust it open)* ALL RIGHT CLASS! My name is Willy. I have an idea of who Willy is. The idea of Willy *Is*! *(Beat)* Other people call me Willy. I must be Willy. Willy? WILLY? *(Screams)* WILLY! *(Pause, calls out)* Simon? *Simon?*

SIMON *appears from behind the counter.*

Simon	Willy?
Willy	*(Getting his bearings)* Historian. January 5th, 2003. That was yesterday.
Simon	*(Writing in his dupe pad)* And the day before yesterday?
Willy	The day before eternity doesn't exist. Is that when you were born? *(Pause)* I'll take a check.

SIMON *rips off a check and throws it at* WILLY. WILLY *drops behind the counter.*

Simon	*(Writes his thoughts in his journal)* What does he mean? Is that when you were born. Don't cast me out. I fit into all of this. I'M IN! I know everything that goes on. It's very clear that you are never going to get past zero at this rate.

I'm trying to get your numbers moving, but Willy, you are locked. Your mind is corroded by bad thinking and bad attitudes. You were filthy when I met you and I'm scraping off that filth from your grey matter. Willyboy you are a scab. I'm trying to give you the time of day and you act like I don't exist. Well I've got news for you Willy, *Simon is*!

SIMON walks to the edge of the orbit. He hears the calls of monkeys and becomes agitated. Unable to control himself, he imitates their calls—screeching and grunting—in answer to them. WILLY, SIBYL and LUCY suddenly pop up, catching SIMON making monkey sounds.

Sibyl	You need a vacation. TAKE IT!
Simon	I can cook anywhere. You want the place? *Take it*. Dish it out. Let someone else take the orders.
Sibyl	Who?
Simon	Whoever can.
Sibyl	Willy, you do it.

WILLY hops over the counter and takes over SIMON's spot as short-order cook. He snaps his fingers, LUCY hands him a dupe pad.

Willy	I'll take'm, I'll make'm, I'll dish'm out and put'm in the book. *(To LUCY)* How about a Sominex special? Ha-ha.
Lucy	*(Taps one for yes)*
Simon	Cup of java.

WILLY gives him the pot.

Sibyl	TAKE MY ORDER! *(WILLY runs over)* I HATE THEM! I hate those cocksuckers. They want me to eat the shit they serve up the crap tube and call it leadership. Those colon-head generals and president's sons—they want me to believe that they are on the side of right. Fucking A, they are on the side of desperation, the sucking crooks, bleeding the poor; vampires eating up the air and earth and sucking up humanity with their corporate leeches. What do we live in, the Dark Ages? Who's running things? Whose got a script? Nobody that I know. The Congress doesn't have it. The newspapers don't have it. Why isn't anyone talking? I want a part. I WANT TO SEE A SCRIPT!
Willy	This is filth, it's just plain fucking filth and I'm not going to write it.
Sibyl	THE TRUTH IS DIRTY! WRITE IT!
Willy	I need time.
Simon	YOU NEED A STORY! Take it down.
Willy	Again.
Simon	From the top.
Sibyl	I HATE THEM! I hate those cocksuckers. They want me to eat the shit they serve up the crap tube and...
Simon	*(Interrupting)* WILLY! What's wrong?

WILLY is fixated on the dupe pad, turning page after page in horror.

Willy	There are monkeys on every page!

He slams the pad on the counter. SIBYL picks it up.

Sibyl	MONKEYS! They even look like you. *(Pointing to SIMON)*

SIBYL and LUCY break into hysterical laughter.

Simon	*(To SIBYL)* RIGHTBRAIN! Would you like some meat loaf?
Sibyl	Sure. I'll have a slice.
Simon	Willy? *(No response)* Willy?
Willy	*(Taps two for no)*

SIMON puts on his jacket and safari hat and jumps on the upstage counter. Back to the audience, he looks out into the distance as if he has left The Orbit behind him.

LUCY combs WILLY's hair.

Sibyl	If you part his hair down the middle he will appear indecisive. If you part his hair down the side, the question will be, which side? If his hair is combed back, straight over his forehead, is that a retreat or an attack? If his hair is not combed at all, is it a sign of resignation? Does he have enough hair to produce an outcome? Willy—just a yes or no—do you want me to do your nails?
Willy	*(Taps two for no)*

LUCY and SIBYL slowly sink from view. SIMON approaches, walking along the top of the counter.

Simon	Now Willy. You were born January 4th. One for yes; two for no.
Willy	*(One tap)*

Simon	That was yesterday.
Willy	*(One tap)*
Simon	Yes. It seems like an eternity ago. *(Pause)* And the day before yesterday?
Willy	*(One tap)*
Simon	The day before eternity doesn't exist.
Willy	*(Two taps)*

WILLY slowly sinks from his chair.

SIMON walks to the downstage edge of the counter. He slowly sinks down. His body vanishes inch by inch as if he were being sucked into a dark hole. His fingertips grip the edge of the counter, then as the final gesture, his fingertips release and they disappear from view.

Blackout.

*

Scene 2
LUCY's Story

Sibyl	*(Calls out)* LIGHTS!

Lights up. WILLY, LUCY, SIMON, and SIBYL seated around the counter.

Sibyl	*(Announces)* "Lucy's Story."

Willy	He can't remember anything that happened forty-eight hours ago. His memory is shot.
Sibyl	He blew a fuse. Too much monkey brain on the brain. Too much crap in the cage.
Willy	*(To Lucy)* Would you mind getting me a cup of java?

Lucy hesitates, then with a newfound sense of power, climbs into the center of The Orbit. She gets the pot and pours Willy a cup.

Lucy	*(Picks up the phone)* Hi, Lucy at The Orbit. Twenty free-range chickens, four racks of baby lambs, ten twelve-ounce New York strips, twenty pounds of burger, half 'n' half, and a loin of pork.

Willy and Sibyl drop out. Simon surfaces.

Lucy	Coffee?
Simon	*(Taps one for yes)*

Lucy pours him a cup.

Lucy	Nice night.
	(No response)
	We've got a meat loaf special tonight. Would you like to try it?
Simon	*(Taps two for no)*
Lucy	*(Lifting the cover of the cake dish)* This must be Willy's birthday cake, left over from yesterday. You make a beautiful cake Simon. Would you like a slice?

318

Simon	*(Taps one for yes)*

SIBYL surfaces and takes a seat.

Sibyl	Willy wasn't born yesterday! Come on. If ya believe that one, listen to this: I've got land in Florida. *(No response from LUCY)* Whatsa matter? Can't take a joke? *(Turning to SIMON)* I say fuck 'em fuck 'em if they can't take a joke.

WILLY surfaces.

Willy	Cup a java.
Sibyl	Like I said, I've got a nice marsh for swimming and some pet snakes.

She and WILLY burst into hysterical laughter. LUCY is silent and pours coffee for WILLY and SIBYL.

Sibyl	*(To LUCY)* I'm not the villain Lassie, so get down.

LUCY places a slice of cake in front of Simon.

Lucy	It's chocolate.
Simon	*(Taps one for yes)*
Willy	THAT'S MY CAKE! *(Pause)* That cake is not a leftover. THAT'S MY CAKE! I'd like a slice.
Lucy	That's the last one.
Willy	*(To SIMON)* Why aren't you eating *it*?
Sibyl	He's saving it.

Willy	You're not eating it because it's mine! MINE!

WILLY lunges for SIMON. They tumble behind the counter.

Simon	MY THROAT!

Growling and barking sounds.

Willy	*(Screaming)* MY ARM! MY ARM!

WILLY and SIMON pop up from behind the counter—
WILLY's arm is about to be clamped by SIMON's jaws.

Lucy	GET OUT! GET OUT!

They drop out. Pause. WILLY emerges in his seat.

Sibyl	You can't just come in here and take every piece of cake you see. I used to take every part that came along. But not anymore. I'm waiting for the part that fits me like a skin. No more public humiliation for me. (*Beat*) What kind of cake was it?
Willy	Chocolate.
Sibyl	That's too bad. Would you like a Haldol?
Willy	Why not.
Sibyl	Helps me get over the bumps.
Willy	Will it help the drops?
Sibyl	What are the drops?
Willy	If I try to take one step, just one step outside of the present moment, a trapdoor suddenly springs; my feet drop, my

	brain hits the top of my skull and I'm plunging thirty-two feet per second with no ground in sight. Now that's a drop. A person with vision doesn't have to worry about the drops. *(Pause)* Do you have visions?
Sibyl	Yes.

WILLY slides along the counter until he is lying right under SIBYL's nose.

Willy	I thought so. I'll get to the point. I'm looking for someone, someone who has a presence—who knows how to seize the moment. *(Pause)* Have you ever baptized anyone?
Sibyl	I'll get my robes.

WILLY follows SIBYL and they drop from sight. SIMON emerges at the stove and positions an egg within the jaws of the vice. LUCY records his actions in the journal.

Lucy	*(Writing)* His sense of time is so affected, that events, instead of appearing in an orderly sequence of past, present, and future, occur simultaneously. He sometimes spends long periods of time positioning eggs within the jaws of his vice. Gauging the amount of pressure to bear on the surface of the egg occupies him in deep and total fascination for hours. The result of all the eggs eventually is found within the omelette. That's all he could make anymore, so he stopped cooking, but he can't stay out of the diner.

WILLY emerges.

| Willy | That's all he could make anymore, so he stopped cooking, but he can't stay out of the diner. |
| Lucy | OUT! |

WILLY drops from sight. SIBYL's clawing hands appear over the top of the counter, she pulls herself up and takes her seat.

Sibyl	How's Simon?
Lucy	Not here.
Sibyl	TAKE MY ORDER! AND GET IT RIGHT! I'm sick of being mis-quoted. Ready?
Lucy	SIMON!

SIMON emerges with a bottle of Haldol and pours out the entire bottle before SIBYL. Hundreds of Haldol tablets hit the counter.

| Lucy | *(Noting the event)* Haldol, coffee back. |

SIBYL's head falls to the counter.

SIMON returns to the stove and LUCY slips him into his jacket. SIMON leaps to the counter and assumes a Muybridge static running position.

| Lucy | *(Recording her actions)* The night was picking up speed. The boulevard was glistening with lights, the cars were cruising by and the stars were flickering like a hundred eyes in the sky. When I walked into the diner I saw Sibyl slumped over the counter. *(Runs over to her)* I looked around, nothing. I |

ran to her side, I turned her over—she was still breathing. I could smell the coffee and spot the symptoms of a Haldol overdose. She was not a victim yet. A pattern was beginning to emerge. Someone was out to get her. Simon had been seen running from the diner earlier. It had to be *Simon*.

She pushes the unconscious SIBYL *back in the chair and carefully leans her over the counter, propping her chin with her hands.* WILLY *comes in as the D.A.*

Willy *(To* LUCY*)* Java.

Lucy The D.A. had arrived.

Willy *(Turning to* SIBYL*)* Hi. You look tired. *(Beat)* Where were you on the night of January 4th? If you need more time, okay, but don't sit on the fence on this. *(No response from* SIBYL*)* Okay sister, but if I don't get some answers I'll have to pull you in for questioning. You're a nice kid—I wouldn't want to do that. Just remember what I said. I won't say another word about it. *(Drops behind the counter)*

Lucy *(Placing a phone order)* Hi—Lucy, from The Orbit. I want game. Yah. Any venison? How about rabbit? Okay, twenty. No, I'll skin them.

SIMON breaks his running stance and leaps from the counter. SIBYL *returns to consciousness.* WILLY *and* SIMON *surface and play cards.* LUCY *hangs up the phone.*

Sibyl *(To* LUCY*)* Cup a Java. *(LUCY pours her a cup)* Your story's not bad and my character is coming along, but you need more—more locations. So who's gonna get it in the end?

Lucy	You.
Sibyl	ME! That's a bad idea.
Lucy	Somebody has to die.
Sibyl	I don't play corpses. Besides, you need someone to tell your readers what really happened. I'm the one to do it. It's okay that everyone thinks that he's gonna get me, but I need to come out on top. If someone's gotta go, make it Willy. If someone has to be sacrificed for a good story, make it him. *(Beat)* I don't want to be in your story.
Lucy	It's too late for that now. *(Steps to the podium and records her story)* I came back later—the D.A. had been there.
Willy	Java.
Lucy	She was stretched out on the counter. They wanted me for questioning.
Sibyl	I'll have the Breakfast Special.
Lucy	They knew I had information about Simon and about Sibyl.
Simon	LUCY!
Lucy	He was into strange experiments. Used a lot of monkeys.
Willy	What is the Breakfast Special?
Lucy	In 1969 he gave his first Tourette patient Haldol.
Simon	Meat loaf and coffee.
Lucy	Tourettic patients must have their dopamine lowered.
Sibyl	Who do you have to fuck around here to get a cup of coffee!
Simon	LUCY!
Lucy	He found out the real properites of Haldol—how it could silence.
Willy	You have a filthy mind.
Lucy	It could be the next mass tranquilizer next to the media.
Sibyl	Lucy.
Lucy	Sibyl was dangerous to them.

Simon-Sibyl	Lucy.
Lucy	She talked raw stuff.

Willy-Simon-Sibyl

	Lucy.
Lucy	Deadly silence, he was.
All	Lucy?
Lucy	I had to find out.
All	LUCY!
Lucy	If there was anybody behind him.
All	LUCY!
Lucy	The science of silence was thriving!
All	*(Screaming)* LUCY!
Lucy	This is going to be the perfect mystery and I'm going to the core!
All	*(Screaming in silence)* LUCY! LUCY! LUCY!

Blackout.

*

Scene 3
SIBYL's Story

Sibyl	*(Calls out)* LIGHTS!

Lights up. LUCY, WILLY and SIMON are seated at the counter. SIBYL stands in the center of The Orbit.

Sibyl	*(Announces)* "Sibyl's Story." *(Beat)* I have never seen so many

people in one place without any money, or any prospects of money. Anybody can sit at this counter. WHAT A DUMP! No process, no selection, no choice, just come as you are, have a cup of coffee, dump your brains, shit, and goodbye. Get out. No show today.

She slaps down a check in front of each one, and one by one they reel backwards, falling from sight. SIBYL picks up a large knife and begins chopping vegetables.

Sibyl   They've gotta play it straight with me—I'm not gonna be around forever. I'm auditioning all the time. Never know where I'll end up and I never know the words I'll be saying. I don't have time for the programmed response— for the wordlocks, mind-sets, subjokes, and non sequiturs. I am on a mission. And the mission is getting the part in *thee* play. I'm ready to move, and they better be ready to move. Gotta know when to press and when to tuck. I may even take this place with me. Doesn't hurt to have a little something on the side. *(Hacking the vegtables furiously)*

LUCY enters panting.

Lucy   Take my order.
Sibyl   *(Checks her out)* Why are you so dirty?
Lucy   I've been underground.
Sibyl   The subways are a good thing. Tearing through the urban belly the third rail sizzles going down, and overhead, the giant metro brain hangs from the strap—rush hour—human

hemispheres knock from side to side. All contact is taboo. Everybody knows the threshold, how far to press, where to put your hand, how far to tuck, where to place your eyes, and it is perfect. Everything fits. And then the doors open and I'm swept down the street and everybody forgets. What goes wrong? Where's the press and tuck?

Lucy   LISTEN! There's an all-points bulletin out on me.

Sibyl   What for?

Lucy   Questioning. The police think that I have inside information, but I'm nowhere near the core. Simon is a suspect.

Sibyl   I see.

Lucy   I want to wrap this case up, but I need a witness.

Sibyl   Like who?

Lucy   Like a doorman.

Sibyl   Don't bring in a new character now.

Lucy   A doorman would know who goes in, who goes out, and at what time.

Sibyl   Where ya going to find someone like that?

Lucy   You just have to keep looking, eventually a body turns up.

Sibyl   Talk to Willy.

Lucy   WILLY!

Sibyl   He could be your man.

Lucy   He's crazy. He comes in here and stares at me all the time and makes these funny tapping sounds. If you were a little more selective you'd get a better clientele coming in and they'd spend more.

Sibyl   Talk to Willy.

WILLY pops up from behind the counter.

Willy	Cup of java.

SIBYL pours.

Willy	*(To LUCY)* Any luck?
Lucy	What do you mean?
Willy	You know, about finding someone.
Lucy	About finding someone?
Willy	I get it. I know how you writers are. Zipped lips until the end—don't like to let anything out of the bag until its ready. *(Pause)* I'm looking for him, too.
Lucy	You mean you're looking for him, too?
Willy	Yes.
Lucy	Let me get this again. You mean you are looking for the *doorman*, too?
Willy	Yeah. I guess you could call him that.
Lucy	Are you a religious fanatic?
Willy	No.
Lucy	Who are you working for?
Willy	NO ONE!
Lucy	*(Shouting)* TELL ME!
Willy	I'm not working for anyone.
Lucy	*(Shouting)* HOW COME YOU KNOW SO MUCH?
Sibyl	*(Shouting)* STOP SHOUTING! YOU TRYING TO RUIN MY BUSINESS?
Lucy	*(Loud whisper)* Who's your source?

She lunges for WILLY knocking him off his feet. They fall behind the counter in a struggle.

WIlly	*(Offstage screaming)* HELP ME! I don't know this woman.

HELP ME!

They both surface for a moment, LUCY gripping him by the throat.

Lucy   *Who?*

They fall behind the counter. Growling, panting, and squealing sounds are heard.

Willy   DON'T BITE!

They pop up.

Sibyl   You two are bad for business. GET OUT!

They drop from sight.

Sibyl   *(Placing a phone order)* Hi, Sibyl at The Orbit. Give me a rack. Lean. Not like last time. Yeah, and I'll take a shoulder, and a loin. *(Hangs up)* I know the right play is out there and its gonna find me and I'm going to be ready for it when it comes. I'm not going to get fat while I wait for it. *(Picks up a menu and reads it as if it were a script)* Okay. From the top—I can make anything play. My memory is as sharp as a razor: *(In a Southern accent)* "The Rhode Island": fresh tuna salad, melted Swiss, sauteed onions, and tomato on grilled rye. "The Indiana": broiled sausages, melted American cheese, tomato, sauteed onions on a toasted roll. "The Montana": grilled ham, what a ham! WHEEW! I'm stuffed.

SIMON appears from behind the counter wearing his safari hat and holding a bloody bag. He lies on the downstage edge of the counter.

Sibyl   Why are you so dirty?

Simon   I don't know.

SIBYL pulls herself up on the counter, alongside him, and closely inspects him.

Sibyl   You have mud on your shoes and you smell like grass.

Simon   I don't know.

Sibyl   You have blood under your fingernails! Where were you?

Simon   Out.

Sibyl   What's in the bag? *(Tries to grab the bag)*

Simon   My vice. How's Willy?

WILLY and LUCY jump on top of the counter and begin moving in, lapsing at times, into apelike stances.

Sibyl   The same. Nothing sticks. He doesn't have anything to come back to except his briefcase or what he gets from other people. I suggested that Lucy write him in as doorman in her mystery, but she doesn't see him that way.

She grabs the bag again. SIMON grabs her.

Simon   How's Lucy?

Sibyl	Fine.
Simon	Is she writing me in?
Sibyl	She's writing you out. Right now you're missing.
Simon	Help me.
Sibyl	How?
Simon	*(Grabs her jaw)* I have to find the gibbon man. I need a disguise. I need a living mask.
Sibyl	*(Struggles in his grip)* That's tricky because you have to know who to come back to. There has to be someone waiting inside. I don't know if your man exists.

SIMON rises, ascending in stages to a bipedal stance, recalling images of the stages of man from ape to Neanderthal man.

Simon	*He is. He is.*

LUCY and WILLY rush for the bag and viciously struggle for possession. SIBYL gets the bag and jumps into the center of The Orbit.

Sibyl	GET DOWN! GET DOWN!

SIMON, LUCY, and WILLY stop fighting and return to their seats, all the time making bestial sounds while randomly calling out for "java," "The Meat Loaf Special," etc. SIBYL speaks over their undercurrent.

Sibyl	I'm getting out of here. You customers are crazy. When I took the part—I mean job—I thought it would be good to get out of town, but I don't like it here. Things are sliding

around. I wanted a part, a job, that I could really sink my teeth into. If only there were rewrites on this one, so that everything works perfectly, even when things appear to go wrong. *(Beat)* I'll be alright. I need a new agent, someone to book me in the right plays at the right time with the right people with the right words. I can do any part they dish up because I know who to come back to. You have to know who to come back to and I know, *(Beats her chest)* I know, *(Beats her chest)* I know, *(Beats her chest)* I know.

Blackout.

*

Scene 4
WILLY's Story

Sibyl	*(Calls out)* LIGHTS!

Lights up. SIBYL, SIMON, and LUCY sit at the counter. WILLY stands in the center of The Orbit holding up a machete.

Sibyl	*(Announces)* "Willy's Story."
Willy	My thoughts seem to bob up to the surface as if they were propelled by a random impulse. The Mayans were suddenly right there. Right in my forehead.
Lucy	You mean you suddenly had an impression of them.
Willy	Yes. Slashing and burning their fields. The brush had to be cut and dried before the rains. Miscalculation of a few days

could lose a year's crop. Exact timing was critical. This led them to create a very precise agricultural calendar. A ceremonial calendar followed, and then, there was a third and secret calendar, one which marked a hidden order below the level of conscious awareness. It controlled what the populace did and thought and felt on a given day. The ancient Mayans possessed one of the most precise hermetic calendars ever created on this planet. *(Pause)* Real history *is* this third calendar.

Simon   Willy, can I borrow a large kitchen knife.

Willy   How about my machete?

SIMON reaches with outstretched arms to receive the machete. WILLY returns to the podium.

Willy   *(Tries to notate his memories)* When I first met them, they were, they were—*how the hell did that go?* Who cares? I'll cut that. I'm taking it from the top. From now on I'm looking at a new calendar beginning with January 4th. HELLO! This is Willy number two speaking. If I'm going to keep records I've got to step free of self-imposed restrictions and see all life as fact. The world as a direct gaze. Hello. Hello. Willy number two bringing it to you.

Simon-Lucy-Sibyl

A new calendar. That's a wonderful idea. It'll get us all in step.

Willy   I'll get a large piece of blank paper. *(Drops from sight)*

Simon   Willy's our boy.

Sibyl   I don't know if he's up to the part.

Simon   What part is he playing?

Sibyl	The victim.
Simon	The victim?
Willy	*(Offstage yell)* I'm coming.
Simon	And what do I play?
Sibyl	Are you sure you want to play?
Simon	I'm in.
Sibyl	Okay. You're the hunter.
Lucy	IT'S PERFECT! PERFECT! IT'S A FIT!
Simon	He's got nothing to lose.
Sibyl	Never had a story.
Lucy	WHAT A LAMB!
Simon	He won't feel a thing.
Sibyl	The head's already gone.
Lucy	Finish him off.

*SIBYL assumes an iconic pose. LUCY and SIMON line up
behind her creating the image of a high priestess with six
undulating arms.*

Sibyl	As the Mayan high priestess I search for the consecrated ground where the pursued and pursuer become one— where the dialectic rests upon the altar for all to see. The truth will sear the senses and wash the veil from our eyes. I will prepare the sacrifice and exhume the cosmic plot.
Lucy	*(Screams)* MURDER!
Sibyl	MONOLOGUES!
Simon	PLACES!
Willy	*(Emerges)* Hello hello. Willy number two.
Simon	Willy? *(Beckoning him closer)*
Willy	Yes.

| Simon | We're gonna have a celebration for all the people who were not born yesterday—sort of a season wrap-up—end-of-the-year thing. We'd like the celebration to coincide with your new calendar. We would like you to host the event, say a couple of words, and to be a bridge between the old and new. In many ways you really embody the event. |
| Willy | I'll place an order. *(On the phone)* Hi, this is Willy at The Orbit. I'd like a side of veal for—of course we have an account with you. Are you new? I've never given you an account number. No, I don't have one branded on my loin! Don't use that tone of voice with me! HELLO! HELLO! |

SIBYL and SIMON drop out. LUCY removes the phone from WILLY's hands and hangs it up.

| Lucy | I have been plagued by strange occurrences which lead me to doubt my own mind. |
| Willy | Lie down. |

LUCY lies on the counter. WILLY plays the shrink.

| Lucy | In the night I wake up and find snakes crawling around the bed, then the toilet begins flushing again and again like a high-speed public latrine. I have to get out. I move toward the door. IT LOCKS! What the fuck is happening? Enough of this weird crap! I want to wake up but I'm not sleeping because I catch a glimpse of myself in the bedroom mirror and my eyes are open. Am I dead or what? What do I do next? So I think, I better go back to sleep, nothing could be worse than this, and I jump into my bed and the toilets |

are flushing and flushing and the floor is covered with dark S's and I shut my eyes and I wait and I wait. It's gotta be better, gotta cross over I think, and bingo! Suddenly the door springs open and I made it. Whataya think of this Willy? This is new calendar material. What's wrong Willy?

WILLY is back at the phone, listening.

Willy	Nothing.
Simon	Nobody home Willy?
Willy	*(Hangs up the phone)* No.
Simon	It's a busy time.
Willy	Yes.
Simon	The coming of the new year makes me want to cook again. Open the doors and feed all the people.
Willy	I'm afraid.
Simon	Fear is a biological necessity, like sleep and dreams. And we all have fear, all of the time, because death is tucked away, inside, waiting to be let out. Danger keeps the blood moving.
Willy	If you leave your old calendar behind, you will be like me.
Simon	Time to slash and burn.

SIBYL surfaces.

Sibyl	Get the new crop in. Lie down.

WILLY lies on the downstage edge of the counter. LUCY grabs a bottle of Mazola oil from the stove and gives him a rub-down, then anointing him with the oil.

Willy	Ummmm, ummmm, that feels ummmm, delicious.
Sibyl	You have a clear forehead.
Willy	Ummmmmmm.
Lucy	Clear.
Willy	Ummmmmmm.
Sibyl	Swept.
Lucy	Smooth.
Simon	Nothing.
Lucy	Pure.
Simon	Innocent.
Lucy	No riddles.
Simon	No once upon a time.
Sibyl	No play.
Lucy	No end.
Simon	Our man.
Lucy	*(To SIMON)* Give me his hand.

SIMON passes WILLY's hand to LUCY. LUCY holds his arm upright from his lying body. SIBYL clasps her hand around the arm, then SIMON, as if all three were united around this outstretched limb, forming a pact.

Sibyl	Thirty-two feet per second. That's the law of the falling body. That's a fact Willy.
Willy	Ummmmmmm.

WILLY rises to a sitting position, his arm remains raised in the air.

Willy	Are you sure there isn't anything I can get for you?

They all nod "no" and back away from him.

WILLY lies back down, then rises again, his arm remains raised.

Willy   Cup a hot chocolate?

They all nod "no" again. He lies down again and then rises again, his arm remains raised.

Willy   How about a coffee?
Sibyl   We're dieting.

WILLY lies back down.

Willy   *(Pause)* It seems like days.
Simon   We're ready when you are.

WILLY's arm drops and he lurches forward to stand on top of the counter. SIBYL, LUCY, and SIMON remain clustered in the center of the ellipse. WILLY walks around them, peering over the top of their heads.

Willy   I'm not the right person for this. You should find somebody else. I can't get this calendar started; I don't know where the day begins. I can't find that precise moment. I'm not a Mayan. If I stuck around long enough, maybe I could work my way up to that position where I could look around and see what was happening, but I don't think I have that kind of time. I have to make my pieces fit first. I've got to take care of myself. Gotta put my man together. Gotta put Willy back together first. Maybe I should start with my autobiography. THAT'S IT! *(Picks up the phone)* Hello, this is Willy from The Orbit—FUCK OFF!

Blackout.

*

Scene 5
The Send-off

Lights up. SIMON, LUCY, and SIBYL seated at the counter watching WILLY at the podium. He is trying to write, literally pressing his writing hand to the page with his other hand.

Simon	Get out there Willy.
Sibyl	We're ready for you.
Willy	I'M BUSY!
Lucy	Maybe he's not the one.
Sibyl	*(Chants)* Willy Willy—take our order.
Willy	*(Indicating to LUCY)* Let her write 'em up.
Sibyl	She only does fiction. *You* understand the importance of facts, dates, and times.
Simon	Take our orders.
Willy	I'm taking Willy's order first. I'm doing an autobiography. Names, dates, places—got to put my man together.
Sibyl	WILLY! You'll never find him.
Simon	WILLY! Where's your briefcase?

Lucy	WILLY! Death must be like forgetting. You simply cannot remember life.
Simon	Life trades for more life. That's a fact. No life. No more life.
Lucy	Write *us* up. *(Whispers)* Later you can write yourself in, no one will ever know.
Simon	It's yours Willyboy, all yours. You are the living end. NOW WRITE!

WILLY begins writing.

Simon	*(Dictating)* Chapter one: I was always interested in the big blend—how people came together—how they mixed. WRITE! I watched living portraits emerge—I conjured up the tastes buried deep in the mind. WRITE! The more I tasted, the hungrier I became. WRITE!
Sibyl	WRITE! I began my career as an actress, perfecting my command of languages—all languages.
Lucy	WRITE! I have always tried to come face-to-face with the characters in my stories.
All	WRITE! WRITE!
Simon	WRITE! Which is why I became a psychiatrist, until I discovered cooking. WRITE!
Sibyl	WRITE! I studied ancient Greek, Latin, and Egyptian— I searched for hidden words. WRITE!
Lucy	WRITE! Sometimes they would make me forget that it was me who was writing the story. They are very clever that way. WRITE!
All	WRITE! WRITE!
All	*(Speaking simultaneously.)*

340

Simon	WRITE! My hunger was insatiable. WRITE! I ate everything and found myself meeting my clients in restaurants, fish markets, and butchers. WRITE! I knew I had to do something! My hunger was insatiable. EAT! EAT! EAT!
Sibyl	WRITE! The language of the subways fascinated me. WRITE! Words are spoken through the skin and eyes. Write! I have considered tattooing as an alternative pursuit to acting. WRITE!
Lucy	WRITE! Sometimes I'd be real quiet, just to lure them out. WRITE! Then I'd start writing like a jackhammer. WRITE! They would feel the ground shift and I'd run to open spaces and I knew that I had them. WRITE!

Note: In the previous round, Simon's part takes slightly longer which makes this round end with Simon's EAT! EAT! EAT! EAT! Simon then launches into the next round in which speaker follows speaker, underscored with EAT! EAT! in sotto voce by the others.

Simon	Opening The Orbit seemed a way of combining my patients with my desire to cook. EAT!
Sibyl	I wanted to find those words that lie deep, beneath the surface of the body. EAT!
Lucy	They couldn't stop once they were released, their words erupted and their sounds rang in my ears. EAT!
All	EAT! EAT! EAT!
All	*(Speaking simultaneously—brandishing machetes, sabres, and scythes)*
Simon	It's important to know who you're cooking for—if they are biters, chewers, or swallowers. EAT! EAT! EAT!

Sibyl	I have in the past found some very good playwrights in tattoo parlors. EAT! EAT! EAT!
Lucy	The earth was moving. I was dizzy following their words—irrepressible vertigo. Then it's thirty-two feet per second. EAT! EAT! EAT!
Willy	I'M STUFFED! I'M HOT!
All	HERE IT COMES WILLY!

WILLY takes the offensive and attacks SIMON, grabbing his arm as if he were trying to rip it off.

Simon	*(Screams)*

Blackout.

*

Scene 6
The Birthday

The sound of military taps.

Low blue light comes up revealing WILLY playing taps with knives on the downstage edge of the counter. Before him is a bloody arm wrapped in a sheet, a pencil remains in the fingers. SIBYL and LUCY sit at their places holding black umbrellas.

SIMON slowly walks around the downstage perimeter of

counter. One arm of his coat is empty. He passes by WILLY *and continues. He disappears. Taps stop.*

Full light.

Willy	So what'll it be? I got some chops tonight, mashed potatoes, baby peas?
Sibyl	I'm stuffed.
Willy	*(To* LUCY*)* What about you?
Lucy	Cup a java.

Pours her a cup and returns to the arm.

Willy	I don't know anything about cooking. But I know that first, you have to put someting in the pot. Sometimes you gotta trim off the fat and more. Gotta leave a few things behind. It's a tight fit any way ya slice it. *(He removes the pen from the fingers)* I'll take this now.
Sibyl	Willy, put that away.

WILLY *puts the arm under the counter. He takes his place at the podium, opens the journal and with pencil in hand begins writing.*

Lucy	It was about eleven-twenty. The night was closing in; somehow he slipped through our fingers.

Lights slowly fade on LUCY *and* SIBYL *as one hand suddenly appears on the inside downstage edge of the counter.*

SIMON slowly rises.

He slides the pedestal cake dish in front of him. He removes the top, revealing the piece of birthday cake.

He lights the candle.

Simon   Goodbye, Willy.

He blows out the candle.

Blackout.

The End

Disgrace

by John O'Keefe

Disgrace *was first presented at the 14th Annual Padua Hills Playwrights Festival, Woodbury College, Los Angeles, California, in 1994. The play was directed by the author with the following cast:*

Katherine: Denise Poirier
Simone: Dahlia Wilde
Christine: Susan van Allen

Escape

Run One

*The lights rise as three women dressed in long, white
dresses with black choke collars, parasols and wide hats
(Gibson girls) run across the stage. SIMONE is carrying a
picnic basket. They are laughing.* **Note: they always enter
from stage right—as if moving in one direction. The stage
is always empty.** *They are running fast, holding down
their hats. The lights fade.*

Run Two

*There is a pause. The lights rise. Again the three women
enter stage right running and exit stage left. They are
laughing. They're trying to keep their hats on. The lights
fade.*

Run Three

They enter running and exit.

Stretch Marks

They enter running.

Katherine	Hurry up.
Christine	Come on. Come on.
Simone	I'm hurrying. Let's stop here.
Katherine	No. No. Farther.
Christine	Yes, yes, farther.
Simone	I'm tired, my legs are hurting.
Katherine	That's how you get the fat off your thighs.
Simone	I don't have fat on my thighs.
Christine	I don't want the fat off my thighs.
Katherine	Why not?
Christine	It leaves stretch marks.
Katherine	I don't have stretch marks.
Simone	Yes, you do.
Katherine	I do not.
Simone	Yes, you do, you have them all over your face!

They laugh and run off.

*

Basin

They amble in.

Simone	This is nice.
Christine	I don't like this place.
Simone	Why not?

Christine	It's at the bottom of a hole.
Simone	No, it's not. It's a valley.
Katherine	It's a basin.
Christine	I don't want to be in a basin.
Katherine	Look up there. That hill. Let's go up there.
Simone	No, it's too far up.

KATHERINE starts to run. The others stay behind.
KATHERINE stops and turns around.

Katherine	Come on. Please. Pretty please. You'll like it up there. We'll be able to see everything.
Christine	Oh, all right.

CHRISTINE starts running, too. Stops, then turns around to SIMONE.

Christine	Come on.
Simone	I don't want to climb up there.
Katherine	If you stay down here it'll get dark.
Simone	It's morning.
Katherine	I'm going.
Christine	I'm going, too.
Simone	You're cruel. You're both cruel.
Christine	It won't hurt you, you're young.
Simone	I'm not young.
Katherine	You're not old.
Simone	I'm old in the middle.
Katherine	Then move the stuff on either end.

Laughter. KATHERINE *and* CHRISTINE *exit running. They speak offstage.*

Christine	Kathy, Kathy don't run so fast. You'll muss your dress.
Katherine	It'll get full of the ground. It's good. It's good.

SIMONE *is alone. She looks around. She becomes apprehensive.*

Simone	*(Screams)* DON'T LEAVE ME ALONE! *(Runs after them)*

*

Orchard

They stroll on stage leisurely.

Katherine	Look, an old orchard.
Simone	It's dead.
Katherine	It was an apple orchard.
Simone	Dead orchards are sad.
Katherine	Look, there's an old building. It looks like it's burned down.
Simone	No, it's just broken down.
Katherine	Broken down?
Christine	By the wind.
Katherine	Yes, and the water.
Simone	It was a convent.
Christine	It had arches.
Katherine	An orphanage.
Simone	With a lot of nuns.

Christine	Nuns are crazy.
Simone	I always wanted to be a nun.
Christine	That's because you had a thing for Jesus.
Simone	Staying in dark rooms.
Christine	Praying in cubicles at night and during the day taking care of the children.
Simone	Nursing them.
Christine	Without sex.
Katherine	Like Mary.
Christine	Like Mary.
Simone	Becoming virgin again.
Katherine	Somehow.
Christine	Yes, somehow.
Katherine	And keeping that way.
Christine	Until we're dead.
Katherine	Where we lived is much like that.

CHRISTINE *suddenly smiles.*

Christine	Yes, except for François.
Katherine	François.
Simone	François.
Katherine	This is a disgrace.
Simone	I don't want to be a nun. I want to be a whore for animals and women.
Katherine	Oh, good God.
Simone	It's true. I want to disgrace them, and myself as well.
Katherine	In heaven's name why?
Simone	I want them to look at me like they did those women in France who slept with the Nazis. I want them to shave

dirty words in my hair. I want them to sneer and spit at Simone: me, and I want to smile at them and look at them with frightened eyes, I want to see the desire in their faces.

Katherine	Desire?
Simone	Yes, the desire one has for a fallen, despicable beauty.
Katherine	You just want respect.
Simone	Respect? Hell no, I want to be feared.
Christine	I think we're in Africa some place on some rich white man's ranch.
Katherine	I think we're in Spain.
Christine	You do?
Katherine	Yes, I can feel it in the air. Can't you? (*She strikes a pose*) Olé!
Christine	(*Strikes a pose*) Olé!
Simone	(*Strikes a pose*) Olé!

Laughter. Lights out.

*

Ambling

Lights come up. They are lying on the ground, resting.

Christine	I think love is a primary quality.
Simone	No, love is a diversion.
Katherine	Love, sisters, is the salt of life.
Christine	It's the sugar of life.
Simone	I hate sugar.
Christine	Then it's the salt of life.

Simone	Yes, salt in the wound.
Katherine	Which wound are you talking about?

They laugh.

Christine	*(Sings)* Love is a dress
	that takes me off
	and puts me on,
	the woman looking back
	in the mirror.
	Whoever she watches
	I watch.
	When I kiss her
	she kisses me.
Katherine	Where did you learn that?
Christine	I just made it up.
Katherine	I thought so.
Simone	I think love is a good kill.
Katherine	That's sick. What do you think?
Christine	I don't think.
Katherine	You do.
Christine	I don't. I don't think a minute. That's how I get places.
	That's how I meet people and do things.
Katherine	You're crazy.

They look at each other.

*

Picnic

The lights come up. KATHERINE *appears. She's out of breath and filled with delight.*

Katherine Hurry! Hurry! You've got to see this!

SIMONE *appears. She's quite exhausted.*

Simone My God, at last.

Katherine Look, look, you can see everything.

Simone I can't see anything.

Katherine Why in heavens not?

Simone I have too much blood in my eyes.

Katherine *(Laughs)* Blood in your eyes! Blood in your eyes! Let me see your eyes.

KATHERINE *takes* SIMONE'S *face and holds it between her hands.*

You're not bleeding. You look beautiful.

They take each other's hands and begin to spin around.

Katherine Beautiful. Beautiful. Beautiful.

Simone Stop. Stop. My knees are going to break off.

Katherine No, no they won't.

They stop.

Katherine They're in your skin, buried in your legs.

KATHERINE picks up SIMONE'S hem and holds it up.

Katherine   See.

KATHERINE grabs SIMONE around the legs.

Katherine   Come on and dance. Dance.

KATHERINE takes SIMONE into her arms and begins dancing the polka. They dance in circles faster and faster. They fall on the floor out of breath.

Katherine   I love you, Simone, even if you are a thief.

Simone   A thief?

Katherine   Yes, you stole François from me.

Simone   I did not.

Katherine   Did too.

Simone   Did not.

Katherine   Did too.

Simone   Did not.

She grabs KATHERINE and they begin to roll in each other's arms, laughing.

CHRISTINE appears over the hill looking bedraggled.

Christine   I'm soaked. I've soaked all over myself. My dress, look at my dress.

KATHERINE gets up.

Katherine	It will dry.
Christine	Yes, and it will stain.
Katherine	Then we'll wash it off in the river.
Christine	What river?
Katherine	The one over there.

She runs and stops at the edge of the hill and points.
SIMONE *whines.*

Simone	That's down in the valley.
Christine	It's not far. We can fly there.
Simone	You fly.
Christine	*(Flaps her arms)* Fly. Fly. Isn't it wonderful? I've never been to any place so wonderful.
Simone	I have.
Katherine	Where is that?
Simone	At home in bed.
Christine	It's too late to be in bed.
Simone	It's never too late to be in bed.
Christine	What time is it?
Katherine	I don't know what time it is, you silly bird.
Christine	I know what time it is.
Katherine	You don't know how to tell time.
Christine	I do. I did. I just forgot. Not from a watch head, but from the sun, from there—

She points at the sun.

Christine	I can tell. It's nine A.M.
Simone	No. It's eleven.

Katherine	Right.
Christine	*(Distraught)* No, it's not that late. It's nine.
Katherine	It's not nine. It's eleven. It's probably even later.
Christine	Don't say that.
Simone	I think it is later. Look, the sun is almost in the top of the sky.
Christine	The sky is moving, not time. It's late down there and it's early up here. It's only nine up here.
Katherine	The sky is not moving.
Christine	The sky is moving. The sky is moving. Look, look at it move. Birds, we're up with the birds.

She traces the bird's flight with her finger.

Christine	I don't care what time it is.
Katherine	Let's have our picnic. Come and sit.
Christine	Oh, I don't want to get up. I want to look at the sky.
Katherine	Christine, please.
Christine	Oh, all right. What about her?

SIMONE *is looking out watching the horizon. Her fingers are in her hair. She is euphoric.*

Katherine	She's coming. Aren't you?
Simone	*(Not taking her eyes away from the view)* Yes.
Christine	What do you see?
Simone	Everything.
Katherine	Come and eat. Look. I have sandwiches.
Simone	What kind?
Katherine	What kind did you fix?

Christine	I think I fixed peanut butter, banana and honey.
Katherine	Yes, here they are.
Christine	The bananas haven't gone black?
Katherine	No.
Christine	What did you fix?
Katherine	Eggs.
Christine	*(Wrinkles her nose)* Ooh.
Katherine	Simone, what did you make?
Simone	I didn't make anything.
Katherine	Then you can't eat anything.
Simone	I don't care.
Katherine	That's not fair.
Christine	You can have some of mine.
Katherine	Aren't you going to eat? Please.
Simone	"Eat!" What an ugly word!
Katherine	Not if you're hungry.
Simone	I'm fed.

CHRISTINE spreads a tablecloth on the ground. KATHERINE takes out the food: two sandwiches. CHRISTINE crosses and looks at the spread.

Christine	Where's the rest of it?
Katherine	Rest of what?
Christine	The food?
Katherine	That's it.
Christine	That's all of it?
Katherine	Yes.
Christine	That's not enough.
Katherine	She's not hungry.

Christine	She will be.
Katherine	That's all of it.
Christine	Simone, she only brought two sandwiches.
Simone	Then let's divide them up.

SIMONE pulls out a knife.

| Christine | Where did you get that? |
| Simone | I had it since I was a child. |

SIMONE crosses and sits on the ground. She opens the napkin and pulls out the sandwiches and begins cutting them on the napkin.

Simone	We shouldn't argue. Especially us. We've come to make amends.
Christine	You're right.
Simone	We could be enemies but now we're becoming friends. When women make up with each other they become everything their lovers fear. (*She is cutting the sandwiches. As she speaks she cuts the sandwiches more intensely*)

| Simone | We've traveled so far to get away from him. To this hill. And now we are arguing as if he were here slumped over his plate. But he isn't here. Only our thin bodies are here and our thin appetites. We don't need much food. We are thin as the wind. Thin boats. There, everything is cut. |

She holds the napkin up with the sandwiches in shreds.

The lights fade.

*

Simone's Story

The lights rise. The women have arranged themselves casually. KATHERINE *is lying on her back. They are just finishing up their sandwiches.*

Simone	I want to tell you what happened between us.
Katherine	Let's talk about it later.
Christine	No, I want to hear about it now. We promised we'd tell everything. That afterwards we'd become friends.
Katherine	We didn't promise that.
Simone	We met on Friday afternoons. We met together after lunch.
Katherine	Today is Friday.
Simone	I went to a café and waited for him.
Katherine	Café Trieste.
Simone	I won't tell you the name of the café.
Katherine	It was Trieste.
Simone	He'd pick me up in his motorcar.
Katherine	The red one.
Simone	Which one doesn't matter.
Katherine	It was the red one.
Simone	And I would go with him into the country.
Katherine	So that no one would see you, right?
Simone	We didn't talk. We just sat and looked at the road and the pastures and orchards moving by us, feeling the wind blow.
Katherine	Did he wear that beautiful touring cap, the plaid one?

Simone	Yes.
Katherine	I thought so.
Simone	We always went to the same place. But we went there by different routes. Some would take us an hour, some less. And once, once we spent the whole day getting there.
Katherine	I can't stand it! I can't stand it!
Simone	You said you wanted to know.
Christine	She does. Don't you Kathy?
Katherine	I hate my name. My name belongs to the kind of person you'd say something like that to. "Don't you, Kathy? Don't you, Kathy?"
Simone	And when we got there, we'd park the car off the road and bring the picnic basket and a blanket.
Christine	A picnic basket?
Katherine	Like this one?
Simone	Yes.
Katherine	I hate picnic baskets.

KATHERINE *gives the basket a kick.*

Christine	What about the blanket? Aren't you worried about the blanket?
Katherine	I'm not worried.
Christine	No, she's excited.
Katherine	Talk to me when you're talking about me. I'm not a bug.
Christine	You're as cute as a bug.
Katherine	I'm not cute. I hate cute.
Simone	He'd bring soap and towels.
Christine	*(Begins laughing)* Soap and towels?
Simone	He'd wait in the trees away from the lake.

Katherine	The lake?
Simone	I'd strip and go into the water. I'd swim out to the middle of the lake. And then I'd call to him.
Christine	*(Mockingly)* François? *(Begins laughing)* François?
Katherine	Stop that.
Christine	It's such a stupid name. I always called him Frank.
Katherine	Frank? Now that's a stupid name. It has nothing to do with François.
Christine	At least it's a man's name. That's how I treated him. *(Disdainfully)* François.
Simone	He'd come out of the trees with nothing on and he'd stand there on the beach, looking for me. And I'd see him, his frame, his thighs, his strong, long arms.
Christine	Yes, like an ape.
Simone	Then he'd spot me and quietly, he'd slip into the water and disappear. I'd watch for him. He never once came up for air.
Christine	I'll bet.
Simone	The longer he took to reach me the more frantic I got. Once I waited a whole half-hour. But then I'd feel them, his hands on my ankles, gripping them, pulling me down. That part was always inflamed me. Knowing what was coming, wondering how long he was going to hold me under before he released me. And then I'd feel his hands climb up the curves of my body.
Christine	Curves?
Katherine	Shut up.
Simone	And then he would pull me down, pull my face down into the water to his. And he'd kiss me. We prolonged this kiss, sometimes to the edge of consciousness. A deep dark kiss. A kiss of profound significance.

Christine	"Profound significance?"
Simone	When we broke the water's surface it was with a lust for life, like the dying gasp of a soul reaching for the light.
Christine	Oh my God.
Simone	The air was so clear, so sweet, the trees like dark dreaming cows, the water like the skin of an eye.
Christine	*(Convulsing with laughter)* Oh, stop, stop, please stop.
Katherine	Stop it yourself, it's beautiful. Go on Simone.
Simone	And then he'd...he'd...
Katherine	Yes?
Simone	He'd wash me.
Katherine	What?

CHRISTINE *begins laughing again.*

Simone	From head to toe.
Katherine	He what?
Simone	He'd run his slippery bar of soap all over my body.
Katherine	You're making fun of me?
Simone	I'm not, he really did it. Didn't he do that with you? Didn't he wash you first?
Katherine	No, I washed myself.
Christine	Maybe he didn't trust Simone to do it.
Simone	No, it was the way the soap squeaked on my skin and how the lather covered certain parts of my body.
Christine	Yes, like steak tartare.
Katherine	Stop it both of you. He was my lover.

CHRISTINE *rolls over on her stomach.*

Christine	Mine, too.
Katherine	I'm thirsty. And I'm depressed.

She fishes around in the basket.

Christine	Now that he's dead we might as well tell the truth about him. It was well known that he was kinky, Kathy.
Katherine	Don't call me Kathy. Call me Katherine.

She pulls a can of Coca-Cola from the basket, pops the top and takes a long, slow drink as the lights fade.

*

Christine's Story
In the dark.

Katherine	*(Wailing)* I don't want to hear anymore.

The lights come up as if they're in the middle of the scene.

Christine	...Yes, but he was always good to me.
Katherine	Please stop.
Christine	He'd play with my hands and tell me that they were like small birds just out of the egg and he'd kiss them and tell me he wished they were his. He begged me sometimes to give him my hands. And I promised him that if I died he could have them. He'd take my hands and put his hands

	over my hands and we'd wiggle our fingers together. We never kissed. In all that time we never kissed. I had a child by him. It was a small girl.
Simone	I didn't know you had a child.
Christine	Yes, it was a secret.
Simone	When was this?
Christine	Remember when I looked so terrible?
Katherine	Never, I've never seen you look terrible.
Simone	I did. You looked like somebody had beat you up.
Christine	Pregnant. A difficult pregnancy. With much blood. I had to put a basin between my feet at breakfast. And the strong smell of my mother's milk. Didn't you notice how wet my chest was?
Katherine	No.
Simone	Yes.
Katherine	But you always looked so flat-chested.
Christine	I put a strap across my breasts. I knew that he would be punished if he were caught being the father of my child. And so I waited, waited patiently for the thin moon to rise in my August month and when it did I went to a cottage he built for me deep in the woods where he kept his cars and his tools and I gave birth the child.
Katherine	Whatever happened to her?
Christine	She ran away.
Katherine	Oh, how terrible.
Christine	Yes.
Katherine	You never saw her again?
Christine	I did. She came to visit me only a few nights ago. She came very near the window and I heard this tiny "tap-tap-tap-ping." The moon was in full stride so I could see the yard in

the sword silver light and there on the edge of the window I saw her tiny fingers creeping up the pane like a young unmarried spider. Those fingers that looked so much like mine. I knew Frank would not be able to bear it. Her hands were in peril. I saw her breath stain the glass, "Mother! Mother! Come with me. I've found a hole in the world and I'm going there. We can run and play with our hands and no one will ever find us." I knew that world was not for me. It was for children who had run away from home at a very early age. I bowed my head and sobbed. Then I heard this sad cry. When I raised my eyes to the window she was gone.

Christine

Simone	How terrible.
Katherine	How ugly.
Christine	It is terrible...and ugly but true.
Katherine	It is not true.
Christine	When Frank came in with my breakfast I knew he sensed something had happened and then he saw them, the tiny prints and finger streaks on the windowpane. And he put his large head on my lap and cried. Then he made this inconceivable request.
Simone	Yes?
Christine	Do you want to know?
Simone	I do.
Katherine	I don't.
Christine	Then I'll tell *you*.

She whispers in SIMONE's *ear.* SIMONE *nods her head solemnly.*

*

Hand-clapper

Hand clapping sequence between CHRISTINE *and Simone.*

Christine and Simone:

> How do you kill a man?
> Hit him in the head with a pan.
> Kick him in the wick.
> Stick him with a stick.
> Trick him with a trick.
> Tickle him with a tick till he twitches.

They laugh. KATHERINE *enters out of breath.*

Katherine Simone? Christine?

Blackout.

*

Traveling Toward the Storm

They are on the move again, KATHERINE *leading.*

Christine I don't understand why we had to go. That was a perfectly lovely place.

Katherine It was too lovely.

Christine How can anything be too lovely?

Katherine Too much loveliness is inebriating. It dulls the senses. It makes you stupid.

Simone You're stupid.

Christine	I want to stop.
Katherine	No, we can't stop.
Christine	I want to stop.
Katherine	*(Not shouting)* We can't.
Christine	*(Not shouting)* Don't shout at me.
Katherine	*(Not shouting)* I'll shout at you whenever I damn please.

CHRISTINE *starts crying.*

Katherine	Good God, what's wrong now?
Christine	Now you're swearing at me.
Katherine	I'm not swearing at you. I'm waking you up. I'm using sounds that will awaken you.
Simone	Oh, good grief, Kathy.
Katherine	*(As if she had just been called a bad name)* I don't mind if you call me Kathy even though I asked you to call me Katherine.
Simone	We want to rest.
Katherine	Are you speaking for her?
Simone	Yes.
Katherine	What are you resting from? We live to move we move to live. If we don't move, we won't live, don't you see?
Christine	Don't be scary.
Katherine	I'm not. I'm just telling the truth. We shouldn't stay in a place like this. And look, it's getting dark.
Christine	It isn't getting dark.
Katherine	It is.
Christine	It is not. It's not even late afternoon yet.
Katherine	What has that got to do with anything?
Christine	The sun goes down behind the world and it gets dark or a

cloud gets stuck in the sky and it gets dim. It's neither dim nor dark. The sky is empty and there aren't any trees to cover it up. And we're not going up a hill so it's fine.

Simone You just don't want to tell us about François.

Katherine I do. I just want to move from where we started.

Christine Where was that?

Katherine The house in the valley.

Christine House?

Simone I don't remember any house.

Katherine Residence.

Simone "Residence?" It sounds like skeleton.

The sky darkens. There is the sound of distant thunder.

Katherine Look.

Christine Where should we go?

Katherine Let's go up.

Christine We'll be strangled by lightning.

Simone You're not strangled by lightning.

Christine Yes, you are. Way down deep you are.

SIMONE and CHRISTINE laugh.

Katherine Let's climb up into it.

Christine Let's have an adventure.

Simone I don't want an adventure.

Katherine Yes, you do.

Christine I do.

Katherine I do, too.

KATHERINE and CHRISTINE grin at SIMONE.

Simone   I do, too-too.

They laugh and run up the hill. The lights fade.

*

Wild Flowers
They enter. There are a number of artificial flowers sticking out of the stage.

Christine   Look, a flower patch.
Simone   Wildflowers.
Christine   I hope they're not catching.
Katherine   What do you mean?

She sneezes. They laugh.

Christine   Should we go in there and pick some?
Simone   We might go to sleep.
Christine   Like the Lizard of Was.
Katherine   Wizard of Oz.
Christine   Sleep. Sleep. Sleep. I want to lie down and go to sleep. I want to sleep forever.

She runs toward the flowers.

Katherine   Stop. We should keep going.

Simone	Where? This is a picnic, not a commute.
Christine	Yes, it's an old-time get-together, for ladies.

She is poised, paused ready to rush into the flowers.

Christine	Please let me go.
Simone	She's not keeping you.
Christine	Yes she is. She's making all of the flowers dull.
Katherine	They are dull. They're not bright. They're strange. They're drugged.
Simone	They're not drugged, you're drugged.
Katherine	*(Suddenly screaming)* I DON'T TAKE PILLS!
Simone	*(Screaming back at KATHERINE and attacking her)* You do. You do. You do take pills. Pills. Pills. Pills.
Christine	I'm going in.

She runs in the middle of the flowers. She calls back to the two struggling women.

It's wonderful. It's beautiful.

She begins eagerly picking flowers.

Come on pick some.

The speeches go on simultaneously.

Simone	*(Panicked)* Let go of my hair. Let go of my hair.
Katherine	*(Screaming in rage)* No. No. No. No.
Christine	*(Hugging the flowers she has gathered)* Wonderful. Wonderful.

Simone	*(Pleading)* Please. Please. Please. Please.
Katherine	You're so beautiful. You are, you're so horribly beautiful.
Simone	Please Katherine. Stop Katherine. I didn't mean anything by it.
Katherine	You didn't mean anything by it? You screwed my lover.
Christine	I know you're worried. I know you think that we're going to get caught. But if we have fun we may never get caught again and if we do we might not even notice it. I love you Katherine. I love you Simone.
Katherine	*(Mimicking CHRISTINE)* "I love you Katherine. I love you Simone."

KATHERINE releases SIMONE and breaks into tears.

	I hate you, I hate you both. Now I'm gonna get in trouble because I got mad.
Christine	No, you're not. Is she, Simone?
Simone	*(Terrorized)* She hurt me.
Katherine	*(Burying her face in her hands)* I'm sorry. I'm sorry.
Simone	Don't say you're sorry.
Katherine	*(Shouting at Simone)* I AM SORRY!
Simone	*(Cowering)* DON'T! DON'T HURT ME!
Katherine	*(Wailing with frustration)* I'm not. I won't. Please, please forgive me.
Simone	You can't make it undone like that.
Katherine	*(Wailing)* HELP ME! HELP ME!
Christine	Don't you see what's happening? We're getting magical. François is with us even though he's down in the basement underneath the stairs. Kathy's got him in her left foot and in her right eye.

Imitating the sound of a man dragging his bum leg as she gathers the flowers.

Crack-slip, Crack-slip, Crack-slip. Coming down the hall. Can't you see him? Crack-slip, crack-slip. (*Imitating his big deep voice*) You in there alone, Kathy? You need Franky's fat pink bat?

Katherine (K̲ATHERINE *and* S̲IMONE *begin laughing. She imitates a bat flying*) Pink bat, pink bat.

Christine See? He's already flown away. You got to watch him, else he'll be coming up the hill with us walking in our feet, talking in our mouths.

Simone (*She looks at her feet, looks at her hands and murmurs as she rises*) Up the hill. Up the hill.

Christine Come on and pick these.

She holds up the flowers. The lights fade.

*

By a Stream

C̲HRISTINE *enters first.* K̲ATHERINE *and* S̲IMONE *enter skipping. They have their arms around each other's waists. They all have some of the wildflowers in their hair.*

Simone Look, a stream.

Christine LOOK!

Katherine It's beautiful.

Simone Let's bathe.

| Christine | *(Looks into* KATHERINE's *eyes)* Bathe. |
| Katherine | *(Looks back)* Bathe. |

They laugh with delight. The lights fade. In the dark.

Katherine	Ooh, it's cold.
Christine	It's white.
Katherine	No, it's not white, it's clear.
Simone	Clear.

*

Garden of Eden

When the lights rise the women are all lying on the ground. They talk to each other as they gaze at the sky.

Simone	I could stay here forever.
Katherine	The sun's so big and fat I could lick it.
Christine	A garden just for ourselves. Look, maybe we could find things to eat.
Katherine	Maybe we don't have to eat any more.
Simone	They kicked Eve out of the Garden of Eden.
Katherine	They kicked out Adam, too.
Simone	No, he could have stayed.
Christine	Do you think so?
Simone	Oh, yes.
Katherine	I think so, too. I think God would have fashioned another woman out of his other rib. And she would have been just fine.

Christine	But he didn't.
Katherine	I know.
Simone	And so he got us.
Katherine	Yes.

They laugh.

Christine	Do you think it happened that way?
Katherine	I think there was another Eden, outside the "garden," the Land of Mermaids where a young girl or an old woman could dress herself in bark and roots. She could let her hair grow long and matted and she could rub her body with charcoal and palm oil until she was black. She learned the language of the Mermaids, unintelligible to Adam. It sprang spontaneously to her tongue. And when the time came she escaped from the garden with her companions and they all turned completely wild. Adam wandered outside the garden in search of them until he was returned, pale and stupefied to the land of fences.
Simone	That's so stupid.
Christine	I liked that story.
Simone	Adam can go there, too. Adam can go anywhere. And he knows how to talk Mermaid.
Christine	No, he doesn't, he's too stupid.
Simone	Mermaid isn't so hard.
Christine	Do you know how to speak it?
Simone	Yes.
Christine	Then speak it.
Simone	I am. It's called "I wish upon, I wish upon." It's called, "I wish there was something else." It's called, "I wish I could

fill the hole in my body." It's called, "I wish I could get away." It's called, "I'll never be alone or I'll always be alone." It's called, "Help me." It's called...

Christine	Stop it.
Katherine	Yes, stop it, you're ruining the afternoon.
Christine	*(Sitting up, disturbed)* Is it afternoon?
Katherine	Yes.
Christine	Why does it always have to go that way?
Katherine	Which way?
Christine	Why does it only get later?
Simone	Why does everything have to get so philosophical? Why can't we just lie here like big snakes on a rock?
Christine	I don't like snakes.
Simone	You would if you were a snake.
Christine	I'm not...a snake.
Katherine	*(Alarmed)* Let's go.

CHRISTINE *begins gathering their things.*

Simone	I don't want to go.
Katherine	Look, we can still climb up that hill over there.
Christine	That's no hill, that's a mountain.
Katherine	No, it's just a high hill. When we get there we'll be able to see everything. Come on.
Simone	Why don't we just go back?
Katherine	We can't go back.
Christine	Why not?
Simone	There's nowhere to go here. Soon we'll be trapped on the top of the highest mountain in the world and there won't be anywhere to go, not anywhere to go.

Katherine	We can't go back.
Simone	Then let's just stay here, stay here in the Garden of Eden.
Katherine	There isn't any Garden of Eden.
Simone	Then let's just stay here. He's coming. I know he is. Let's just stay here until he comes.
Christine	*(Frightened)* He can't come. He's dead. He's dead as an old rat.
Simone	He's close.
Christine	*(Rising panic)* No he isn't.
Katherine	Please, please come.
Simone	Haven't you felt him? Following us behind each branch? Haven't you heard his feet breaking the leaves?
Katherine	Let's go.
Simone	Tell us about François and I will.
Katherine	Nothing happened. He never touched me.
Simone	I'll bet. Tell us.
Christine	I don't care if I hear it.
Simone	Yes, you do. It's only fair.
Christine	You're not trying to be fair. You're trying to be evil.
Simone	Yes, I am.

She makes a scary face and laughs.

Christine	*(Frightened)* Stop it.
Simone	*(Talking in François' voice)* Make her tell us.
Christine	Stop it.
Simone	*(Gets up and approaches Katherine)* What did he do? What did he really do?
Katherine	*(Screaming)* HE BEAT ME! HE BEAT ME! He locked me in a dark room and beat me.

Christine	Stop it! Stop it!
Katherine	He did. Now, let's go.
Simone	*(Shaken)* Which way should we go?
Katherine	Up.

The lights fade.

*

Nearing the Storm

A crash of thunder. The lights come up as KATHERINE is running across the stage. She enters then exits on the other side. There is laughter offstage, then SIMONE and CHRISTINE enter. They are talking and laughing. CHRISTINE is swinging the picnic basket.

They laugh and skip after KATHERINE as they sing.

Christine and Simone

It's raining, it's pouring
the old man is snoring
he bumped his head
on the side of the bed
and couldn't get up till the morning.

Lights fade.

*

Katherine Comes to a Precipice

KATHERINE comes running alone. She's out of breath. The lights have gotten dimmer. SIMONE sings the popular oldie, "You, You, You, I'm In Love With You."

Simone	*(Singing)* "You, you, you I'm in love with you, you, you..."
Katherine	Christine?
Simone	No, silly.
Katherine	*(She can't locate where SIMONE is)* Simone?
Simone	*(Singing)* "Won't you make my dreams come true. Let me cling to you, you, you."

SIMONE dashes out of the trees and grabs KATHERINE and whirls her around, laughing. KATHERINE struggles free.

Katherine	Where's Christine?
Simone	Back there.
Katherine	Where?
Simone	By the marsh.
Katherine	You just left her there?
Simone	I couldn't drag her with me. Besides, I didn't want you to get lost.
Katherine	I know where I'm going. How is she going to find us?
Simone	The path.

SIMONE looks behind her at the path. KATHERINE is surprised to see it.

Katherine	Oh.
Simone	You didn't know there was a path?
Katherine	*(Lying)* Yes.
Simone	Any one can find us. All they have to do is follow the path.

SIMONE laughs. She rushes at KATHERINE and clutches her to her.

| Katherine | *(Struggles with SIMONE)* LET GO OF ME! |
| Simone | You're not strong now, are you? Have you become a girl again? Have I become a man? Am I your man? I look like him, don't I? |

(Suddenly screaming enacting François) "What's the matter with you, are you stupid?"

(She shoves KATHERINE back and struts toward her) "What are you gawking at?"

KATHERINE looks at SIMONE, bewildered.

| Simone | *(As FRANÇOIS)* "Come here. I said, Come here!" |

KATHERINE backs away from SIMONE, bewildered.

Simone	*(As FRANÇOIS)* "Come on, Kathy, come out of your cell and make a baby with me in the sink."
Katherine	STOP IT! STOP IT!
Simone	*(As FRANÇOIS)* "Come on and be my girlfriend."

*They struggle. They fall on the ground and begin rolling
and fighting. SIMONE overpowers KATHERINE.*

Simone (*As herself*) Do you think I killed her? Do you think I did?
Do you think I pushed her into the marsh and killed her?
Do you? Do you, my darling?

Katherine Did you?

Simone Do I look like the kind of person that would do a thing
like that?

Katherine You look beautiful. You always look beautiful.

Simone Beautiful. Beautiful. Beautiful is what you beat. Look at
me.

Katherine You have a scar on your throat.

Simone Isn't it beautiful?

Katherine Who did it to you?

Simone Who do you think? Kiss it. Kiss it and make it better.

KATHERINE runs her lips over SIMONE's scar.

Simone We didn't kill anybody. We killed a shadow.

*Laughter. SIMONE and KATHERINE start. CHRISTINE enters.
Her face is dirty.*

Christine I forgot it.

She holds the basket up.

*

Cleaning up Christine

KATHERINE is wiping CHRISTINE's face off with a napkin.
SIMONE is cleaning CHRISTINE's muddy dress.

Christine	If our fathers were here they could clean me up.
Katherine	How did you get so muddy?
Christine	I forgot about the water.
Katherine	What do you mean?
Christine	There wasn't any.
Katherine	What?
Christine	Is my dress dirty? I made this dress just for this.
Simone	We all did. Just be quiet.
Christine	I haven't had my pill.
Katherine	What pill?
Christine	The pill that François gives me at noon at three at nine.
Katherine	You don't need a pill.
Christine	Oh, I do.
Katherine	You know about this?
Simone	Yes.
Katherine	You didn't say you took pills.
Christine	I did.
Katherine	I didn't hear you.
Christine	I said it softly. I wanted to go, too. I wanted to go. Don't you take them?
Katherine	I take them but I don't need them.
Christine	I do.
Katherine	What happens if you don't get them?
Christine	I don't remember.
Simone	Look at her hands.
Christine	My hands are too beautiful to look at.

SIMONE suddenly runs a little distance away and shouts into the sky.

Simone   THE WORLD IS RUNNING DOWN! With every gesture I make smoke. Look at the sky. It's cracking. The heat's going up into the stars. Look, they're sucking all the water away.

Christine   *(Touching her face)* My skin is bad now. Now we can't make up.

Katherine   We've made up.

Christine   Have we?

Katherine   Yes, haven't we, Simone?

Simone   Oh, yes. *(Screams it angrily at the sky)* WE'VE MADE UP!

SIMONE runs back and gazes at CHRISTINE's hands.

Look at her hands.

Katherine   What's wrong with your hands? *(She holds CHRISTINE's hands up. They are paralyzed)*

Christine   They're being shellfish.

Katherine   Why didn't you tell me she was this bad off.

Christine   I'm not bad.

Simone   Everyone knew it. If you weren't so bad off yourself you would have noticed it.

Christine   You're talking about me. You don't need to talk about me. I helped you just like everyone else did. I helped hit him in the head. I helped put his face in the water.

Katherine   *(Shouting)* But you didn't say you needed pills!

Simone   You're the one who needs pills. You're the one they always locked up.

Katherine	*(Shouting defensively)* That's because I killed my husband!
Simone	It's because you didn't behave.
Katherine	It's because François loved me the most.
Simone	Yes, that's why he locked you up in a room.
Katherine	He put me there to keep me away from the lights.
Simone	*(Shouting)* Stop acting crazy! He took you in the room because he wanted to play. And you liked it! We all did!
Christine	I liked it. Didn't you Katherine? I liked it. We all liked it. We liked it under the table, in the john, on the stairs, in the examination room, in the basement, late at night in the cells with his hand over our mouths. We liked it up the pooper. I had a baby by him. I had it in the toilet!

CHRISTINE looks at them and begins laughing. They look at her and begin laughing back. Gradually they stop laughing; then slowly they look up as if at a door at the end of a set of stairs. They are speaking to their captor, very seductively.

Christine	François, François, come here.
Simone	Do you like our dresses?
Christine	Aren't they pretty?
Katherine	We made them ourselves.
Simone	Especially for you.
Katherine	Come on down in the basement.
Simone	And have some fun.
Christine	Did you hit him?
All	No.
Christine	Did you ever hit him?
All	No.

Christine	Are you lying?
All	Yes.

They make striking gestures in unison.

All	BANG!

BANG!

BANG!

They begin laughing, laughing and laughing. The lights go down.

The lights rise.

The women run across the stage. This time there's a mood of feverish, incipient hysteria about, and a savage joy of beings who are just beginning to understand that there is nowhere else to go, that there is nothing to hide.

*

Simone's Baby

The thunder rolls, the lights flash, when the lights come up it is darker. They fall on the ground, out of breath.

Christine	Let's sleep under a rock.
Simone	We'll get buggy.

Christine	Bugs don't touch me. They cry when they see me. I've killed bugs. I killed them in my husband's house.
Katherine	You killed your husband, not your bugs.
Christine	I killed them both.

They laugh.

Christine	Who did you kill, Simone?
Simone	I didn't kill anybody.
Christine	We've all killed somebody. Kathy killed her husband. Didn't you?
Katherine	Yes.
Christine	I killed mine two times.
Katherine	You mean you killed two husbands?
Christine	They're all the same.
Simone	I never had any husbands.
Christine	You had girlfriends.
Simone	Yes. I killed my baby.
Katherine	What?
Simone	I killed my baby.
Christine	You're not supposed to kill your baby.
Simone	Why not?
Christine	Because babies don't do anything.
Simone	Babies do everything. They're smart. They're so smart they can't even talk. They make you goo and coo, they pop their eyes and drivel on their chins, they poop in your hands. They scream all night. They scream all day. Because they hate this world. They hate the creatures from this world. Because they're from another planet. And they yearn for their planet. They scream for their planet. They scream in

hatred for the women who stuffed them in their bellies and pulled them down into this dirty, pointed world, stuffed them in bags in their bellies, and ran away with them into this dirty, pointed world. So what do they do? They do the only thing they can. They grow, grow and scream and make you hold them and clean them. They make juice come in your chest and they suck it out of you. And then they hide, hide away and make this big meat body that walks around and shouts and talks and drives away in cars.

Katherine What were you?

Simone A nurse.

They laugh. SIMONE gets up, crosses to the picnic basket and picks it up.

Simone We're not going down again, are we?

The other two look at each other, then look at her.

Katherine No.

CHRISTINE shakes her head "no."

They embrace. Lights out. Thunder and lightning.

*

Eye of the Storm

*Thunder and lightning. C*HRISTINE *enters first.*

Christine   LOOK! It's gonna storm. Let's get killed.

*The lightning flashes, the thunder cracks. C*HRISTINE *holds up her dress in her gnarled hands.*

Christine   FRANÇOIS! FRANÇOIS! Come on down and let's fight.
(*She laughs*)

Katherine   Christine, get down from there.

Simone   No, let her die.

Thunder crashes.

Christine   (*Shouts after it*) FRANÇOIS! FRANÇOIS! Look at him, there he is. See him stumbling out of the clouds?

Thunder crashes.

HERE HE COMES!

*S*IMONE *becomes frightened.*

Simone   Let's get out of here.

Katherine   There's nothing to worry about, let him come. If he hits me there's gonna be storms, earthquakes, starvation, no children will be born.

*S*IMONE *starts screaming.*

Simone	He put my head in the water! He put my head in the water so I couldn't breathe!

Flashes of lightning. The thunder cracks. SIMONE and KATHERINE hold each other.

Christine	Look! He's coming! Coming! *(Screams up into the storm, shaking her fist)* François! François! FRANÇOIS!

Crash of thunder. Darkness.

Marriage

They are sitting together in moonlight.

Katherine	They say that women and the moon go together.
Simone	That's bullshit.
Christine	Let's get married. Simone, give me your hand.

SIMONE puts out her hand. CHRISTINE takes out the knife, grabs SIMONE's hand and cuts it.

Simone	*(Screams)* How did you get my knife?

Christine	I took it. Give me your hand, Kathy.
Simone	Never.
Christine	Don't be afraid. I'm good. Even with my hands this way.
Katherine	Don't kill me! Don't kill me!
Christine	I'm not going to kill you. *(Laughs)*
Simone	I'm bleeding. I'm bleeding.

Christine   Here, hold your hand over this.

She holds the empty coke can under SIMONE's hand.
SIMONE is trembling.

It's like a kiss, full of symbols.

She lifts SIMONE's hand above the can.

Christine   Look at it in the moonlight, black as a snail's back.
It's the soul.

Katherine   You can't have my soul.

Christine   Yes, I can. *(Gently)* Give it to me, Katherine.

KATHERINE looks into CHRISTINE's eyes. CHRISTINE leans
forward and gives KATHERINE a kiss. The kiss lingers.
KATHERINE gives CHRISTINE her hand. CHRISTINE cuts
KATHERINE's hand.

Christine   I learned to do this from my husband.

Katherine   Ow!

She holds KATHERINE's hand over the Coke can.

Christine   Here, take this napkin. *(Gives SIMONE and KATHERINE*
napkins.) Now it's my turn. *(She cuts her hand and holds*
it over the Coke can. When she's done she puts the can on
the ground) Now we drink it.

Simone   Oh, come on.

Christine   Yes.

Katherine	Not me.
Christine	No, look it's fine.
Simone	I don't want to.
Christine	It's our last night on earth. Don't you understand?

KATHERINE and CHRISTINE rise up on their knees. SIMONE gets up and runs stage left and searches for a way out.

Simone	I'm getting out of here.
Katherine	Where are you going to go?

SIMONE looks about her, then at them. She crosses and kneels with them.

Christine	I, the despised, the despicable, the desperate, the displaced, the disgraced...
Katherine	We're not that bad.
Simone	We are.
Christine	...do take thee as my lawful...
Katherine	Unlawful.
Christine	...unlawful wife...
Simone	Husband...
Katherine	And wife...
Christine	...And wife and husband till death do us part.
Simone	What does that mean?
Christine	Don't worry about it.

CHRISTINE gives SIMONE the Coke can.

Simone	How much?

Christine	Well, not too much, there's just a little.

SIMONE takes a sip, grimaces and passes it on to KATHERINE. KATHERINE drinks from it. She seems to like it. She hands it to CHRISTINE. CHRISTINE drinks from it.

Christine	Yuck.
Simone	What's wrong?
Christine	I don't like blood.
Katherine	*(Gets up)* Let's go.

They get up. They take each other's hands. The lights fade.

Flight

Blackness. KATHERINE makes a soft, lonely wind sound in the dark. The lights come up, they are lying on their stomachs looking out at the vista from the top of the hill.

Katherine	Woooo, woooo. You hear the wind coming up from the bottom? Look at the stars. You can see everything here. Everything in the world. Look there's a football game going on over there. There's a horse show. There's a strongman's place and a working heart dance hall where all the high-heeled girls go. And a "Good Guys" camp stall where they're all drinking cocoa around a campfire. There's a graveyard and a night-time cemetery scene. There's a church singing in a deep, black hole. *(Wailing softly)* "Hallelujah. Hallelujah." This is called Baldy Rock Mountain. Except that one side of its head's caved in. *(Suddenly)* GO OVER THERE!

Simone	*(Alarmed)* Where?
Katherine	Over there. Both of you.

They turn and walk forward cautiously.

	Don't dawdle. Hurry.
Simone	What's wrong?
Katherine	HURRY!

They walk cautiously forward, looking in front of them and then looking back at KATHERINE. Suddenly they both scream and back away. SIMONE falls to the ground. They have just about fallen into an abyss.

Katherine	SURPRISE!

SIMONE crawls away from the ledge on her hands and knees, then lies on her back, gasping. CHRISTINE walks to the edge and peeks over.

Katherine	Take a good look, Christine.
Christine	I can't see anything.
Katherine	That's because there's nothing there.

CHRISTINE looks at KATHERINE, then looks back down at the abyss, then looks back at KATHERINE, smiling.

Simone	Katherine, I can't fly.
Katherine	Did I say fly?
Simone	Kathy, stop it.

Christine	Fly?
Katherine	I found this place in my dreams. It's a great place.
Christine	It's a great idea.
Simone	Kathy, please.
Katherine	Don't you go to places in your dreams, Simone?
Simone	Yes, but they're not real.
Christine	How do you know?
Simone	Because every time I woke up I was locked in my cell.
Christine	*(Looking down the hill on the other side)* LOOK! LOOK! Lights. They're coming after us. I'm so excited. It could be a lot of fun, Semi.
Simone	Semi?
Christine	Yeah, that's your name. *(Runs toward the edge and stops just short, teetering on the brink)* Yes or no?
Katherine	Not yet.

CHRISTINE pulls her back. They fall into each other's arms and laugh. They begin dancing and spinning.

Simone	STOP! STOP!

KATHERINE and CHRISTINE stop and run upstage.

Christine	Did you hear that?
Katherine	Voices?
Christine	Look.
Katherine	They're getting close.

Christine	*(Shouts down the hill)* Come on up, we're having a party.
Simone	Shut up.

Christine	*(Holds her hands up. They're not gnarled anymore)* Look, my hands are coming back! I've got wings, Simone.
	CHRISTINE and KATHERINE charge at SIMONE. They pull her from the ground and begin swinging her around near the edge of the drop.
Simone	No, no, I'm not going to go. *(Struggles free)*
Christine	Don't go then. Stay here and let them lock you up. *(Shouts down the hill)* NOT ME!
Simone	You won't get away this way. You'll just be dead.
Christine	How do you know? That's what they told you. And look, they're coming after us. They're going to pull us down in a pit in the dark and lock us behind the fences of Eden. How can they know what's there when they don't even know what's here? *(Points at herself)* They don't believe in magic.
Simone	I don't either.
Christine	I do. *(Looks up and make a spreading motion)*
Simone	I want to touch something. I want to touch something. *(Begins crawling, moving her hand over the ground)* I don't like heights.
Christine	Yes, you do. You like them too much.
Simone	Too much, too much, maybe that's it.
Christine	*(Takes SIMONE in her arms and helps her to her feet)* You're in love with them. They're your girlfriends.
Simone	The heights?
Christine	*(Laughs)* Yeah, all of them.
Katherine	*(Singing down into the abyss, the first lines of "Indian Love Song")* "I hear you calling, calling me."

She holds out her hand to SIMONE.

SIMONE gazes up at her. She takes CHRISTINE *and*
KATHERINE *in.* KATHERINE *and* CHRISTINE *smile at her.*
SIMONE *takes their hands. The women stand together,*
stage center, SIMONE *in between them.*

Simone   *(Laughs)* Why am I always the reticent one?
Katherine   Because you're the leader.
Simone   The leader of what?
Christine   Our squadron. *(Runs to upstage right and shouts down*
            the hill) Yes we did it! We did it all! Hurry! *(Runs back*
            and takes her place next to SIMONE)

KATHERINE looks at CHRISTINE *and* SIMONE.

Christine   Won't they be surprised?
Katherine   Yes. *(Looks at* CHRISTINE *and* SIMONE) Enough?
Simone   Yes.
Christine   Ready?

They run downstage toward the abyss, holding hands and
fling their arms up. Black out.

The End

Understanding the Dead

by John Steppling

Understanding the Dead *was first presented at the 14th Annual Padua Hills Playwrights Festival, Woodbury College, Los Angeles, California, in 1994. The play was directed by the author with the following cast:*

Skip: John O'Keefe
Sandborn: Mick Collins
Karen: Priscilla Harris
Dead Woman: Kathleen Cramer
Local Man: Shelley Desai
Nigel: Clive Saunders

The play takes place somewhere on the Gulf of Mannar,
Tamil Nadu, South India.

"...day and night blazes the funeral pyre:
The ashes of the dead, strewn all about,
I have preserved against thy coming,
With death-conquering Mahakala 'neath thy feet
Do thou enter in, dancing thy rhythmic dance
That I may behold thee with closed eyes."

—*Sakata Bengali Hymn, author anonymous*

*Darkness. Sound of small bells, chimes, woodblocks.
Sounds fade.*

*Light up on Demon's face—genderless, painted bright col-
ors—grotesque, mouth open in silent shriek.*

A man's voice in dark.

Sandborn   Over there, almost everyone knows someone died this
way. It is not unusual. They wake up screaming—covered
in sweat—screaming, see, and they'll sit up, often anyway,
and they're screaming, and then they fall back. Dead.

Light on Demon begins to fade.

(Pause) They just die. There is no reason. They die, that's
all. *(Pause)* There is a belief that an evil female spirit
comes and seduces them, and then destroys them.

Lights up gradually on SANDBORN—*seated at small wood
table. He's about 45 or 50, wearing light cotton slacks and
pastel shirt. Tropical attire. Standing behind* SANDBORN *is a
man of about 45 in more Western-looking clothes. This is* SKIP.

In Indonesia, Vietnam, Laos, Thailand, they all have their
names for it. And you'll see young men with long nails
on their pinkie finger. They'll paint them, see, paint their
fingernail because they think the bad female spirit will be
fooled by the nail—she'll think these young men are actually women—and she'll pass them over. *(Silence)* Here

the men paint their nails—but it's just 'cause they like it—
far as I can tell.

Silence.

These deaths. There is no scientific explanation, see—
none. They die. They fall back, and they're dead.

Skip takes a couple of steps forward.

Skip   You remember we spoke? *(Beat)* Yesterday. We spoke on
the phone.

Sandborn looking at him. Pause.

I'm with the hotel.

Skip takes out card and hands it to Sandborn.

We have hotels throughout many developing nations.
(Pause) We spoke on the phone.

Sandborn   Yesterday.

Skip   We spoke on the phone, yesterday. You suggested I come
by—we could tour the area. *(Beat)* Discuss "Revitalization."

Sandborn   I remember that part.

Skip nods, steps downstage—his back to Sandborn.

He's looking out at the landscape.

Silence.

Skip   You're an American?!

Sandborn   I'm American. *(Pause)* There is no tourist bureau here. *(Beat)* There's only me.

SOUND of bells and woodblocks.

I still believe America is a great country.

As lights fade on SANDBORN and SKIP, the sound of bells and drumming increases. A middle-aged Indian or Asian man begins lighting mosquito coils, placing one every few feet around the stage. Another light comes up on blonde woman (KAREN). She's wearing shorts and skimpy halter top. She stands, listening to the music, swaying slightly.

Music stops—she stops, a little startled. The LOCAL MAN steps over...

Karen   I can't do this—I can't have mosquitoes everywhere.

He stares at her.

The mosquitoes.

Local Man   Mosquitoes.

Karen	Can you see my legs? Can you see the bites?

MAN says nothing. She bends over, looking at her leg.

Should we count them...one, two...three, four, five, six, seven, eight...

She looks at him.

That's just one leg. Eight.

LOCAL MAN nods.

Lights coming up more to include SANDBORN, seated as before. KAREN indicates mosquito coils.

Sandborn	Mosquito coils.
Karen	Mosquito coils.
Local Man	Yes, you burn the coils—and this will keep the mosquitoes away.

KAREN looks over at SANDBORN.

Karen	What about rehearsal?
Sandborn	How's that?
Karen	Can we burn coils while I rehearse?
Sandborn	Uh-huh. I don't see why not.
Karen	I'm a professional.
Sandborn	You have to tell me that? I can see what you are—you're a professional. I could see that right off.

KAREN looks back at LOCAL MAN, stares at him a moment.

Local Man   There will be no mosquitoes... not for you.

Lights fading/changing.

Sound of blocks, bells, etc. KAREN sits, tying bells to her ankles. SKIP stands, watching her. SANDBORN stands next to him.

Skip   So. What we have here, are authentic regional dances, dances of the indigenous peoples.

KAREN looks up at him, then resumes tying the bells to her ankles.

Sandborn   Sure. Uh-huh.

Skip   The Hill Tribes can set up stalls—along the seashore there. Sell "folk art."

KAREN is finished and stands up.

That way, with the stalls, people can get a look at these tribes—up close—see the way they live and behave.

KAREN stands, listening to the drumming start. SKIP's attention is mostly on SANDBORN now.

Sandborn   The people don't produce much, nothing you could call "folk art." Nothing that you can really move, anyhow.

The local stuff just doesn't move.

Skip   …We'll put the good shit in the hotel shops—get some of that clunky jewelry from Tibet—Nepal—Doesn't matter. It doesn't matter.

Skip swats at the air a couple of times.

(Beat) Lot of fuckin' mosquitoes.

Blackout. Drumming continues.

Lights shift. Skip and Sandborn on road.

Sandborn   Those dogs—about one in four carries rabies. They can appear quite normal—but if it happens they lick you— you maybe just pet the little guy's head and he licks your hand—that's all it takes.

Skip   And they eat these dogs.

Sandborn   They eat the dogs—they'll eat some of the dogs.

Skip   Rabies. You catch rabies if you eat, like, dog curry?

Sandborn   I don't know. Never heard of it.

Skip   Guess if it's cooked. If they cook it enough.

Sandborn   If it's cooked, sure.

Skip   Cooking would just kill the virus.

Sandborn   I'd say it would. Cooking kills about everything.

Skip   Uh-huh. *(Pause)* But this lagoon. The mosquitoes.

Sandborn   Well, it's home to a lot of mosquitoes. Sure.

Skip   These cottages. Until a point later in time—until that point mosquito nets seem essential.

Sandborn   Sure they do. I think they do.

Skip	Just in these first cottages.
	SANDBORN nods in agreement.
	What we're looking at are package tours. Germans, Danes, Italians—maybe some Americans.
Sandborn	I been here a lot of years.
Skip	Uh-huh.
Sandborn	It's mostly been budget travelers. Kids with backpacks— seekers—long as I been here.
Skip	I understand that.
Sandborn	I was in that first wave of tourist development. Fifteen years ago. *(Pause)* The plans were never very grand. I'm only a friend of the government. *(Pause)* I have permanent residence here. *(Pause)* I'm an American citizen. *(Pause)* I live here. *(Beat)* I just live here, that's all.
	Silence.
Skip	When you came, did you plan on staying? *(Pause)* Did you plan to stay this long?
Sandborn	I live here. *(Pause)* And this is what became of the great adventure of my life.
Skip	*(Pause)* When you've left...
Sandborn	I don't leave anymore.
Skip	When you've gone home...
Sandborn	*(Beat)* When I have, yeah, what?
Skip	Do you feel lost?
Sandborn	A long while ago, when I went home, I felt lost.
Skip	And now you don't go home anymore.
Sandborn	That's right, I don't go home anymore.

SKIP nods vaguely. Silence.

Skip   You know, really, I don't like this heat.

Sandborn   Nobody likes it.

Skip   *(Beat)* Not even you?

Sandborn   For me it's not a question of "liking" things. *(Pause)* It's hot, it's hot all fuckin' year—that's how it is here.

SKIP nods.

SKIP stepping over.

Karen   I don't understand how these people dance.

SKIP sits.

Skip   Let's freshen up that Mai Tai, huh—

He waves LOCAL MAN over—points at her drink.

Once more, amigo—and one for me.

LOCAL MAN nods and departs.

Years ago—they tried to develop this beach as a resort—but a couple from Scotland, I think, and then this American woman—they got some bad shellfish, I don't know—and all three died. Today we could cover that up—we could sidestep that kind of issue. But at that time it just queered the whole deal.

Local Man brings their drinks.

Thanks, boss.

Local Man departs.

Three white corpses.

Karen Yeah.

Skip All Westerners.

Karen Yeah.

Skip downs his Mai Tai. Beat.

Skip It's always been a tough tourist sell. *(Pause)* The beaches are all covered in excrement—or they smell like fish. *(Pause)* How did you come to be here?

Karen Too old and not enough talent.

Skip Don't say that—what's talent, anyway?

Karen *(Smiles)* It's what I don't have.

She gulps some of her Mai Tai. Silence.

Skip turns to look out toward audience.

Skip It's dirty, the whole place is dirty. It's dirty in a way I didn't know about—those walls there, there's a thousand years of dirt on them—ten thousand years—there is so much dirt that light doesn't reflect off them—it just gets sucked into some other dimension. *(Pause)* The first few beach cottages the Conroy Group built—this was fifteen years ago—the

cement mix was wrong—the walls just kind of melted—
they slipped...slipped so slowly...they slipped into the dirt
streets. Onto the street edges where the waste accumulates.
And after a while it became the best place to urinate—the
cement mush being so absorbent. And all the men here
pissed all over what had once been the walls—every day—
for over a decade—pissing into the bad cement mix that
the Conroy Hotel Group had paid for. *(Beat)* Somehow
somewhere someone had imagined a beautiful sun-drenched
stretch of sand—with happy, smiling, pale people playing,
laughing and drinking. What they got was urine-soaked rubble.

Lights shift.

LOCAL MAN *standing with* DEAD WOMAN. *They stand in
the dim light.*

Local Man	Do you know about the thieves?
Dead W.	I know to be careful.
Local Man	There are associations of crime. *(Beat)* Gangs.
Dead W.	Young men. *(Pause)* In the train stations there are many thieves. *(Beat)* Skinny, frightening young men.

Silence.

I don't miss many things. I don't miss riding trains—or my
fears of the night—I don't miss my family, or much of anything. *(Beat)* I miss physical desire.

Local Man *(Silence)* I am an adult. I sleep with my brother in one bed.
My wife and children sleep outside. My mother cooks for

us and she pushes the food up through a hole in the floor. She lives beneath us in a room—with its own entrance. On my brother's birthday you will come to dinner at our house. My mother will cook special sweets for after dinner. It will be an honor to have the dead come to our house.

Dead W.   *(Smiles)* Thank you. I would love that.

Lights shift.

*

Lights up on KAREN *rehearsing her dance. Far upstage the face of the* DEAD WOMAN *in demonic grimace. The face gradually fades as rehearsal continues.*

SKIP *is to one side, Mai Tai in one hand.* SANDBORN *is next to him.*

KAREN *stops dancing, watching from upstage.*

Skip   I've been in the hotel business for almost twenty years.

Sandborn   Sure, good thing.

Skip   Worked in the Gulf States the last six, seven years. Dubai, the Emirates, Oman.

Sandborn   Uh-huh. Sure. Sure.

Skip   The Conroy Group has eight three-star hotels in the Gulf.

Sandborn   Didn't know that.

Skip   The Arabs—that's a tough one. Muslim world—that's a

	tough arena.
Sandborn	Sure it is.
Skip	That's some very uptight shit—Islam—very uptight.
Sandborn	I wouldn't know, really.

KAREN *approaching along the perimeter.*

Skip	This is a promotion. How I'm supposed to look at it. *(Beat)* This... *(Indicating area all around them)* ...coming over to this. *(Beat)* The Conroy Group...They believe in the area, that tourism can be a factor here.
Sandborn	I guess it could happen.
Skip	What is this tourist thing, anyway? You know what I'm asking? Do you?
Sandborn	Tourism?!
Skip	The reality of people going on vacation—going someplace to have fun, to be entertained—and these people, these fucking people, and they actually show up, and they got cameras, and maps, and travel books...and sometimes I think, I think I don't fuckin' understand. *(Downs his Mai Tai. Pause)* They have no real wants—no deep needs. They have only their thirst for distraction. That's all.

Lights shift.

KAREN *seated.* DEAD WOMAN *stands nearby.*

Karen	I can't dance when I have dysentery. *(Pause)* The first tourist package is due in ten days. *(Pause)* I can't dance like this.

	(Pause) The Local Man—and man here—that man, he has a brother, and it is his brother's birthday. He invited me to his house for the birthday party.
Dead W.	Hmnnn.
Karen	His brother is so quiet.
Dead W.	His brother is very quiet.
Karen	I'm afraid to eat anything—that the cramps will come back.
Dead W.	His brother, his brother is very, very ugly.
Karen	That's too bad. I guess.
Dead W.	Very, very ugly.
Karen	If I eat anything—the cramps come back. *(Pause)* Do you blame anyone? You know, about your death?
Dead W.	It's nothing we can speak about. Let's speak of other things. *(Beat)* At dusk, have you seen the bats? In the shore caves—right at sunset...
Karen	I keep my back to the caves. *(Beat)* The way they've put up the stage. When I dance.
Dead W.	Then you'll miss the bats. For the most part.
Karen	I face the jungle.
Dead W.	*(Pause)* Are you homesick?
Karen	*(Shakes head)* I've traveled a lot. I don't seem to care any more where I go.
Dead W.	I was homesick before I died. While I was sick. *(Beat)* I fell sick and died quickly. Fuckin' shellfish.
Karen	I'm homesick when I dance. That's the only time.

Lights shift/early morning light. The Local Man *squats, blanket wrapped around himself. The* Dead Woman *walks near him.*

| **Dead W.** | The smoke, this morning, it doesn't disperse, it stays close |

416

to the ground.

Local Man The smoke from the dead is always unusual.

Dead W. But with children...You don't cremate children.

Local Man No. The child is to be buried.

Dead W. This morning they burn three adult bodies.

Local Man From lower castes—it is cheap wood. There is little special about it.

Dead W. *(Pause)* The smoke.

Local Man The cemetery for children is behind the pyres. It is for Hindu, Muslim, Christian, all together.

Dead W. Yes.

Local Man You may visit it.

Dead W. *(Nods. Pause)* In these villages, they drown girl babies.

Local Man There are many small graves for baby girls, yes.

Dead W. Drown them mostly, or smother them, or feed them unhulled rice.

Local Man Yes, there are many ways. It is unlucky time for the girl child.

Dead Man It is a country that does not have much luck for anyone.

Local Man No. *(Beat)* It is not because they are not loved that they are killed.

Dead W. I had a child. A boy. A very sickly child. The only child I had.

Local Man A boy child is always a blessing.

Dead W. He became very ill when he was ten years old. He was in the hospital for many months. I believed he would die.

Local Man But he did not die.

Dead W. *(Beat)* No. No, he survived. *(Pause)* He has survived.

Local Man Is he a good son?

Dead W. *(Shrugs—beat)* He was quite separate from me. *(Pause)* Do you have children?

Local Man I have one girl, and one boy.

Dead W.	*(Beat)* So you did not kill your girl child?!
Local Man	*(Beat)* It is a great financial burden—a girl, there will be a dowry and it may create a debt that I will never be able to pay off. But that is how it is. I love her.
Dead W.	I think that's good.

Lights shifting.

SANDBORN walking down toward LOCAL MAN. LOCAL MAN nods greeting. SANDBORN seems not to notice DEAD WOMAN. He nods to LOCAL MAN.

Sandborn	There's going to be a couple of gentlemen from the hotel here today.

LOCAL MAN nods. He looks at the DEAD WOMAN. She's backing away. Far upstage the face of a demon appears.

We have to have things looking neat here.

LOCAL MAN nods. The demon's face is fading.

It's been suggested to me—maybe we could keep the beggars a little out of sight. At least the aggressive ones. *(Beat)* You know the ones. Who I mean.

Local Man	*Aap janteho. Unki jarurat kaise hai.*
Sandborn	*Mei samajta hunh!*

LOCAL MAN nods. SANDBORN seems weary.
(Beat) This is how business works. I didn't invent it.

Lights shift/on: KAREN. Far to side is SKIP—a fresh Mai Tai in hand, listening.

Karen   Up on the rocks—the hill—behind the caves, there are goats.

SKIP kind of vaguely nods. Sips his drink.

I go up on the top—and there are maybe fifteen, twenty goats. And I feel like the shepherdess—the goat girl, with my flock. It's the best thing to pretend. And I know they watch my show.

Skip   Who? The goats? That who you mean?

Karen   My flock of children.

Skip   Goats.

Karen   I dance for them. *(Pause)* I have to dance for someone.

Lights shift/on: SANDBORN—SKIP steps over to him.

Skip   Beggars. They're all beggars.

Sandborn   You don't have to give them anything.

Skip   Always with their hand out.

Sandborn   *(Pause)* Here you are with things they don't have.

Skip   Fucking country will never be able to develop tourism.

Sandborn   *(Beat)* We'll keep most of the beggars—the diseased ones, out of sight.

SKIP takes a long gulp of his Mai Tai.

Skip   Why are you here? What about your family?

Sandborn   I don't have much contact with any of them.

Skip	*(Pause)* Why here?
Sandborn	This is where I stopped. That's all.

Silence.

Skip	This development—you don't want it here, do you?!
Sandborn	Doesn't matter.
Skip	If they build a real hotel—if this preliminary package goes well, we'll create a lot of jobs—help the local economy.
Sandborn	*(Pause)* I started, back in Chicago, I was in computers. That's what I did. One year my vacation time came up and I wanted to go somewhere far away—so I went to Thailand—and I just never went back. Never used that return ticket. Sold it, in fact, and I just kept moving around.
Skip	*(Beat)* Computers. What did you do with computers?
Sandborn	I forget, really. *(Shrugs)* Something.

Skip sips his Mai Tai.

Skip	Not many Americans over here.
Sandborn	Not so many.

Pause.

Skip	Maybe you've been here too long.

Sandborn looks at Skip. Pause.

People who come here, they don't want these beggars—cripples, these lepers, crawling after them—deformed limbs reaching after them…fingerless hands…sunken eyes—voices cracked and weak. (*Stops, finishes his drink. Pause*) The Conroy Group, they expect things of me. The Conroy Group Hotel is a three-star establishment—throughout Asia and the Near East… (*Pause*) The Conroy Group, they expect things— why they sent me, I know you understand. You're not unsympathetic, you're not an un-experienced man—I know that. I can see that.

Lights change/on: DEAD WOMAN *and* KAREN.

Karen   I'm afraid.

Dead W.   That's all right.

Karen   I'm afraid of it becoming cold. I'm afraid of night. I'm afraid of this man's brother, and of being touched.

Dead W.   Who do you dream will touch you?

Karen   The Muslim butchers—in the Muslim market, the ones who kill the goats and sheep—unthinking little goats the butchers lead out back of their shops where they sever their heads and carefully skin the bodies. Then, I believe, they will lead me out back—and will kill me, and my head will hang next to the bleeding goat heads—in the stall of the Muslim butcher.

Dead W.   That is only a dream, that will not happen.

Karen   I'm afraid I'm gonna die here—dancing—while dancing. (*Pause*) I don't believe the tourists will be watching when I dance. They won't see much, but the dead watch, all the time, they watch.

Dead W.   That's all we can do. All we can do is watch.

Lights on: British tourist, NIGEL, standing in swim trunks, towel over his shoulder. He looks around, then takes seat at table.

SANDBORN walks over and sits at table with NIGEL.

Sandborn   My name is Sandborn.

Pause. They look at each other.

Did you get your complimentary drink?

Nigel   Complimentary drink.

Sandborn   Compliments of the Conroy Group. Inside next to the registration desk. One of the attendants will get it for you. Maybe a Beefeaters and tonic, we use quality tonic— and a large slice of lime. Lots of ice. Very refreshing. Maybe take it out on the beach with you.

Nigel   Sandborn?!

Sandborn   Yes, Sandborn.

Nigel   Are you the manager?

Sandborn   Manager?

Nigel   Here at the resort.

Sandborn   I'm, ah, a consultant.

Nigel   *(Pause)* The missus and me, we seem to be the only guests.

Sandborn   The first—you're the "first" guests.

Nigel   *(Pause)* We didn't want to go on down to Brighton again.

Sandborn   No—

Nigel   We wanted a change this holiday.

Sandborn   Something a little different.

Nigel   Eight years. Eight consecutive holidays at Brighton.

You come to feel you've had all the fun you can there.

Sandborn   I would imagine.

Nigel   This trip—this was a kind of "package" holiday. *(Beat)* The resort here, it doesn't seem to have a lot of potential for nightlife. You think?

Sandborn   I believe there is entertainment planned for this evening. A dinner show.

Lights changing as LOCAL MAN *brings out another chair, with* SKIP *following.* SKIP *nods, smiling toward* NIGEL. NIGEL *smiles back.*

Nigel   *(To* LOCAL MAN*)* Beefeaters and Schweppes, please, garçon.

Music plays as KAREN *enters, in costume. She stands, ready to dance. She bows to audience (*SKIP, NIGEL, SANDBORN *and* LOCAL MAN*) who applaud politely.*

Karen   Thank you, thank you very much. Thank you all for coming tonight—and let's give the Conroy Group a big thank-you for making all of this possible. *(Gives "thumbs-up" sign to* SKIP*)* Thank you, Conroy Group!

More polite applause.

It's just great to be here, isn't it. Exotic India! *(Beat)* What I'd like to try and do this evening. *(Pause, hesitates)* What I want...

Lights change/silence.

... is...*(distracted, hesitating)*...is to demonstrate...
the...ah...basic hand symbols of...classical, ah...

Holds up "Pataka Hasta"—first single hand gesture.

... of...Classical Indian dance. Just a little introduction to,
ahm, to help you enjoy tonight's performance. *(Pause)*
Pataka Hasta, the first of the mudras—indicating the confidence of divinity—and the beginning of discourse. *(Pause)*
When lifted upwards it is offered to the gods—twisted
downward it is meant for the lower and underworlds.

*She holds up second hand, "Tripataka." She grimaces,
fighting off stomach cramps.*

Tripaka—the triple flag—originating from Shiva—evoking
the descent of the gods or avatar. *(Pause)* Shit. *(Grimace—
Pause)* It is also used for holding weapons...*(Beat)* or to
apply sacred marks to the forehead...or...or...to wipe the
tears from the face.

*She pauses, looking around. Grimaces from worsening
attack of dysentery.*

Number eleven is "Suchi Mukha."

Holds up hand in eleventh position.

The tusks of the elephant. It may also mean the world. The
circle...Fuck. *(Grimace—recover)*...or the flame of a lamp.

She holds up several more hand positions—a little frantic and confused.

The Hansa Paksha—Swan Wing—accepting, embracing... or small child...or...ahm...a covering. *(Pause)* Or...or the snake's head; Sarpa Sirsa—offering water. The snake is often the conveyance for Lord Vishnu...and also, at times, the snake represents empty space, and...in some cases it is meant as eternity. And in some cases it is meant as eternity.

Longer pause, as she loses energy. The cramps subsiding.

Dance was a gift to man from Brahma the creator...

She tries and holds a few positions then stops, the energy gone.

That's all I know...I learned more, I've forgotten. I learned fourteen words of Tamil, but I've forgotten them, too. I learned a prayer to Kali—a song, but I've forgotten that as well. I've forgotten so many things in my life. *(Pause)*

Lights fading on all but KAREN as she begins several ballet positions.

I can't remember all the little girls in my ballet class, I can't remember the voice of the gray woman who taught us. *She holds one more ballet position. Silence. She releases.*

Pause.

I don't know how many days I've been hurt and rehearsed anyway. *(Pause)* Thousands of faces I can't recall, hands in my mouth I don't remember—taste I can't bring back—or the order of things, the year, the month...*(Beat)* and to come here to feel so damaged...So imperfect...

Pause.

Lights slowly begin to fade.

...Forgetting more and more...until finally there is nothing more to forget. *(Beat)* For those of us who wander unprotected, we are left only the waking dreams of the mute; all the animals—the religiously intoxicated, the uncertain figures in the sunlit distance, who appear wrapped in blankets despite the heat—noiselessly looking toward heaven, and already blind.

Blackout.

Lights coming up on: SKIP and SANDBORN.

Skip	The flies, the flies alone. How do I explain that? *(Pause)* If I'd had another month—an extra month, I think we could have turned the corner. *(Beat)* But I'm dealing with people who do not realize where I am. And so I end up looking bad. I don't come out looking so good on this one, believe me.
Sandborn	One day—my first week in Bangkok—I was walking around and I thought, okay, okay, I can let it go.
Skip	Let what go? Your old life?

Sandborn	Not old or new. I could just let go of my life. A couple of years later in Calcutta—I was selling books, English language paperbacks, off a table I set up on the street. That's when I started to really figure it all out.
Skip	I've seen guys like you before.
Sandborn	I'd make a hundred rupees a day, tops.
Skip	I've seen guys like you—I've heard these stories before.
Sandborn	You've never seen anyone like me.
Skip	*(Pause)* Okay—if you say so. *(Pause)* I just can't think about it anymore.
Sandborn	What I figured out—I figured out that I had no way left to divert myself. *(Beat)* Time passed. Crowds passed. Sometimes someone bought a book. I felt I had no immediate enemies— only myself—and I've always been my first best enemy. *(Pause)* Different times, I'd start to cry. At some point, just about every day, I'd be made to cry.
Skip	What? Why'd you cry, Sandborn?
Sandborn	I've never been able to decide completely. My best guess, I was crying because time was passing.

Silence. Lights shifting. LOCAL MAN, *wrapped in blanket, enters.*

Skip	It's late.
Local Man	It is my job.
Skip	Aren't you tired? Go home, go to sleep.
Local man	*(Nodding)* When I have to, I will sleep.

SKIP *nods wearily. Pause.*

Skip	We only have one guest. You and Sandborn—you can both go home.
Local Man	At my house, it is my brother's birthday.
Skip	I don't know your brother.
Local Man	My brother is well known in some places, though he is not an important man.
Skip	Well, I don't know him. *(Beat)* Sandborn, you know him?
Sandborn	I know who he is.
Local Man	*Aap jante ho. Arvind.*
Sandborn	*Arvind, boat achha.*
Local Man	When my brother was eighteen, he had traveled north to Madhya Pradesh, to work for my uncle in Agra. This was only weeks before the surrender of Phoolan Devi—the famous woman bandit. So my brother traveled for several days to arrive in Bhind the morning of the surrender. Thousands of people had come to watch—mostly poor villagers and my brother stood among them that morning waiting to see India's bandit queen. When Phoolan Devi came out, she stood on a stage where they had placed photographs of Mahatma Ghandi and the goddess Durga or Kali. She had wanted in some way to surrender to them, and not the government. She was from the Sudra caste, same as my brother and myself. She was charged with the murder of twenty-two high-caste men in the Uttar Pradesh. *(Pause)* A low-caste woman responsible for the death of Brahmin men is an unthinkable outrage and people began to see her as the avatar of Kali.
Skip	You think she is?
Local Man	Kali is the goddess of retribution. It is possible. *(Pause)* You know the image of Kali. *(Beat)* Kali stands upon a corpse holding a severed head. From her neck hangs a garland of

skulls. Kali is the power of time. For when the veils of our world are gone—then only naked time remains. Only eternal night.

Skip   You think gods usually give up and go to jail?

Local Man   *(Beat)* Women and schoolchildren cheered her as she was led away.

Skip nods. Silence.

My brother invites everyone for the celebration of his birthday.

Lights shifting.

Nigel and Skip.

Nigel   Man like yourself. *(Beat)* I'd wager on boxing, hockey, one of the tougher sports, If you were British, I might even have said rugby.

Skip   You'd say that—just off my appearance?

Nigel   Brutal game rugby. But the way you carry yourself, I think it's that type of thing that tells you the most about someone. Their carriage, the angle of the head when addressing someone.

Skip   I was a wrestler—in high school. *(Pause)* One year of college, I wrestled there, too.

Nigel   There, there, you see. Can't fake things of this sort. Man like yourself. *(Beat)* In my business a man can't get away with a whole lot of this sort of nonsense…Where I grew up—East End, All Saints—Whitechapel—when the Kray

	twins ran things—Reggie and Ronnie, a man wouldn't think to try a lot of nonsense over there. Course, things aren't like that now, and I'll tell you a lot of people wish gangsters like Reg and Ron would come back. They miss the days of real organized crime. Where I'm from. *(Pause)* Man has to know where he stands. That's what I'm sensing with you. You have to be treated like a man, otherwise…
Skip	…Otherwise you don't have anything.
Nigel	Otherwise you got a load of cac. *(Beats)* And then a man can become embarrassed. It feels embarrassing. You lose your bearings.
Skip	I've always tried to do the best I can.
Nigel	I don't know, if I'm wrong you just tell me. I look around and what I see is not what I was promised in the brochure. *(Pause)* There is a degenerate element at work here. *(Pause)* Man like yourself, must cause you pain.

Skip nods very slowly.

Must cause you to suffer.

Light shifting.

Sandborn, upstage is Dead Woman. The demon face appears far upstage, then fades. Sandborn is undoing his tie, taking off his "Conroy Group" coat. Dead Woman approaches, watching him.

Dead W.	Will you leave here?
Sandborn	I have no will to leave.

Dead W.	Have you become disenchanted?
Sandborn	*(Pause)* When the monsoons come, much of this area will flood. *(Pause)* I have no new ideas. No plans.
Dead W.	But you're going to leave?!
Sandborn	*(Beat)* I resigned my position with the Conroy Group. *(Pause)* Each summer when the rains come, and it floods, thousands are forced out of their homes and must live as refugees until the waters recede. Then they return and begin to rebuild their homes, knowing that it is unlikely they will be spared the floods the following summer. *(Beat)* They are spellbound by the routine of their lives— the lives of their families before them. *(Pause)* We've never spoken, until tonight, though I know you've been here.
Dead W.	Everything changes, even the dead change.
Sandborn	Okay.
Dead W.	*(Beat)* I often become tired of the things I see. *(Beat)* Very few people remember the person I was when I was alive. And the ones that do—I hardly remember them anymore. *(Pause)* I have so much to learn.

Light shifting.

Skip stands, holding Mai Tai. Nigel stands upstage, listening.

Skip	I have these terrible dreams. Dark, unsmiling women come to steal from me. *(Beat)* They smell of smoke, their hands stained with henna. *(Pause)* I wake, disoriented, momentarily, and there are giant cockroaches on the walls of the cottages, and on the wall of the office, and the mail has arrived, full of cancellations... *(Beat)* And the stones we laid in, to form

a walkway, have cracked and yellowed—and the only place to cool off is in the caves, along the water where the bats live. *(Beat)* But these women come for me when I close my eyes, they float toward me...

Nigel   You must not close your eyes, Skip.

Skip   I won't. *(Pause)* I'll carefully watch myself—I'll stay awake, alert, on guard.

Nigel   You must always be on guard, Skip, always.

Lights on: KAREN walking slowly. LOCAL MAN watching.

Local Man   Karen?

KAREN stops.

Karen, you may not be safe on this road at night.

Karen   Who will come to hurt me?

Local Man   *(Beat)* Night wanderers—all the various Raksasas—servants of Yama, the King of the Dead.

Karen   *(Beat)* Maybe just bad men.

Local Man   Maybe. *(Pause)* Low emotions allow some spirits to influence otherwise good men.

Karen   Fear, anger, loathing...

Local Man   Yes, and then the good man cannot be recognized for who he was.

Karen   Everyone is afraid. Everyone is angry.

Local Man   *(Pause)* At my house, you may stay the night safely. There is a party, and we have prepared food.

Karen   I can't go any farther. Dust blows into my eyes constantly, no matter where I turn. There is a ringing in my ears. *(Pause)*

If I lie down, when I lie down, I know those who have nothing will crawl in the dark and tear at me while I'm still awake but unable to resist and nobody will hear me call for help. I'll be found in the morning, without hands or feet, my useless body to be collected and put on the cart provided for the nameless dead and wheeled to the site of immolation. As my body begins to burn, the fire tender with his long stick will poke at my corpse to keep it in place on the pyre. My ashes will fly away in the unfamiliar haze. *(Beat)* This will conclude my career—this will be the end of all my dancing.

Lights shifting on: NIGEL *and* SKIP.

Nigel	Nobody wants excuses. The Conroy Group—you think they're gonna want excuses?
Skip	*(Beat)* No.
Nigel	I worked all my life, Skip—and I've been in jobs, places in which I was surrounded by weakness. And it's always the lads in the trenches, Skip, it's the lads what get blamed when the wheels come off.
Skip	It's not the big shots.
Nigel	Big shots don't take the blame.
Skip	Not how it works.
Nigel	I'll tell you something else; this country, these people, they've always been a conquered people, Skip. They don't really know who they are. *(Beat)* I mean, we did a lot for these people. Built their railroads—taught them mining. A lot of 'em wouldn't mind the return of the British. *(Beat)* Wouldn't mind a little of our discipline come back.
Skip	*(Pause)* All the kitchen staff left. *(Beat)* I'm too old to blow

Nigel	it this way—this kind of thing, I can't recover from this. There are things you can't control—man can't cry about it, you grit your teeth and take it on your feet, and…this is my point, Skip, you at least leave 'em with something to remember you by.
Skip	*(Pause)* There's nobody here but you and me—and your wife—nobody else. The whole fuckin' place is deserted, the goddamn generator isn't even working right, and everything is starting to smell. *(Beat)* Even I'm starting to smell bad.
Nigel	I'll stand by you, Skip—I'll tell 'em how it was.

SKIP *is taking off his shirt.*

Skip	My clothes smell— *(He's taking off his trousers)*
Nigel	Skip…
Skip	Doesn't matter how much you wash—the smells get worse anyhow. *(Beat)* The smell—like garbage, it gets in your mouth…You start tasting it, and every breath you take is rotten.
Nigel	Insidious stuff.
Skip	I don't think there's much else I can do—
Nigel	I'll tell your story, I'll tell everyone just the way it came down.
Skip	…just walk out to the water, just past midnight, isn't it? Just dive in, start swimming.
Nigel	It's a bold choice, Skip.
	SKIP *has socks and shoes off now—stripped down to his shorts.*
Skip	Just keep swimming—headed out to the caves across the lagoon—with the carvings in them, in these caves, they tell me they got ancient carvings.

Nigel	Carvings of what?
Skip	I don't know, but they're very fucking old, and it's dark in the caves, and nobody will ever find my body. Nobody.
Nigel	Nobody's gonna recover any body here.
Skip	Lost in cool dark water...disappeared...lost and gone in absolute obscurity...absolute...obscurity...absolute.

Lights shifting. DEAD WOMAN approaching LOCAL MAN.

Local Man	You have come, after all.
Dead W.	Of course.
Local Man	My brother is inside. He's been so impatient—hoping to meet you.
Dead W.	*(Smiles)* And there are sweets left?
Local Man	We prepared extra, to be certain we did not run out. We had heard about the sweet tooth of the dead. *(He extends his hand)*
Local Man	Please...
Dead W.	Thank you.

Lights fade.

The End

Demonology

by Kelly Stuart

Demonology *was first presented at the 15th Annual Padua Hills Playwrights Festival, U.S.C., Los Angeles, Califronia, in 1995. The play was directed by Robert Glaudini and Kelly Stuart with the following cast:*

De Martini: Bob Gould
Gina: Lola Glaudini
Collins: Jan Johnson
Child: Kathleen Glaudini

Act 1

Lights up. Fortieth floor of an office building. DE MARTINI's office. Spare and cold high-tech decor. A large sleek desk. A computer built into the desk occasionally casts a green glow. Behind DE MARTINI's desk, an opening through a glass wall. Behind the glass, a corridor is visible which winds around to the doors of an elevator directly visible through the glass, upstage center.

DE MARTINI sits at his desk. The elevator doors open. GINA steps out. She looks confident at first but immediately loses it, stepping into the corridor. DE MARTINI seems oblivious to her entrance. She's lost, walks off one way then reenters, winds her way around to DE MARTINI's office. For the first time, she sees DE MARTINI and tentatively steps into his office.

Gina	I'm looking for Joe De Martini.
De Martini	And you are?
Gina	Gina...
De Martini	Then, that would be me.
Gina	Oh, you're Joe De Martini.
De Martini	Yes.
Gina	Gina...

De Martini	Gina...Yes.
Gina	They said in personnel I should report to you.
De Martini	Uh, to me...yes...Excuse me...uh—
Gina	Gina.
De Martini	Gina, yes. May I suggest you do something with your hair? Your current hairstyle, it's a bit casual.
Gina	I'm sorry.
De Martini	No need to be sorry. You just have to change it. I'm sure that's easy enough for you.
Gina	Oh...of course.
De Martini	It gives you a fluffy headed appearance, and, we like our people, that is...we prefer, rather, a...glossy helmet of hair as opposed to...what your hair looks like now. Grooming and neatness are extremely important Gina.
Gina	Oh.
De Martini	So, why don't you just, take a couple minutes to try and look a little more...presentable. Hair must be swept back from the face and out of the eyes.
Gina	I understand.
De Martini	So, why don't you go do that right now.
Gina	Okay. Sure.

She goes off. He waits. She reappears in a corridor behind him, frantically pulls her hair tightly up, slicks it down, regains her poise and then reenters DE MARTINI's office. He looks at her, pleased.

| De Martini | Very good, Gina. *(Beat)* Now, regarding the telecommunications protocol. If you were to answer the phone, you use a warm, modulated tone of voice. Make sure you don't |

pitch your voice too high; that shows a lack of confidence Gina. However, since I'll be out of the office two weeks... whether or not you'll be here when I get back, I don't know... but...all of my calls will be handled by voice mail, so there is no reason to answer my phone. Nor will you need to make personal calls from this phone. There is a pay phone conveniently located on the first floor in the cafeteria. That should suffice for all personal calls which should not be made on company time. Is that understood?

Gina Yes, sir.

De Martini You are always required to display on your person an authorized security badge. Very good...I see you are wearing it. Now, your specific duties...

Gina I can type eighty-five words per hour.

De Martini Per hour?

Gina I mean, per minute.

De Martini In any case, you won't be doing much typing. You have microfiche skills?

Gina Fish?

De Martini Microfiche. Microfiche. Document retrieval.

Gina Oh. Micro *feesh*. Microfiche. Microfiche. Yes.

De Martini You'll need to print up P.O.'s from microfiche, match them to invoices and file them correctly. Your work will be audited on a random spot-check basis, by a designated supervisor assigned by personnel. You will also be required to do upkeep of data entry as provided to you by your designated supervisor.

Gina Yes, sir.

De Martini And...you really don't need to carry that briefcase Gina. Briefcases often camouflage things like, inappropriate

reading materials or snack foods which are better left
at home.

Gina Yes, sir.

De Martini *(Gestures off)* Your workspace is—there.

Gina Yes.

De Martini We use only black pen, or blue if you must, but no other
types of colored ink should be used on any documents,
especially your time card. In fact, time cards should be
rendered in number two pencil so that your supervisor can
make appropriate corrections.

Gina Yes, sir.

De Martini Well, all set...Do you understand your duties?

Gina Yes.

De Martini Well then, go ahead and get to work. And if I don't see
you when I get back, nice meeting you.

Gina Thank you.

*He exits. GINA stands there looking at the stack of papers.
She look completely baffled. The phone rings. She turns
and looks at it. It continues to ring. Lights fade out.*

*Lights up—a week later, JOE DE MARTINI sits at his desk.
COLLINS stands holding a coffee cup.*

Collins You can see her coming a mile away with that bright red
slit for a mouth. Veronica has a red bikini. She only wears
red or white or black. Those are her colors. Veronica parks
on level B, and I fucked my wife's sister in that parking lot
once. So when I saw Veronica there, Veronica...Well. I knew
it was fate. Veronica, Veronica, in the jacuzzi. Oh, what a

	pleasure she was on the eyes. Her breasts always seem to be pointing at me. It's as if there were laser beams blasting me...And now I get this.
De Martini	Jesus Christ.
Collins	In my email this morning. There's something new going on...something strange.
De Martini	Yes. Yes there is.
Collins	I know what it is. Women admire me.
De Martini	How do you know it's from a woman?
Collins	This is from Veronica. Veronica in marketing.
De Martini	Twelve other executives have come to me with similar messages. It ruined a perfect vacation in Tahoe. *(Beat)* Someone's in the hall.

De Martini grabs a file off the desk. The two men study it and murmur over it with feigned importance as Gina enters.

Collins	Let's look at those assets.
De Martini	Have you checked these with Johnson?
Collins	Yes, we should run these up Johnson's pole.
Gina	Excuse me.
De Martini	Well, uh...
Gina	Gina.
De Martini	Very good, Gina, you can put those files away please.
Gina	Yes sir.

She walks to the filing cabinet. Bends down to put away the file. Collins leers at her. She's unaware of it.

Collins	How do you like the view?

Gina	Beautiful today, isn't it.
Collins	Oh, yes.
De Martini	You can see all the way to Mt. Baldy. And that down there is downtown Glendale.
Collins	Gina, that skirt is so tight. Uh-oh.
Gina	Is this?...Is this skirt?...Is this against the dress code?
Collins	Not my dress code at least. In my dress code, my dear, all you need are two Band-Aids and a cork. Nice meeting you, Gina. *(He exits)*
De Martini	I'd like to apologize.
Gina	No problem.
De Martini	I think there is a problem.
Gina	No, not at all.
De Martini	I'm not so sure.
Gina	It's not a big deal.
De Martini	Remarks of the nature that Collins just made, constitute a hostile work environment.
Gina	I'm not the kind of person to sue someone for sexual harassment just because he's an asshole.
De Martini	Alright. Good.
Gina	Is that it? Cause Veronica wants me to type the report.
De Martini	Veronica can wait. I have to ask a few questions. But I don't want to offend you. Okay?
Gina	Okay.
De Martini	There have been some unusual events. Security breeches. Where's your security badge?
Gina	Security badge?
De Martini	You were given one by personnel. Were you not? What's that there. Your security badge. It is to be worn by you at all times. Not crumpled in your hands. Please put it on.

Gina	I know, but I wrote something on it. Something I shouldn't have written.

He grabs the badge from her.

Gina	It was a joke. Please don't read that.
De Martini	*(Reads)* I am dying?
Gina	I'm not anymore.
De Martini	This simply expresses a temporary sentiment?
Gina	Yes, but it's already over. I don't feel that way now.
De Martini	What agency are you with? You're not from Talent Tree are you?
Gina	No.
De Martini	Snappy Girl? Star?
Gina	No, I'm from Budget Temp sir.
De Martini	Budget Temp. Hmmmn. Budget Temp. Well then. Do you feel inclined to sabotage, Gina?
Gina	No.
De Martini	Are you a person who harbors bad feelings, I wonder?
Gina	No. I only harbor good feelings.
De Martini	Because if you do harbor such feeling I'd rather press matters through company channels than through an insidious crusade of sabotage.
Gina	What?
De Martini	Ten thousand pounds of baby formula were shipped to Bolivia just last week. The original order was to go to West Covina.
Gina	But they check the orders after I input them.
De Martini	Someone is going into the mainframe and changing the orders after they're checked. Okay? Here's what I think. Someone is into some sabotage here and I'm wondering why.

Gina	I have no idea.
De Martini	Someone is trying to injure the company.
Gina	It looks that way, sure.
De Martini	It does. It does look that way, Gina. I think somebody's misrepresenting herself. There is someone here who gets off on the intrigue, who finds it exciting. You look at her face and you think she's one thing, but what's really happening is not what you think and I hate that.
Gina	Well sir, I've never done anything wrong. On purpose. I have a new baby, I don't get much sleep.
De Martini	And do you—breast-feed this baby?
Gina	Yes, I do.
De Martini	And do you consider yourself to be a breast-feeding advocate?
Gina	I don't give her formula, if that's what you mean.
De Martini	So, that's why you're always running to the bathroom. To excrete your milk.
Gina	Yes.
De Martini	And this..."breast" milk is in the freezer? Here? On the premises?
Gina	Yes.
De Martini	I can get you free formula.
Gina	No thanks. No thank you sir.
De Martini	Why not?
Gina	Because I have my own milk.
De Martini	You also have a spot on your blouse. A wet spot there.
Gina	Oh.
De Martini	Why don't you borrow my jacket?
Gina	Thank you. *(Pause)* I know about this company. What this company did. But, I'm hoping that was an accident. I like working here, it's a really nice building.

De Martini	What did this company do?
Gina	Oh, you know, bad baby formula.
De Martini	No, I certainly don't know about that. Where did you hear it?
Gina	I don't remember...somebody...just some friends of mine knew and they wondered how I could work here. Ethically you know, morally.
De Martini	Yes.
Gina	But I hope...it was just accidental. Right? Maybe...Bad judgment. Some misunderstanding which caused...some death, some babies to die. Some, hundreds of babies. Am I right?
De Martini	People here don't talk about that.
Gina	I'm sure they don't. It's a little unnerving.
De Martini	Why are you talking about it to me?
Gina	I just felt like saying, like it's something unsaid. Everybody thinks about it but nobody says it.
De Martini	What makes you think they think about it?
Gina	All the bomb scares maybe. Last week I brought a briefcase to work and it...
De Martini	So that was your briefcase there with the bomb squad.
Gina	I don't know how it got down there. I think someone took it and put it in the lobby.
De Martini	Then phoned in a threat.
Gina	Yes, that's what I think.
De Martini	Why didn't you speak up?
Gina	When I saw that robot, trying to detonate my briefcase, I thought...I was sure I'd be fired.
De Martini	Some very provocative items in that briefcase.
Gina	Yes, and that robot ripped them to shreds.
De Martini	Why did you bring those items to work?

Gina	I think that's all, sir. That's all I want to say. I think I'd better go to the ladies room now. Thank you for the temporary use of your coat.

The light is changing to something otherworldly. Seductively she slips his coat off her shoulders and hands it to him. She steps into the corridor. He follows her into the corridor and watches as she exits. He puts on his coat, reaches a hand in his pocket. He pulls out a note, silently reads it.

De Martini	What's this?...Jesus Christ.

COLLINS enters.

De Martini	Look at this! *(Hands COLLINS the note)*
Collins	This is a very explicit note.
De Martini	She must have slipped it in the pocket of my coat.
Collins	Maybe she got our coats mixed up.

COLLINS and DE MARTINI walk around the corridor and stand in the area in front of the elevator. COLLINS reads the note. His voice is excited by what he reads. At the same time, GINA enters DE MARTINI's office. The lights have dimmed. She puts her briefcase on his desk, sits in his chair, she has a mysterious expression on her face.

Collins	*(Reading the note)* "I am here, and I know you are there in your office. I press myself against the wall and I sense the warmth in your body. When you are at lunch I sit in your chair and I open and close your desk drawer and I

put my fingers on all the pens and pencils that you have been touching. I want to devour you. I want to choke to death on you."

De Martini   That's enough, give it back. Ever since she came to work here, things have really gone to shit.

Collins   Who, Gina?

De Martini   Yes. Gina, what if it's her?

Collins   And she's writing these notes to all the men here.

De Martini   To all the important men. And she's waiting to see how we respond. So, how do I respond?

Collins   I call Veronica on her extension, and when she answers, I just hang up.

De Martini   But, there is a higher moral question here. Gina is a person. She's my employee. I have power, over Gina...

Lights cross fade to DE MARTINI's *office. Music plays.*

GINA *opens the briefcase, takes out a plastic funnel and breast pump. She unbuttons her blouse and begins to pump her milk. She gets up and pumps her milk to the music, dances as she pumps then takes a bag of milk she's pumped and puts it into the briefcase. Sits down, puts everything away. Quickly buttons up her blouse. Snaps the briefcase shut. Sits with her eyes closed as if napping.*

Music stops as COLLINS *and* DE MARATINI *enter, are surprised to see* GINA. *She opens her eyes.*

Gina   Sorry...Joe...Mr. De Martini. I thought...I'm sorry, I thought you were at lunch.

De Martini	What are you doing here?
Gina	Taking a break.
De Martini	In my office?
Gina	I needed somewhere, quiet and dark.
Collins	Why?
Gina	So I could think about things.
De Martini	You didn't think about going through my desk? Looking through confidential files?
Gina	No.
Collins	What were you thinking about?
Gina	My thoughts are my own private property.
Collins	I made a mess of myself last night, just thinking of you.
Gina	*(Good naturedly)* You really are a pig, aren't you.
Collins	Oh, yes, yes I am.
Gina	Better go take your mud bath then.
Collins	You look really nice today, Gina. *(Exits)*
De Martini	I'm more than surprised to find you in here.
Gina	When you're in the file room for three hours straight, the letters and numbers start marching together. I needed a quiet place to sit down. That's all. It's perfectly innocent.
De Martini	It sounds like you're not very happy in your job.
Gina	Are you?
De Martini	That's a personal question.
Gina	But that's what you asked me.
De Martini	As it pertains to your work performance, which in regards to me, is none of your concern. I see that you've got a new briefcase Gina. What's in it?
Gina	My personal items.
De Martini	I think there's something more. I think you hate this company. You hate the people who work for this company. You think

	you're different from everyone. Better. You imagine yourself with a soul. A precious quivering beautiful soul that shrinks each day you are forced to come work here. You imagine your soul emits horrible screams which only you yourself can hear. Like a lobster dropped into boiling water, and what you want is some kind of revenge.
Gina	The truth is, I love working here. I've learned a million things about the world, from typing, from data entry, from filing. Everything inside those files represents something. Something immense. Tons and tons of powdered formula. Thousands of cows and people and grass and land. Packaging. Factories. Retail stores. The trucks that drive there. And I get to see it all through the computer. Millions of people buying and selling all over this country. It's like a giant crystal ball. Even this building, it's more than a building. All that glass and marble and steel. The way it juts up into the sky, so erect, so shiny and hard. I get this feeling it's almost alive, and it's trying to say something to us.
De Martini	I really just need to see the contents of your briefcase, Gina.
Gina	I told you, it's personal.

He grabs briefcase, they struggle.

De Martini	You signed a confidentiality agreement when you came to work here, did you not? You promised to submit your belongings to inspection of authorized authorities. *(He gets it open, gasps)* These implements. This funnel, this vial...is...is this what you use to collect your milk?
Gina	Yes.

De Martini	If I've invaded your privacy in any way, please accept my sincerest apologies. This I presume is your milk? It's so warm.
Gina	That's the way it comes out.
De Martini	And you just did this? Here, in my office?
Gina	Yes. I take it home to my baby.
De Martini	Why? Why here in my office?
Gina	I just needed a quiet place.
De Martini	And you felt that being here, in my office is conducive.
Gina	Yes, it's very conducive.
De Martini	I don't recommend that you let people know about, what you do—in my office or otherwise.
Gina	Someone could get the wrong idea about our relationship.
De Martini	Which is strictly professional...Gina, I got your message.
Gina	What message?
De Martini	The message.
Gina	Did I leave you a message?
De Martini	Did you?
Gina	I don't remember that I did.
De Martini	Are you saying you never gave me a message?
Gina	Right.
De Martini	And if you did give me a message, I shouldn't consider it?
Gina	I don't know what you're talking about.
De Martini	No message then, the message is canceled.
Gina	Was this an unsigned phone message?
De Martini	All messages are to be signed with your initials, is that understood?
Gina	Yes.
De Martini	Please, in the future...please, Gina, please: Don't leave me any messages that you cannot acknowledge.

452

COLLINS sticks his head in the office.

Collins	Send them to me. Joe time for lunch.
De Martini	You may continue to sit at my desk as long as you wish.
Gina	Thank you.
De Martini	And would you—answer the phone? For me?
Gina	Of course.
De Martini	Answer it—*(Italian accent)* Joe De Martini's office, may I take a message. Only don't use that accent.
Gina	Yes, sir.

COLLINS and DE MARTINI exit. Pause. GINA sits at his desk. She picks up the telephone and dials.

Gina Hello Mark?...What's wrong?...Are you sticking pins in her Mark? Why is she crying like that?...I know you'd never do that, so why do you say that? I'm working. Understand? I'm here because I am working. You are not. Mark? Mark, don't do that to me. Don't you fucking do that to me! Don't hold the phone to the baby's mouth when she's screaming. You bastard. Goddamn you shithead. You hear me?

The other line starts ringing. She puts MARK on hold, picks up the other line.

Gina This is...uh...Joe De Martini's office. May I take a message? Hello?...Hello?

She hangs up. DE MARTINI enters.

De Martini	Gina...that was me. I was checking to see how you'd answer the phone. You've passed the intelligence test.
Gina	That's good to know.
De Martini	And you exhibit a...genuine interest in your duties. *(Suspicious)* Why is that?
Gina	Because of you, sir.
De Martini	Because of me?
Gina	You make working here an interesting thing.
De Martini	Do I?
Gina	You do. I'm a temporary here. I'd like to be a permanent.
De Martini	That could be arranged. How would you like to be my assistant?
Gina	Would this be considered a promotion?
De Martini	You could consider it that.
Gina	How about financially?
De Martini	That could be done.
Gina	I'm making seven dollars an hour, I'd like to make fifteen, for a start.
De Martini	We'll simply...upgrade your skill rating, which up until now has been vastly underrated.

She moves towards him.

Gina	I'm really grateful to you, I want you to know that.
De Martini	Thank you, and I do know that, Gina.
Gina	I'm going to show you how grateful I am, you'll see, you've made the right decision.

He sees the phone. A line on hold.

454

De Martini	Gina, this line...
Gina	Excuse me. I'll be right back. *(She starts to go)*
De Martini	This line on hold here—
Gina	I have to go to the ladies' room, sir.
De Martini	This line here, on hold—this red light blinking like a demon's eye.

She exits. He picks up the phone, at first there's no sound.

De Martini	This is Joe De Martini.

Then the sound of a baby's whimper.

De Martini	Who's there?

Now the sound of a baby's crying.

De Martini	Who is this goddamn it!

The crying gets louder and louder. DE MARTINI hangs up. Silence.

De Martini	Jesus Christ.

DE MARTINI's eyes fix on GINA's briefcase. He opens it, takes out the bag of milk. He cradles it in his hands for a moment then puts it in an accordion file. COLLINS enters.

Collins	You look like the cat that's had the canary.
De Martini	I can assure you I've had nothing but plain dry cat food.

Collins	So, what was Gina really doing in your office?
De Martini	*(Clutching the file)* Nothing...nothing at all.
Collins	Joe, are you alright? You look pale.
De Martini	I feel like the blood has drained from my head.

GINA enters.

Collins	Yes, and I know where it's drained to.
De Martini	I just made Gina a permanent employee. Assigned to my office.
Collins	Well, I've heard she takes excellent dick-tation.
De Martini	Get us some coffee please. Would you Gina?
Gina	Surely. *(She moves to get coffee. Stops)* Milk?
De Martini	What?
Gina	Milk in your coffee?
Collins	Yes, please.
Gina	Mr. De Martini? Milk?

End of scene.

Transition: red special on DE MARTINI, as he hears the word "milk" (voice over by GINA) spoken over and over with music underneath. As lights come up, GINA is walking back and forth in front of his desk as she works. From her workspace offstage to the filing cabinet and back over and over. DE MARTINI watches her as the music with the word "milk" continues to play. Every time he hears the word "milk" DE MARTINI reacts. After several crosses, GINA turns, stops, the lights become normal. Music cuts out.

Gina	Am I bothering you?
De Martini	I noticed you seem to be walking back and forth.
Gina	Yes.
De Martini	Back and forth, back and forth. All day long.
Gina	I'm sorry. Am I making you nervous?
De Martini	No.
Gina	You seem nervous. Your hands are shaking. Sir...are you alright?
De Martini	It's just...all this walking back and forth. Like a duck in a shooting gallery.
Gina	Well, I hope you don't want to shoot me. Do you?
De Martini	Not quite.

DE MARTINI runs offstage, returns pushing her entire table, papers, and all into his office. He runs off again and returns with a rolling chair, puts it in place for her. This should be done with accompaniment to music so it's like a little performance.

De Martini	This should save wear and tear on your shoes.
Gina	Oh, I never would have thought of that myself. I guess that's why you're an executive.
De Martini	You need to conserve your energy.
Gina	Why?
De Martini	Because...there are special demands on your resources.

The lights suddenly dim. The phone rings. DE MARTINI nods to GINA to answer it. She walks over to this desk, picks up.

| Gina | Joe De Martini's office. Oh...How long is that going to |

	take? Okay. Uh-huh. *(She hangs up)* The main frame crashed. They won't have it back on line until two.
De Martini	Jesus.
Gina	Does that happen a lot?
De Martini	Recently, yes.
Gina	It seems like such a big intimidating system.
De Martini	You've seen it?
Gina	The systems guys gave me a tour.
De Martini	When was this?
Gina	Yesterday, before I went home.
De Martini	No one is allowed to go in there except specially authorized personnel.
Gina	The guys authorized me. Anyway, it probably just got tired and shut down. I'd get tired, too, if I was on twenty-four hours a day.
De Martini	Computers don't have feelings, Gina. They're simply machines. Susceptible to tampering.
Gina	Tampering?
De Martini	Yes. Tampering fingers.
Gina	Oh...I see...I need to go to the ladies' room sir. Excuse me.
De Martini	Gina...
Gina	I'll hurry. *(She exits)*
De Martini	Why is it that whenever I'm going to confront an employee, she runs off to the ladies' room? She seems to have so many physical needs.

COLLINS *enters.*

Collins	You weren't in the meeting.
De Martini	No.

Collins	Something remarkable happened during Johnson's presentation. First he spoke of some damaging problems. Things that look like, industrial sabotage. Someone with access into the system, rerouting orders into infinity. Revoking credit to our most trusted customers. Causing havoc. Havoc and chaos. Then as Johnson flicked off the lights, the first image on the overhead projector was a pair of succulent moon-like breasts. And desperately as he flipped through his pages, we saw more and more pictures of breasts and body parts. And Johnson, who was a V.P., has now been suspended without pay. And you'll never guess who was asked to take over after Johnson's departure?
De Martini	You were.
Collins	No. Veronica.
De Martini	Veronica?
Collins	Veronica, she's a very smart girl. She's collected almost six million dollars in payment from accounts in arrears. And now, she's my fucking boss.
De Martini	Yes, and I'd like to know how she did that.
Collins	You think Johnson put breasts in his own report?
De Martini	Of course not. No. *(Quietly paranoid)* The La Leche League. Ever heard of them?
Collins	No.
Collins	These are a group of radical breast-feeders.
Collins	You've seen the movie *Planet of the Apes*?
De Martini	Yes. The apes take over the earth.
Collins	Substitute what for apes?...Planet of the Women.

The phone rings. De Martini *picks it up.*

De Martini	De Martini speaking. Gina? No. She stepped out. Who wants her? Where? What does he want? I'll be right down. *(Hangs up)* Excuse me, Skip. Something's come up.

DE MARTINI exits. COLLINS stands there, toys with items on GINA'S desk. GINA enters. She looks around registers that DE MARTINI is gone.

Gina	Mr. De Martini's not in at the moment.
Collins	Actually, you're the one I came to see.
Gina	I can't print any reports right now. The computer is down. Down again.
Collins	That computer's been down a lot lately.
Gina	Yes. It seems to "go down" all the time.
Collins	It never used to be that way. Something is wreaking havoc on the system. Or someone. We're all curious about you, Gina.
Gina	Who?
Collins	All the men here. You've got us all curious.
Gina	I'm not any different than that rest of you.
Collins	I'd say you are.
Gina	What about Mr. De Martini. What does he really think of me?
Collins	Oh, respects you. Completely respects you.
Gina	And I have a lot of respect for him.
Collins	What's so great about him?
Gina	Large sums of money flow through his hands, like a river, and he directs the flow.
Collins	You're getting to be very business-minded working here.
Gina	There are so many bankruptcies right now. That's fascinating.

Collins	We're seeing a lot of chapter elevens right now, that's right.
Gina	It's like a virus.
Collins	It is like a virus. Yes.
Gina	Why is that? First one and then the other. All of these companies going under. It's almost like it's some kind of wave.
Collins	A wave and a virus, yes. All those things.
Gina	What is going on Mr. Collins.

COLLINS grows more and more flustered.

Collins	Well, basically, what happens is this. One company starts to *go down*, and that makes it *hard* for...company two, uh...Once you're *behind*, you can't get a...*head*. So both companies fall...into the...red. And since company two has reneged on its fees, then company two sucks company three...down under, deep like a stone...because, commerce...uh, you can't do it alone.
Gina	And if someone had the capital to buy out these companies ...while they were down.
Collins	Then that person would be in an exquisite position for an excellent deal.
Gina	That is so interesting.
Collins	I only regret that between us, we haven't got the capital to pool to...
Gina	Is this company going to go bankrupt Mr. Collins?

Elevator doors open. DE MARTINI steps out. He's horrified to see COLLINS and GINA standing so close together. He rushes around the corridor to get to the office.

| Collins | Oh, no...not this company, no. |

DE MARTINI enters the office.

De Martini	There's a disheveled young man in the lobby asking to see you.
Gina	Oh, my God.
De Martini	He's got a small bundle, and I assume from the noises emitted, this bundle contains some type of human infant. I told him that per my request, you would call him on the lobby extension.

GINA picks up the phone. DE MARTINI gestures to COLLINS to stand out in the corridor. They watch GINA through the glass.

Gina	Why do you have to be so lame? Mark? Have you been smoking pot again? Mark? Pot? Around the baby? No. No... It does not help her sleep. You're stupid. You're going to blow your parole. Don't call me that. Fuck you, Mark. Is that what you want? I'll be right down. *(She hangs up)*
De Martini	Everything all right?
Gina	I just have to...take her some milk.
De Martini	She seems to be a ravenous thing.
Gina	I'll go.
De Martini	So, that was your husband?
Gina	Yes.
De Martini	Lucky thing these windows are so thick or I bet some people might be tempted to jump.
Gina	I won't be long. *(Grabs her briefcase. Exits)*
Collins	I've got some reports for Gina to type.

De Martini	You've got your own secretary, Skip.
Collins	She's got an empty slot for a brain. Anyway, she quit. She just quit on me. Some of these girls are so temperamental. I've got these spreadsheets that have to be typed and Gina is fast.
De Martini	Gina's very busy right now. I've got her on this backlog of filing.
Collins	I need someone now.
De Martini	Call personnel, get yourself another girl.

The phone rings. DE MARTINI answers.

De Martini	Joe De Martini's office, De Martini speaking. Hello Veronica. No. Not at all. No Veronica, I haven't seen him. *(Beat)* Well, if I do, I will certainly tell him. What? Gina? She stepped out for a moment. You can tell me. Xerox Each New Account. Okay. Yes I can repeat that back to you Veronica. Xerox Each New Account. What? You want me to...One second. Xerox Each New Account. Yes...Yes...I am writing that down Veronica. I'll tell her. Will do. *(Hangs up)* Xerox Each New Account. What if it's some kind of code.
Collins	You're paranoid Joe. *(Pause, then alarmed)* What did she say about me?
De Martini	Just that she wants to see you in her office. Right away.

GINA enters. COLLINS looks at her, exits slowly. GINA sits down, starts typing. DE MARTINI stands staring at her, her typing slowly coming to a halt.

| De Martini | Am I disturbing you, Gina? |

Gina	No.
De Martini	Why did you stop typing?
Gina	I thought you were going to tell me something.
De Martini	What gave you that impression?
Gina	When someone looks at you...keeps looking at you.
De Martini	Are you accusing me of staring at you?
Gina	I'm missing a bag of milk.
De Martini	That's terrible.
Gina	No, it's just strange. I thought I put it in my briefcase.
De Martini	I hope no one took it and put it in their coffee.
Gina	That would be stupid and infantile wouldn't it.
De Martini	Not if your milk was left unsecured. That would've been naive on your part, at best. And at worst, a provocative act.

COLLINS appears, waiting in front of the elevator. He can't hear what DE MARTINI says through the glass. COLLINS gives DE MARTINI a friendly wave. DE MARTINI waves back. It's clear DE MARTINI is indicating to GINA that COLLINS is probably the guilty party.

De Martini	What if some employee possessed—a twisted sense of inter-personal relationships. To an idiot like that, seeing your milk, such an idiot may believe that you want your milk taken.

The elevator doors open and COLLINS steps in. The elevator doors close.

Gina	I'd feel sorry for that person.
De Martini	Yes. Such a person as that is obviously sick. And in need of your pity. *(Pause)* You know—I've got a special little

freezer in the lounge, the executive lounge...I think your milk would be safer in there.

Gina   So, what do I do...just give it to you?

End of scene.

Transition: a red special up on DE MARTINI. *Other lights change to greenish otherworldly light. There is a green light from the desk computer glowing on his face. Music plays, and a taped voice over with the music of* GINA's *voice saying "Give it to you...Give it to you..."*

DE MARTINI *takes out the bag of milk hidden in the accordion file. He stares at it intently.*

De Martini   Xerox Each New Account. Xerox Each New Account.

He lets a little of the milk drip out onto the glass of his computer. He draws the letters onto the glass.

De Martini   X.E.N.A...X.E.N.A.

He inadvertently puts a finger in his mouth. He tastes the milk on his finger. His expression becomes one of demented understanding.

De Martini   *(Pronounces the word)* XENA. What does that mean.

XENA!?

He suddenly bites into the bag of milk and drinks. He finishes the bag, looks out.

De Martini XENA!!!

Lights fade out.

End of Act 1

Act 2

Lights up. The lighting is otherwordly. DE MARTINI has just finished the milk. There's a CHILD demon watching him.

Child	Working late?
De Martini	You could say that.
Child	Why are you drinking the baby's milk?
De Martini	I never had it. I never got to have it.
Child	The mother is going to be mad at you.
De Martini	I'll refill the bag with coffee creamer. She'll never know.
Child	The baby knows.
De Martini	Lucky for me, babies can't talk.
Child	Everything talks when you learn how to listen.
De Martini	Is that what's happening to me?
Child	You can't stop thinking of Xena.
De Martini	Yes. Xena.

GINA appears. She carries files, she seems to be doing ordinary office tasks. Her mouth moves but the words we hear are taped voice over and completely the opposite of what GINA seems to be saying. She should mouth phrases that are critical of DE MARTINI. The CHILD demon moves her mouth so that she seems to be the one saying the words we hear from "XENA."

De Martini	Gina?
Xena (V.O.)	No. My real name is Xena. It means stranger in Greek.
De Martini	What do you want from me Xena?
Xena (V.O.)	I want an explosion. I want it so bad.
De Martini	I can't give that to you.
Xena (V.O.)	Do you want me to teach you, Joe?
De Martini	Yes...
Xena (V.O.)	I know you. I know your whole life. Meaningless conversations that add up to nothing as numbers gnaw away at your groin. Nothing you say means anything, Joe. You say what you have to say in the moment. You want to please me, that's why you drink. But you've got to prove you can handle it, Joe, you've got to prove that you're really a man.
De Martini	But I am a man, aren't I?

She exits.

De Martini	Xena?
Child	Part of Xena has gotten inside you.
De Martini	Through the milk?
Child	Are you in pain?

The CHILD goes behind DE MARTINI and begins massaging his shoulders.

De Martini	It's a sort of pain. Images inside my head of me and...
Child	Xena.
De Martini	Yes. Who are you?
Child	Child Assassin.

The CHILD grabs DE MARTINI's head, slams it down hard on the desk. Exits. GINA enters. Lights restore to normal office lighting.

Gina   Good morning, Mr. De Martini.

De Martini   Are you on drugs?

Gina   Of course not.

De Martini   How do I know that?

Gina   It's not just me who'd be affected.

De Martini   That is also my fear.

Gina   If you want me to take a urine test, I'll do it, okay? Whatever you want.

The CHILD crosses through the upstage corridor. DE MARTINI sees her, GINA does not.

De Martini   You are on something. Some kind of substance.

Gina   No, I'm not.

De Martini   Then, what was that...that *thing* I just saw.

Gina   Why would you see things if I'm the one on drugs.

De Martini   I am expert at reading facial tics. I noted you had a reaction just then.

Gina   I was only reacting to you, sir, you seem so upset.

De Martini   Do you remember telling me you felt this building was alive?

Gina   Yes.

De Martini   What exactly did you mean?

Gina   It was just something to say.

De Martini   Are you that much of a birdbrain, Gina, that you don't even know what you mean when you speak?

Gina	Nothing we say means anything, sir, we say what we have to say in the moment.
De Martini	Xena.
Gina	Gina.
De Martini	No. Xena. It means, "Stranger in Greek." You told me about it.
Gina	I don't remember that.
De Martini	No?
Gina	Maybe you were dreaming.
De Martini	Did you have any—dreams...last night?
Gina	Maybe.
De Martini	Please, tell me about it.
Gina	I had this dream that...my baby was gone. I looked everywhere for her...Finally I opened the door to the freezer and found my husband had put her in there. She was frozen solid as a rock. Her face was blue, and I held her in my arms. Then I woke up.
De Martini	But that was just...just a bad dream.
Gina	That's right. And it's a brilliant morning.
Child	*(From off, imitates GINA)* That's right, and it's a brilliant morning!
De Martini	Are you concealing a child in here?
Gina	No.
De Martini	I swear to God I just heard one.
Child	Swear to God...
De Martini	Gina, are you toying with my head.
Child	Toying with my head.
Gina	No...not at all.
De Martini	But...didn't you hear that child just then.
Child	Child just then.

470

Gina	No.
De Martini	I swear to God I just heard a child *imitating me.*
Child	*Imitating me.*
De Martini	SHUT UP!...Please. Please shut up.

The CHILD makes a loud slurping sound. DE MARTINI tries to plug his ears.

Gina	Sir? Is there something I can do for you, sir?
De Martini	I can't...spell it out. You've got to just know.
Gina	I've had special training for that, sir.
De Martini	You have?
Gina	I'll take care of you. I'll take care of everything. Excuse me. *(She exits. The CHILD appears)*
Child	There is nothing so encouraging as getting away with your first crime.
De Martini	Are you some type of maniacal force?
Child	The word you search for is manifestation. How are you feeling, Joe?
De Martini	Thirsty.
Child	The more you drink, the thirstier you'll get.
De Martini	Why?
Child	You've got to drink more to find out. Everything has a meaning here, Joe. There is a great significance to signs. *(Gestures to the phone)* This for instance.
De Martini	It's a telephone, right?
Child	And it's about to ring. In ten seconds.
Child	Ten...nine...eight...
De Martini	And who's going to call?
Child	Seven...six...five...

De Martini	Is it going to be Xena?
Child	Four...three...two...*one.*

The phone rings. DE MARTINI *stares at it, excited. He picks it up.*

De Martini	Hello?
	Oh...it's you.
	I'm sorry, Skip. I was expecting a call.
	What is it?
	Just a moment. *(Looks at the* CHILD*)*
	He wants to know if I'm alone.
Child	Yes, you're alone.
De Martini	Yes, I'm alone.
	Yes...Yes...I'm sure I'm alone.
	Oh...I see...
	Where did you get it.
	Well then.
	You'd better bring that right up. *(He hangs up)*
	How did you know that call was coming?
Child	I made it come. I can make everything come.
De Martini	Can you teach me how to do that?
Child	There's a lot I can teach you, Joe, but learning, it's sometimes a painful thing.
De Martini	Can't be much more painful than how I feel right now, can it.

The elevator opens, COLLINS *steps out. The* CHILD *watches as* COLLINS *approaches.*

Child	Excuse me. *(The* CHILD *exits.* COLLINS *enters the office)*

Collins	This is it, baby. We got 'em now. Red level security clearance, custom made by the guys in systems.

Music comes out of the computer and a woman's voice giggling and saying, "Oh...Oh..."

Collins	Virtual Veronica.

Virtual Veronica

Oh...*oh*, It's so *big*!

Collins	Point and click on any object you want her to suck.

GINA enters. VIRTUAL VERONICA continues to giggle and say "Oh! Oh!"

Gina	What's that?
Collins	It's something bad.
De Martini	Mr. Collins.
Collins	I'm a bad man, Gina.

GINA looks at the computer screen. VIRTUAL VERONICA's voice can be heard saying:

Virtual Veronica

You look like you need a blow job, sir. Oh...Oh...

Collins	Virtual Veronica.

DE MARTINI shuts the computer off.

Collins	You're not mad are you, Gina?
Gina	No.
Collins	Why not?

Gina	When you see a cockroach, do you get mad at it?
Collins	No.
Gina	You might step on it, or spray it with poison, but you don't get mad at it for being a bug.
Collins	Oh, no. Oh, no. Not at all. *(Suddenly he realizes this is a put-down. He takes his disk)* Excuse me.

COLLINS exits. GINA has seated herself at the desk and is writing something on a legal pad. DE MARTINI watches her with alarm.

De Martini	What's that you're writing?
Gina	Nothing.
De Martini	Do you write down conversations you hear in this office?
Gina	Why would I do that?
De Martini	For documentation.
Gina	I should, you're so witty.
De Martini	No, as a means to attack us legally.
Gina	I was just writing a note to myself.
De Martini	May I see it?
Gina	Yes. This is my self-affirmation.
De Martini	*(Reading)* "Desire can be transmitted to its physical equivalent."
Gina	That's right. It's from a book called *Think and Grow Rich*.
De Martini	What does it mean?
Gina	Thoughts are things.
De Martini	Thoughts are things?
Gina	Sure. You think about anything enough, you can get it. *(A beat. She opens her briefcase, takes out a bag of milk and slowly walks over to him)* You said you could take care of this?

| De Martini | Yes. I can. |

Transition: a special light on DE MARTINI. *Other lighting becomes otherworldly.* GINA *has exited.* DE MARTINI *takes a bag of milk and drinks it, sucking it like a baby. As he drinks, music plays, the same music from the "Virtual Veronica" computer game.* GINA *enters in the guise of* XENA. *She moves to the music, shimmying her breasts at him as she walks. She dumps an accordion file out on his desk. Instead of papers there are bags of milk in them.*

XENA *walks back and forth from* DE MARTINI'*s desk to the filing drawer, filing away the bags of milk. We hear taped voice over.*

Xena (V.O)	You suffer like a baby in the body of a man.
De Martini	Yes.
Xena (V.O.)	It's intense.
De Martini	Yes it is.
Xena (V.O.)	I can take all your suffering away. Give you what you never had in your life. What you should've had the first day you were born...and you need so much more, because you're a man.
De Martini	Oh!
Xena (V.O.)	I'm going to take care of you. All the way.
De Martini	All the way?
Xena (V.O.)	Yes. *(She's filed all the bags of milk out of sight. She seems to be almost touching him, her breasts right in his face. Then she turns abruptly—)*Excuse me one moment. *(She exits)*
De Martini	Wha! Wha! Wha! *Xena!*

Gina enters. Lights bump to normal lighting. Gina has heard his babylike outburst.

Gina   Gina.

The phone rings. Gina rushes to answer it. As she's on the phone, De Martini is searching through files, looking for bags of milk. He doesn't find any, comes up with only papers.

Joe De Martini's office. Gina speaking... Okay...red hanging file folders. Binders in aqua. Pushpins...I'd better shoot the rest over on email. Mr. De Martini is standing right here. *(She hangs up)* Veronica asked me to thank you.

De Martini   For what?

Gina   The monthly report you prepared was the clearest most accurate ever.

De Martini   But...you prepared that report.

Gina   But you taught me how. You've taught me so much. I wish there was something I could do for you.

De Martini   I wish we could talk without subterfuge.

Gina   So do I.

De Martini   But we can't.

Gina   And that is a horrible, horrible thing.

De Martini   You know, everything we do here is monitored. How fast you type, the percentage of errors, the amount of time you spend on the phone. The sensor wires under the carpet monitor wherever you walk.

Gina   And this is all, like...recorded in a big computer somewhere?

De Martini   Yes. Most employees don't know that. Just keep it our secret.

Gina	That's why I really want to go to computer school. Computers. That's the power. Could you get this department to pay for some classes? Computer classes for me?

COLLINS enters. DE MARTINI moves away from GINA.

Collins	Want to hear a pussy joke?
De Martini	No.
Collins	Come on. Pussy jokes are funny.
Gina	Because you don't have one.
Collins	Joe—what's the difference between pussy and sushi? *(Beat)* Sushi comes with rice.

GINA sits down at her computer.

Collins	You weren't offended were you, Gina?

GINA gives him a blank stare.

	'Cause, if you have a joke you want to say to me about...penises or something. Then we'd be even.
Gina	That's okay.
Collins	Taking the moral high ground?
Gina	I'm not taking any ground at all. I just...haven't heard any appropriate jokes worth repeating.
Collins	Okay, how about an inappropriate joke?
Gina	What's the difference between you and a bucket of vomit?

Beat. The phone rings. GINA answers it.

	Joe De Martini's office. Gina speaking.
	Yes. He's here.
	Chartreuse.
	Nine-and-a-half inches.
	I'll tell him. *(She hangs up)*
De Martini	What is it?
Gina	Veronica wants Mr. Collins in her office.
Collins	Regarding what?
Gina	I don't know.
Collins	Why didn't you ask? You're a secretary right? Isn't that what secretaries do? They ask, "And what is this regarding?" Don't they? Isn't that part of your job?
Gina	I'm not a secretary, I'm a personal assistant.
De Martini	Excuse me, Gina, you are a subordinate. You will offer your secretarial services to any guest or visitor of this office.
Gina	Yes, sir.
Collins	Thank you, Joe.
De Martini	Get Veronica back on the line and find out what she wants right now. And you can tell her we're in the middle of a meeting.

GINA *dials.*

Gina	Veronica? Mr. Collins is in a meeting at the moment. He'd like to know what this is regarding.
De Martini	Very good, Gina.
Gina	Yes. They really are in a meeting. Yes, that's what they told me to say, but they are, uh, meeting. Standing right here. Yes. I'll tell him. *(She hangs up)* She said you already know what you've done. She sounded mad.

478

Collins	Shit.
Gina	She wants you right now.

COLLINS exits.

De Martini	I asked you to tell her that we were in a meeting.
Gina	I said...I did say that.
De Martini	I hope we are not having a problem with you doing what I need you to do.
Gina	She knew I was lying.
De Martini	I thought you were more skilled at deception.
Gina	No, I'm not. But if that's how I have to be, I'm sure you can teach me.
De Martini	What is that supposed to mean?
Gina	Just what I said. *(Sits down at the keyboard, types furiously)*
De Martini	Sometimes Gina, in the performance of a job, we've all got to take a little criticism. It's nothing to give yourself a headache about.
Gina	Others might give me a headache. I would never do that to myself.

On the wall, a shadow fades up. It seems to be DE MARTINI's shadow, yet it has the unmistakable shape of the Devil, with horns, and a large erect penis. GINA doesn't see it. DE MARTINI is at first not aware of it.

De Martini	You know, sometimes criticism is actually praise. It may not always be possible for me, the employer to reveal the intentions behind my directives, no matter how much I may wish to reveal them. *(Sees his devilish shadow, freezes)*

	But whatever you think of me Gina, I am not the Devil.
Gina	Neither am I.
De Martini	My intentions are good.
Gina	Usually I perceive you as good.
De Martini	Usually...Yes.
Gina	You have your days, but, so does everyone right? It's just human.
De Martini	Yes.
Gina	We're both human beings.
De Martini	And maybe there is more, variety than I'd thought in the scope of what it is to be human.
Gina	I think so.

He looks fearfully at his shadow. GINA *still doesn't see it.*

De Martini	And no matter how much one's behavior may, mirror the personality of—Satan.
Gina	You know, the word for Satan, from the original Hebrew, actually meant an obstacle put in one's path by god...as a challenge. The Devil worked on God's behalf. I learned that in college.
De Martini	That is...very interesting. *(He sees that the devilish shadow has faded)*
Gina	Interesting but useless. I need training in computers.
De Martini	If I arranged for you to be trained, in some aspect of computer operations...
Gina	Yes?
De Martini	You would no longer be my assistant.
Gina	I wouldn't be anyone's assistant would I.
De Martini	No. They'd have you transferred away.

Gina	I'd miss working for you.
De Martini	Would you?
Gina	Of course, if I was promoted...I'd always come visit.
De Martini	I like the way you do things, Gina. Nobody else does things like you. I'd miss that.
Gina	We'd see each other in the cafeteria. We could eat lunch together.
De Martini	You've misunderstood. I wouldn't miss you. *Socially*—I find that you are especially suited to lubricating the daily operations of this office. And without this skillful lubrication, things would dry up, would—fall apart completely. I can't afford to take that chance.
Gina	I just want to really be an asset.
De Martini	Believe me, you are an extremely fine asset.
Gina	So, you won't recommend me for computer training. Or further advancement.
De Martini	It's simply not feasible.

GINA sits down and types. Her typing takes on an irregular rhythm like Morse code. The CHILD appears.

| Child | Can you hear that typing? |

DE MARTINI nods.

Do you know what it means? She's talking to you.
She's typing in code.

As GINA continues to type, we hear a voice over of XENA.

Xena (V.O.)	Dear sir...If you understand this code, come close to me, and open your mouth. I will continue to type, and ignore you.

DE MARTINI gets up, stands near GINA with his mouth open.

	I can see the milk in your mouth. I know that you have been tasting me. I know that the taste is living inside you, and I know you want more.
De Martini	Yes. Oh yes...but, how do I get more?
Gina	Sir?
De Martini	Please, keep typing, Gina.
Gina	It's difficult to talk to you and type at the same time.
De Martini	Then don't talk.
Gina	You asked me a question.
De Martini	The verbal responses you make aren't important. In fact, they're confusing me.
Gina	I try so hard to be a good worker, to do my job well, but sometimes it seems like my real job consists of letting you grind me down.
De Martini	It is not my intention to grind you, be it down or otherwise. *Now type.*
Child	Ignore what she says, that's just decoy speech.
Gina	Let's just forget we had this conversation.
De Martini	Right.
Xena (V.O.)	Milk sucker.
De Martini	What?
Child	Keep listening.
Gina	There is no reason to be so emotional over a trivial workplace exchange.
Xena (V.O.)	Get close to me. Closer, unbutton my blouse.

De Martini	Is...Is that what you want me to do?
Gina	Yes. Let's forget it.
Xena (V.O.)	Reach out and grab me, rip open my blouse. Suck on me, suck on me...

GINA gets up to exit.

Child	Bye!
De Martini	Where are you going?
Gina	I'll just finish those files now.
De Martini	You're not mad are you?
Gina	I am never annoyed with you, sir. Every moment of working for you is a moment of deep professional satisfaction.

COLLINS enters. He has several Xeroxed copies of breasts.

Collins	Look at this! What do you make of this!
Gina	What is it?
De Martini	It seems that someone has Xeroxed her breasts.
Collins	I was standing next to the Xerox machine when all these... breasts came shooting out. The machine was jammed! It wouldn't shut off! And I'm being blamed for it! It was probably one of those goddamned activists...or someone I suspect is both a woman and an activist. Someone is trying to get me fired, and she's doing a pretty good job of it, too.
Gina	Who would want to do that.
De Martini	Xena—
Gina	Gina...
De Martini	Gina, you'd better go take your break.
Gina	What?

De Martini	Legally, you are entitled to a ten minute break every two hours. I think this would be a good time to take it.
	She exits. COLLINS stares at DE MARTINI. There is a note taped to the seat of DE MARTINI's pants that will be noticeable at some point below.
Collins	I want her transferred to the West Covina Office.
De Martini	We can't...can't do that now. This matter requires great strategic thought.
Collins	I am a master of strategic thinking.
De Martini	You are a life-support system for a penis.
Collins	And you are a hypocrite.
De Martini	I am in the process of a deep investigation.
Collins	Is this part of it?
De Martini	What?
Collins	This note here—stuck to your ass. *(Grabs the note, reads)* I want to crawl into your lap and bury myself inside you. Puncture your skin like a screw worm. Submerge myself in a river of your blood. Take your heart in my teeth and eat it.
De Martini	She is under the force of great vast hormonal tides. Whatever the case, we must act like adults.
Collins	Like adults in adult films?
De Martini	Your constant vulgarity grows distasteful.
Collins	I simply came in here to make a request for a verification of employee accountability.
De Martini	You must make your requests with the proper requisition forms. Verbal requests will no longer be honored.
Collins	I'll take my requests to human resources.
De Martini	Do what you must.

| Collins | You are pussy whipped. |

COLLINS exits. XENA enters. She carries an accordion file (as before), reaches into it. Instead of bags of milk there are chicken feet.

| De Martini | Chicken feet! Chicken feet! Chicken feet! |

XENA files chicken feet and pieces of gore.

Xena	Are you suffering?
De Martini	Yes.
Xena	And you think you're the only one?
De Martini	The only one with this quality of suffering.
Xena	Good...that's how you learn. *(Exits)*
De Martini	But what am I to learn? What am I to learn! Goddamnit!

The CHILD appears in front of the elevator with a bundle of dynamite. DE MARTINI stares at the note.

Oh, my God...This note, appears to be in my handwriting.

The CHILD waves goodbye and with a laugh steps into the elevator. DE MARTINI turns, sees her for the first time.

What's that you're carrying.

| Child | A bomb. |

The elevator doors close. GINA enters. She has a paper and pen in hand.

De Martini	Xena?
Gina	If that's what you want to call me, fine. Xena. Call me whatever you want. I have something here I need you to sign.
De Martini	I don't think I'd better sign anything right now.
Gina	Sit down.
De Martini	What are you going to do to me, Xena?
Gina	*(Massaging his shoulders)* We've got to get these knots undone. You're so tense, you're tensile. You're tight. You can't walk around like that...
De Martini	Do you know what it's like to lead a double life?
Gina	I'm sure everyone who works here has some kind of double life, otherwise we wouldn't last a day.
De Martini	Can you admit to yours? Gina?
Gina	Yes. If you sign this authorization for transfer.
De Martini	Transfer?
Gina	For me.
De Martini	Where?
Gina	They want me upstairs.
De Martini	Upstairs? But this is the top floor of the building.
Gina	Upstairs has other meanings, sir.
De Martini	And what makes you think they want you up there.
Gina	I was recommended by Veronica.
De Martini	Veronica...Is this really what you tell me it is? Or is it more likely, some type of...confession?
Gina	If there's something you need to confess to me, sir, I promise to keep it between you and me.
De Martini	Then why do I have to sign anything?
Gina	If there's a good reason for the denial of this transfer, Veronica has asked that you put it in writing.
De Martini	I can't let you go, I told you, Gina. You are indispensable.

*The phone rings. G*ɪɴᴀ *answers it.*

Gina Gina's...I mean...Joe De Martini's office. Oh no, are people stuck inside. *(To D*ᴇ Mᴀʀᴛɪɴɪ*)* The elevators have all stopped working *(Into the phone)* So, what do we do... Okay. Thanks. *(She hangs up)*

De Martini Do you remember when you told me you felt like this building was alive, and then, you pretended not to know what you meant? You really did have a meaning in mind, didn't you.

Gina Maybe.

De Martini What was it?

Gina That, no matter what this company's done, this building is standing up there gleaming. It's there to tell people

I ᴀᴍ ʜᴇʀᴇ.

I'ᴍ ʙɪɢɢᴇʀ ᴛʜᴀɴ ʏᴏᴜ.

I'ᴍ sᴛᴀɴᴅɪɴɢ ᴜᴘ,

ᴀɴᴅ ʏᴏᴜ'ʀᴇ ᴅᴏᴡɴ ᴛʜᴇʀᴇ ꜰʟᴀᴛ.

De Martini I know a certain executive here, he told me—he senses the presence of a bloodthirsty force. He says that we don't see the blood. It's like they have a vacuum that sucks it all up and bleaches it white. There are bones in the walls. He says, sometimes it's as if this whole building is breathing.

Gina He must be a sensitive person.

De Martini He is a horror to himself.

Gina I wouldn't think he was horrible at all...Now, please sign.

De Martini I can't let you go.

Gina You've taught me intricate management techniques. Someone else deserves that chance now, and I should have a chance to *move on.*

De Martini	According to my friend, there is this substance, that transmits thoughts. He has these thoughts, which are not his thoughts, not characteristic of his way of thinking. He's been given this understanding, but, it's more like a weapon. The most destructive weapon. Because he can't operate, not like he used to. Can't operate at all.
Gina	I hope he gets help. Do I know him?
De Martini	He was enticed. Deliberately enticed.
Gina	What does he want from me?
De Martini	He wants...He wants...

The phone rings.

Gina	Hold that thought. *(Answers phone)* Hello? Yes. This is Gina. Oh no. That's terrible. Yes. He's here. I'll tell him. *(Hangs up)* The factory exploded.

Beat—they look at each other.

De Martini	That's it. It's done. It's done...Now, Xena.
Gina	What does your friend want from me?
De Martini	Milk. He's had it. He's had it and he can't get enough. It is so good, so goddamned good...I dream that you come to me at night. You sit on my chest. You breathe into my lungs and you suck the air out. You could stop me from breathing. You could tell my heart to stop and it would. Why? Why are you always so silent? Your silence draws the breath from my body. I can't breathe. I'm talking, I'm talking. I'm saying things I shouldn't say...
Gina	If I could stop you from breathing, believe me, I would.

| De Martini | But I thought something happened between us... |
| Gina | No, nothing happened. Now sign this please. |

He signs.

Thank you sir.

GINA gets her briefcase, is starting to exit. COLLINS enters. A high heel shoe in his hand, a little blood running down his forehead. He's stunned.

Collins	Veronica just hit me in the head with her shoe, when I only just did what she asked me to do.
Gina	Was this a verbal, or nonverbal request.
De Martini	Gina, I love you.
Gina	You don't even know me. *(She exits)*
De Martini	She's gone now...gone forever.
Collins	Good. She was probably a lesbian.
De Martini	You know, there was this certain executive here. Who thought...You see, he thought...he had this temp who was more than just a temp. She was...a woman. But she was more than just a woman. She had a power over him. A kind of supernatural power.
Collins	This guy sounds like an idiot.
De Martini	An idiot. Yes. Because, she was...She was just a woman, and nothing more.

The CHILD appears upstage.

| Child | And nothing more. |

De Martini	And this certain executive was just—He just seemed to be having—
Collins	Having a real fucking problem with reality.
De Martini	Reality. Reality. Reality. Yes. Except that this temp...This woman's appearance here *paralleled* so many *destructive events*. And he wants to know if *she* was the cause of these events or if somehow *he* himself was responsible.
Child	He himself was responsible.
Collins	Wait a minute. This temp. Who was she?
De Martini	I don't know.
Child	Yes, you *do* know.

At that moment, GINA appears. She steps into the elevator. She's brightly lit. Both men turn and stare at her. The elevator doors close. All lights fade except a momentary special on DE MARTINI—he has an expression of understanding.

De Martini	It must have been me.

Lights fade out.

The End

Note on "Freeze"

When I first read Murray's play *Freeze*, I thought of the word "frieze" and mentioned putting mics on the actors and staging it behind a window, the actors arrayed in a flat plane against the glass. This may have been Murray's intention all along, because he said yes right away. The next day we took our "site walk" around the U.S.C. campus. We found a couple of spots that could have worked, but one area in particular stood out. This was one of those forlorn little in-between spaces Padua specialized in animating, a spot you might otherwise walk past on a daily basis and never notice. The building itself was a functional modernist structure with a cement exterior, and close to the north end was this drab little area where twelve-foot windows faced a small, stage-like patch of cement that included two metal grates. We staged the family scenes behind the window panels, the actors speaking into hidden mics, and kept the "Jamie" and "Kurt" scenes out front, each character assigned to one of the grates. The audience sat on risers across a bed of ivy. A few days before we opened, Murray pulled me aside and showed me the path along which the audi- came around the far side of an adjacent building, and in the distance saw "Rick," "Tracy," and "Joan" lit up in their "frieze" behind the win- dows as night fell. More than one reviewer mentioned this as the most beautiful image of the festival, and it remains so in my memory.

Guy Zimmerman, March, 2003

Director

The Playwrights

Neena Beber's plays include *Jump/Cut*, *Hard Feelings*, *Thirst*, *The Dew Point*, *A Common Vision*, *Tomorrowland*, *The Brief but Exemplary Life of the Living Goddess*, and the one-act *Misreadings*, produced by Woolly Mammoth, Theatre J, The Women's Project, The Magic Theatre, New Georges, Gloucester Stage, Watermark, Soho Rep, Ojai Playwrights Conference, ATL's Humana Festival, among others. She is the recipient of an L. Arnold Weissberger Award, Amblin/Playwrights Horizons and Otterbein commissions, a Paulette Goddard fellowship, an AT & T First Stages and NEA Creativity Grant, and an A.S.K. Exchange to The Royal Court Theatre. Beber is a member of New Dramatists, and the HB Playwrights Unit. She grew up in Miami, Florida.

Maria Irene Fornes is one of the most influential and prolific American avant-garde playwrights of our time. Among her most celebrated plays are *Promenade*, *The Successful Life of 3*, *Fefu and Her Friends*, *The Danube*, *Mud*, *Drowning*, *The Conduct of Life*, *And What of the Night?*, *Abingdon Square*, *Enter the Night*, *Summer In Gossensass*, and *Oscar and Bertha*. Ms. Fornes is the recipient of nine Obie Awards, one of which was for Sustained Achievement in Theater. She has received NEA awards, including a Distinguished Artist Award, Rockefeller Foundation grants, a Guggenheim grant, an award from the American Academy and Institute of Arts and Letters, the Chesley Award and a New York State Governor's Arts Award. She conducts playwriting workshops in theaters and universities in the United States and abroad. From 1973-79, she was the managing director of the New York Theatre Strategy. In addition to directing most of her own plays, she has directed plays by Calderón, Ibsen, Chekhov and several contemporary playwrights. Two volumes of her plays have been published by the Performing Arts Journal and other plays have appeared in various anthologies. She was a TCG/PEW Artist-in-Residence at Women's Project & Productions and her work constituted the 1999-2000 season at the Signature Theatre Company, including the world premiere of her latest play, *Letters from Cuba*. It was the first of Fornes' plays to deal directly with her Cuban heritage and garnered her Obie Awards for both writing and direction. Current projects include an adaptation of Gertrude Stein's *The Autobiography of Alice B Toklas* for the Acting Company.

Joseph Goodrich is a writer and actor from Minnesota. His plays have been produced in New York City (HERE Arts Center, The Six Figures Theatre Company), Los Angeles (The Padua Hills Playwrights Festival, Circus Minimus, Theatre of NOTE and others), San Francisco (Core Performance Manufactory Company), New Orleans (Asylum/Zeitgeist Center), Minneapolis/St. Paul (Minneapolis College of Art and Design, Red Eye Collaboration, Study Cow Productions and others), and Portland, Maine (Portland Stage Company). As an actor, he's performed extensively in New York (Soho Rep, Theatre For A New City, The Ohio Theater, The Women's Project and others); Los Angeles (The Lost Studio, Theatre/Theater, Cast Theatre and others), in the Tulane University Shakespeare Festival, The Dallas Theatre Center, and at the Theatre Des Dechargeurs and Le Maroquinerie in Paris. He is a member of New Dramatists.

Murray Mednick is the founder of the Padua Hills Playwrights Festival and Workshop, where he served as Artistic Director from 1978 through 1995. Born in Brooklyn, New York, he was for many years a playwright-in-residence at New York's Theatre Genesis, which presented all of his early work (*The Hawk, The Deer Kill, The Hunter, Sand, Are You Lookin'?* and others). He was artistic co-director of Genesis from 1970 until 1974, when he emigrated to California. Plays produced since then include *Iowa* and *Blessings* (for the PBS series "Visions"), *The Coyote Cycle, Taxes, Scar, Heads, Shatter 'N Wade, Fedunn, Switchback, Baby, Jesus!, Dictator* and *Freeze*. Mednick's plays *Joe and Betty* and *Mrs. Feuerstein* received dual runs in Los Angeles and New York in 2002; *Joe and Betty* received the American Theatre Critic's Association Best New Play Citation in that year. He is also the recipient of two Rockefeller Foundation grants, a Guggenheim Fellowship, an OBIE, several Bay Area Critics Awards, the 1997 *L.A. Weekly* Playwriting Award (for *Dictator*) and a 1992 Ovation Lifetime Achievement Award from Theatre LA for outstanding contributions to Los Angeles theatre. Most recently, Mednick was awarded the 2002 Margaret Harford Award for Sustained Excellence in Theater awarded by the Los Angeles Drama Critic's Circle.

Marlane Meyer's plays include *Etta Jenks, Kingfish, The Geography of Luck, Why Things Burn, Moe's Lucky Seven, The Chemistry of Change,* and *The Mystery of Attraction* (2002). Her work has been produced at the Los Angeles Theatre Centre, The Women's Project, Playwrights Horizons, The Joseph Papp Public Theatre, The Royal Court Theatre and South Coast Repertory, and has received many awards including The Joseph Kesselring Award, The Susan Smith Blackburn Prize and The Pen Center Award for Drama.

Susan Mosakowski is a co-artistic director of Creation Production Company, which she founded with Matthew Maguire in 1977. The company has produced more than fifty original works for the stage, plus works on video and audiocassette. She has been an artist-in-residence at the Long Beach Opera (California), The Illusion Theatre (Minneapolis), the Padua Hills Playwrights' Festival (Los Angeles), The Minneapolis College of Art and Design, and Ireland's Tyrone Guthrie Playwriting Center (Annaghmakerrig). She currently serves on the theatre panel for the New York State Council on the Arts. Her recent play, *Nighttown*, premiered at The Flea Theater, and she is currently working on *Monster*, a play with music by Julia Wolfe. Awards for her work include a Rockefeller Foundation Playwriting Fellowship, a National Endowment for the Arts Playwriting Fellowship, three consecutive Northwest Area Fellowships, and numerous grants from foundations as well as individual and company grants from the NEA and NYSCA. Publications include *Cities Out of Print*, *Ice Station Zebra*, *More Monologues for Women*, and "The Rotary Notary and Her Hot Plate" in *FLESH: Architectural Probes*. Mosakowski is the director of the audiobook program at the New York Public Library; her audiobook productions (for the Library and others) include Ian McKellen's reading of the Robert Fagles translation of Homer's *The Odyssey*, and Claire Bloom's reading of *The Portrait of a Lady*.

John O'Keefe, who began working with the Padua Playwrights Festival in 1982, has written more than 40 plays and has won three Bay Area Critic's Circle Awards, six Hollywood Drama-Logue Awards, three LA Weekly Awards, four Dallas Critic's Circle Awards, the New York Performance Art Award (Bessie), and a citation by the

American Critic's Association. Born in Waterloo, Iowa in 1940, O'Keefe was raised in Catholic orphanages and state juvenile homes throughout the American Midwest. He began singing in church choirs at the age of five and pursued his musical interests, subsequently receiving a vocal scholarship at the University of Iowa, where he earned a BA degree in Philosophy and an MFA in Theater. He continued his experimental work with the Iowa Theatre Lab. His affiliation with the Magic Theater in San Francisco began with their 1972 production of his play *Chamber Piece* and the 1973 production of *Jimmy Beam* and continues to this day, including six full productions, with two more currently in the works. Among these, *All Night Long* won the full round of Bay Area Critics Awards. O'Keefe was co-founder of the Blake Street Hawkeyes, a performance lab ensemble based in Berkeley, California. O'Keefe was one of five writers chosen for a residency at Sundance Film Institute in 1989. His work *Shimmer* toured throughout the United States and Europe and was then produced as a feature film by American Playhouse and broadcast nationally. He performed his one-man show, *The Promotion*, at Lincoln Center in 1991. *The Deatherians*, O'Keefe's musical about sex and euthanasia in Amsterdam, had its world premiere at the Undermain Theater in 1996, sweeping the Critics awards in Dallas that year. The Magic Theater of San Francisco presented an O'Keefe Festival in February 2000, featuring *Bronte, Don't You Ever Call Me Anything But Mother*, a showing of the American Playhouse production of his film, *Shimmer*, as well as readings of several of his other works. *Glamour,* which was nominated for best play by the American Critics Association and had its New York premiere April 9th, 2002.

John Steppling is an original member of the Padua Festival, and former artistic director of Empire Red Lip (Los Angeles) and former co-artistic director of *Heliogabalus* and *Circus Minimus* (both Los Angeles). His plays have been performed in Los Angeles, San Francisco, London, New York, Paris and soon in Krakow. Steppling is a Rockefeller Fellow, two time NEA recipient, MacDowell Colony Resident, and a PEN-West winner. His plays include *Dream Coast*, *Teenage Wedding*, *Neck*, *Contagion: An American Book of the Dead*, *Dog Mouth*, *Standard of the Breed*, *The Shaper*, and *Pledging My Love*. Film credits of note include *Animal Factory* (an adaptation of Eddie Bunker's book, directed by Steve Buscemi). A collection of Steppling's plays was published in 1996 (*Sea of Cortez and Other Plays*) and many other plays have been anthologized. In recent years, he has lived in London, Paris, and now Krakow (with his wife Anna).

Kelly Stuart started her life in the theatre with the Padua Hills Playwrights Festival, and has gone on to write twenty plays. Recent plays include *Homewrecker*, presented at the Schaubuehne in Berlin, and *Mayhem*, produced at the Evidence Room in Los Angeles (March 2003). Other plays: *Furious Blood*, (Sledgehammer Theatre/January 2000), *Interpreter of Horror* (NY Fringe Festival/Padua Hills Playwrights Festival) *The Square Root of Terrible* at the Mark Taper Forum, *The Peacock Screams When the Lights Go Out* at the Sledgehammer Theatre in San Diego, and *Ball and Chain* at Padua. She has had plays commissioned by the Taper, South Coast Rep, Playwrights Horizons, Sledgehammer, and The Guthrie. In the fall of 2000 she received a Whiting Foundation Award. She is proud to be an alumnus of New Dramatists. She lives in New York and teaches at Columbia University.

About Padua

In 1978, Murray Mednick and five other playwrights, including Sam Shepard and Maria Irene Fornes, converged on the old Padua Hills estate in the foothills of the San Gabriel Mountains, just east of Los Angeles. The playwrights, along with a class of playwriting students and a company of actors, were given free reign to re-investigate their creativity, work on writing exercises in the morning, rehearse in the afternoon, and present the results in the evening.

Under Mednick's artistic direction, the annual Padua Hills Playwrights Workshop/Festival became an important cultural event in Southern California that had a lasting impact on American theater. Among the many playwrights of national prominence to emerge from or be nurtured by Padua are: David Henry Hwang, John O'Keefe, Kelly Stuart, Jon Robin Baitz, Marlane Meyer, John Steppling, Julie Hebert and Susan Mosakowski, to name a few.

In 2000, Mednick invited playwright Guy Zimmerman to transform Padua from an annual outdoor festival into a theater company mounting high-quality productions of new work. As Artistic Director of Padua Playwrights Productions, Zimmerman's intent is to sustain and enhance the vital Padua tradition by drawing on the extensive roster of Padua writers for new work.

To date, the company has staged nine productions, including three in New York City. In the space of only two years, Padua has garnered multiple awards including LA Weekly, Garland, and Los Angeles Drama Critics Circle awards; end of the year roundup "top 10" mentions in the *New York Times*, *Los Angeles Times*, *Los Angeles Daily News*, and *LA Weekly* among others, and an American Theatre Critics Association Citation. In March, the Los Angeles Drama Critic's Circle awarded Padua its highest honor, the Margaret Harford Award for Sustained Excellence in Theater.

Requests for permission to stage the plays, in part or in their entirety, should be directed to the following sources.

Failure to Thrive:
Joyce Ketay
The Joyce Ketay Agency
1501 Broadway, Suite 1908
New York, NY 10036

Terra Incognita:
Morgan Jenness
Helen Merrill Limited
295 Lafayette Street, Suite 915
New York, NY 10012

The Chemistry of Change:
John Buzzetti
The Gersh Agency
41 Madison Avenue, 33rd Floor
New York, NY 10010

Disgrace:
johnokeefe.org

All inquiries including requests for permission for *Steak Knife Bacchae*, *Freeze*, *The Tight Fit*, *Understanding the Dead*, and *Demonology* will be forwarded to the individual playwright. Correspondence should be directed to Padua Playwrights Productions, 964 Tularosa Drive, Los Angeles, CA 90026.

Padua Playwrights Press books are available from your local bookseller or visit www.paduaplaywrights.net. Other available titles:

Three Plays by Murray Mednick

16 Routines, Joe and Betty, and *Mrs. Feuerstein.*

Murray Mednick at his darkly comic best.

"A playwright's playwright...Mednick has spent his career at the forefront of avant-garde theater." —Sandra Ross, LA Weekly

300 pages, Paperback, ISBN 0-9630126-3-0

$14.95

Best of the West

Includes plays from the Padua Hills Playwrights Festival by:

Susan Champagne, Martin Epstein, Maria Irene Fornes, Julie Hebert, Leon Martell, Murray Mednick, Susan Mosakowski, John Steppling, Kelly Stuart

312 pages, Paperback, ISBN 0-9630126-2-2

$14.95

The Coyote Cycle

Seven Plays by Murray Mednick

"...it permanently reshaped my vision of what theatre could achieve— ritual, magic, playfulness, and respect for the playwright-actor bond entered my creative vocabulary and have been my resources ever since... in a day when much of the public has come to doubt the power of theatre, Murray Mednick's Coyote is proof that the best of it can still change lives." —David Henry Hwang

176 pages, Paperback, ISBN 0-9630126-1-4

$15.95